THE MOST WANTED MAN IN CHINA

THE MOST WANTED MAN IN CHINA

My Journey from Scientist to Enemy of the State

FANG LIZHI

TRANSLATED BY PERRY LINK

HENRY HOLT AND COMPANY   NEW YORK

Henry Holt and Company, LLC
Publishers since 1866
175 Fifth Avenue
New York, New York 10010
www.henryholt.com

Henry Holt ® and 🄷 ® are registered trademarks of
Henry Holt and Company, LLC.

Frontispiece: Courtesy of Shuxian Li and Ke Fang

Library of Congress Cataloging-in-Publication Data

Fang, Lizhi.
   [Fang Lizhi zi zhuan. English]
   The most wanted man in China : my journey from scientist to
enemy of the state / Fang Lizhi ; translated by Perry Link.
       pages cm
   Includes index.
   ISBN 978-1-62779-499-2 (hardcover)—ISBN 978-1-62779-500-5
(electronic book)   1. Fang, Lizhi.   2. Dissenters—China—
Biography.   3. Scholars—China—Biography.   4. China—
Politics and government—1976–2002.   I. Link, E. Perry
(Eugene Perry), 1944– translator   II. Title.
   CT1828.F47A313 2016
   951.05'7092—dc23
   [B]   2015023833

ISBN: 978-1-62779-499-2

Originally published in 2013 in traditional Chinese characters
by Commonwealth Publishing Co., Ltd. (Taiwan)
First published in the United States by
Henry Holt and Company

Designed by Meryl Sussman Levavi
Printed in the United States of America

10 9 8 7 6 5 4 3 2 1

CONTENTS

FOREWORD

by PERRY LINK

WHEN FANG LIZHI, ONE OF CHINA'S MOST DISTINGUISHED SCIENTISTS, began in 1986 to talk to his students about the "universal rights" of human beings, he knew the risks. In those days, the use of the term "rights" in China was highly sensitive, even dangerous, and three years later Fang would pay the price for his candor. He spent the last twenty-two years of his life in exile from China, but his ideas, on their home turf, were not so easy to stamp out: the concept of "rights" lived on, and it gradually became less perilous to mention the word. In 2003, a "defend rights" movement took root among Chinese lawyers and activists, and by the time of Fang's death in 2012, factory workers, miners, petitioners, and even farmers in small villages had begun to conceive and pursue their interests as "rights." The trend had grown beyond anything China's rulers could reverse. It was a sea change and thus had many causes; no person did it single-handedly, or could have. But if we ask which person, among the many, did the most, the name Fang Lizhi must surely arise.

A brilliant physicist, Fang was recruited out of college to work on Mao Zedong's project to build an atomic bomb. Later he became one of the youngest people ever appointed to China's Academy of Sciences. When he began speaking out about human rights, he was already vice president of the prestigious University of Science and Technology of China. It was the highest position from which anyone in China had ever stepped out to be a "dissident." Fang's admirers have likened him to Andrei Sakharov (1921–1989), the Soviet physicist who, like Fang, worked on nuclear weapons for a Communist state, later turned to human rights advocacy and dissent, and eventually was punished by exile (internal in Sakharov's case, external in Fang's). Sakharov won the Nobel Peace Prize in 1975. The conditions of the Cold War, added to the fact that Russia has closer ethnic and cultural ties to the West than China has, can explain why Sakharov is better known in the West than Fang is. But they are kindred spirits, and Fang's historical legacy is at least as large.

For Fang as for Sakharov, rights were implied by science. This book shows how, step by step, it was the axioms of science—skepticism, freedom of inquiry, respect for evidence, the equality of inquiring minds, and the universality of truth—that led Fang toward human rights and to reject dogma of every kind, including, eventually, the dogma of the Chinese Communism that he had idealistically embraced during his youth.

Fang entered world headlines on February 27, 1989, the day after the Chinese police had barred him and his wife, Li Shuxian, from attending a barbecue banquet in Beijing to which U.S. president George H. W. Bush had invited them. They were in the news again after the Tiananmen Square massacre of democracy advocates on June 4, 1989. Late at night on June 5, staff from the U.S. embassy in Beijing, acting on instructions from the White House, invited the Fangs, who were then at the top of a Chinese government "wanted" list, to take refuge in the U.S. embassy. They accepted and stayed for thirteen months, sealed in a secret location, while "the Fang problem" became a major headache in American foreign policy. (On June 26, 1989, Fang received a note of support from Andrei Sakharov; this was six months before Sakharov died.) In the final chapter of this book, Fang reveals the negotiations that led to his and Li Shuxian's release from the U.S. embassy. They went to England, and then to the United States, where Fang settled at the University of Arizona and resumed his career as a professor of astrophysics. He was teaching full time when he died.

Many histories, biographies, and works of fiction have been written about the saga of the Communist movement in modern China—how it rose, inspired hope, and then brought disaster; how the Party survived, adapted, got rich, and lumbered on. No book, though, does better than this one at giving a sense for what the whole epic experience felt like from the inside. I say this for several reasons.

For one, Fang is a gifted writer. In high school he won essay contests, and the talent shows. His insights are deep, he illustrates them in vivid detail, and he is utterly honest. Other Chinese writers can rival him in some of these regards, but none can match his reach: from his early life in Beijing alleyways to his encounters with top political leaders, it is the same astute, observant Fang Lizhi who is our guide. He explains how water was delivered in premodern Beijing, how farmers catch pigs, and why students at China's leading technical university in the mid-1980s ate their meals standing up. From personal experience of "labor reform," he tells us how wells are dug by hand and how a railroad construction crew rolls boulders down a mountainside without killing anybody. He doesn't flinch when the topics turn hideous: how victims of political persecution select their means of suicide, and how people guard the gates at morgues to prevent wild dogs from eating the corpses of their friends or relatives. The same matter-of-fact voice shows us a vociferous public debate he has with Wan Li, one of China's highest officials.

He is as honest about himself as on any other topic. Other Chinese intellectuals, when they look back at the 1950s and 1960s, tend to see themselves—and rightly so—as victims of Mao Zedong and his regime. They often do less well at explaining their original attraction to Communism. But not Fang. He explains how, as a high school student in the late 1940s, he despised the corruption and incompetence of the Nationalist government, was captivated by the prospect of Communism, and joined an underground organization at a time when doing so could cost one's life. On a rainy night in 1949 he stayed up past midnight at an outdoor stadium, literally dancing in anticipation of his first chance to see Mao Zedong in person. In college, from 1952 to 1956, he fell deeply in love with physics, with Communism, and with his girlfriend Li Shuxian, who was his classmate and herself a physicist and sincere Communist. He saw his shining future resting on a tripod—physics, Communism, girlfriend—each leg sturdy, each supporting the ideals of the other two.

Soon, though, the physics and Communism legs came into conflict. Science asked him to begin in skepticism and to build knowledge by hypothesis, evidence, and proof—from the bottom up. In Marxism class, on the other hand, he was given the right answers on the first day and told to work from the top down. And there were other anomalies: for science, truths are universal; Mao Zedong said that truth has a "class nature." Science thrives on the free flow of information, but the Communist organization directed information only to certain people and only under certain conditions. These anomalies, at first only irritating, grew deeper as Fang's college career moved on. Then, in the late 1950s, intellectual quandary turned into real-world pain as Fang was torn away from physics and from his girlfriend and sent to do labor in a small farming village in Hebei Province. What most shocked him in the village was not his own suffering but the degradation of the "peasants" who—it had been said in Marxism class—were the "vanguard of the revolution." Communist theory was suddenly revealed as a pompous abstraction.

Fang's disillusionment grew deeper a few years later during another stint of labor reform, this one at a coal mine in Anhui Province. There, at the bottom of a mine, his political faith hit bottom as well. He found that the miners—the quintessential "laboring masses" in Communist imagery—were the victims, not the agents, of the "proletarian dictatorship." In this regard they were like the intellectuals: the authorities exploited both groups, only in different ways.

With Deng Xiaoping's "reform and opening" in the early 1980s, Fang gave the Party one more chance. He had been expelled in 1958, but he rejoined the Party and went around making speeches urging young scientists to do so as well. His reason? Not that the Party was doing well, but almost the opposite: the Party holds the reins of power, he argued, and this fact will not soon change; it does govern badly, but this fact will change only if people with better ideas join and work from within.

In 1983, on a trip to Germany, Fang crossed from West Berlin to East and, immediately upon arrival, had the odd feeling that he had been to this place before, even though he plainly had not. The streets were gray, the monuments were pretentious, the border was policed. The whole atmosphere was all too familiar. The guides wanted to sell him East German postage stamps and wanted to be paid in Western hard currency. Marxist culture, he saw, can trump and homogenize national cultures.

Thirty years out of college, Fang was more strongly attached to science than ever, but his attachment to Communism had completely disappeared. The process happened step by step, despite his having granted the benefit of the doubt at every turn. First, Mao was a hero. Then, no, Mao did some absurd things—but can't the Party correct them? No, the Party turned out to be an elite of self-interested power engineers—but doesn't Marxism itself deserve better? No, Marxism is not the answer; it apparently spreads the same shades of gray everywhere. After 1987, when Fang was expelled from the Communist Party for a second time, he found himself a "dissident." There seemed no other way.

In describing the bloody Tiananmen Square repression of June 1989, Fang sets the events against the wartime memories of his boyhood:

> Here's what happened: the central government of China mobilized 200,000 regular troops, supplied them with regular military weaponry (tanks and submachine guns) and used regular military formations and tactics to force an entry into its own capital city, territory that it already held.

After students and other civilians were massacred, Party leaders blamed Fang for starting the whole thing by inspiring the students, and, as noted above, he and Li Shuxian took refuge inside the residence of the U.S. ambassador to China.

Confinement there was tight, but of course it was better than prison, and it provided enough spare time for Fang to draft this book. "It seems a good time," he writes in his introduction, "whether in order to understand the past or to interpret what will come next, to do a review of where I have been so far." He began writing in October 1989 and finished the book shortly after leaving the embassy in June 1990. Li Shuxian has told me that his routine in writing was to conceive one chapter at a time, organize its structure in his mind, and then just sit down and write it out rather quickly. One can only marvel at his memory. Working with no library, no Google search function, and very few notes, he named dates, times, and places, and quoted from letters and documents, in ways that have held up extremely well under my fact checking.

Fang's allies in the struggle for democracy and human rights in China have sometimes misunderstood the depth of his devotion to science. It was always his north star, however the rest of the heavens might spin. When he entered the U.S. embassy, some activists criticized him for not choosing political martyrdom instead; when he exited the embassy, some were disappointed that he turned down leading positions in the overseas Chinese democracy movement in order to be a professor of astrophysics. But these criticisms reflect a misunderstanding of the man. Throughout his life, Fang saw himself as a physicist who had duties as a citizen. At several points in the 1980s he chose physics over opportunities to move upward in Chinese officialdom. Later, during his exile years, he counseled young Chinese democracy advocates against careers as "professional activists." He advised them to be physicists, computer technicians, teachers of Chinese, or whatever—and to be citizen activists on the side.

Fang himself had the capacity to do many things "on the side." His powerful brain enabled him to focus on a wide variety of topics beyond his academic pursuits. He sometimes seemed charmed by his own good luck in having such a super-brain and played with it almost as if it were a toy, pointing it here or there to see what would happen and then noting down the interesting results. In this book he takes us on many and diverse short detours through topics in both Chinese and Western learning. The history of science gets a great deal of comment. He finds, for example, an uncanny convergence between passages in Galileo and in China's ancient *Book of Documents* on a conceptual point that undergirds modern relativity theory; he explains how Johannes Kepler used pitch intervals and rhythms to describe the speeds and oscillations of planetary movements and then relates the theory to problems of perspective in viewing contemporary China; and he compares accounts of the different colors of stars in Sima Qian's *Records of the Grand Historian* (ca. 100 B.C.) to spectral measurements of star color in modern physics. But he also addresses history more broadly. He recounts a visit to Malam Jabba in Pakistan, where the seventh-century Chinese pilgrim Xuanzang, who traveled to India in search of the true Buddhist scriptures, crossed the Karakoram range on his way back to China. Fang's account of Xuanzang, reaching back thirteen centuries, makes an ancient world seem as vivid as today's. On a trip to Japan, Fang learns how Chinese merchants who ventured to Japan in the days when ocean travel depended on the prevailing winds were obliged to spend half of each year, including festive New Year's, in Nagasaki; as he paints their life there, one almost feels that one is walking among those merchants.

About once or twice per chapter, Fang's language turns lyrical, challenging its translator to capture its glow. Here, for example, is how he describes his elation upon arriving at Peking University as a first-year student in 1952:

> It stood at a civilized distance from the racket of the city, from the traffic noise and the hawkers' calls, and seemed elevated to its own plane of purity. When I walked through the campus in the cool air at night, past the semi-somnolent Nameless Lake and the Temple of the Flower Goddess that graced its bank, past the majestic water tower that reached toward heaven, and when I heard the bells that tolled occasionally from the clock pavilion, I had the feeling that all these signs were augurs of my future, which, like the scenes themselves, would be peaceful, harmonious, and boundless.

Fang sometimes turns a bit mystical, almost religious. He wonders at one point, with Immanuel Kant, if "the starry heavens above me" and "the moral law within me" are related. Elsewhere, after he and Li Shuxian hike to a peak in the gorgeous Huangshan Mountains, he writes:

> The top is like a small island that juts out toward space, holding its own, bucking and tossing among the clouds that billow one moment and disperse the next as they blow by. The air is thin, the wind chilly; this is the frontier of the secular world, the edge where the cacophony of human loves and hates melts away. It reminded me of the "Paradiso" section of *The Divine Comedy*, where the highest level in Heaven is

occupied not even by God but only by Dante, his lover
Beatrice, and their limitless joy.

Fang's language is always graceful, and it occasionally soars, but its
most regular delights are its flashes of wit. He shows by example that even
a Maoist steamroller cannot annihilate a good sense of humor. Indeed, satire is his primary weapon in combating—one might say dismantling—his
primary adversary, whose image grows sharper as his account proceeds.
He calls this adversary *dangju*, which I translate alternately as "the
regime" or "the authorities."

Dangju is not necessarily particular people, or the same people from
one time to the next; it is the faceless authority that emanates from the top
and ossifies the thinking of everyone within its system. Here is one of
Fang's many stories about *dangju* mentality: An astronomer at the Beijing Observatory is killed in an auto accident. The police want to record
it as an "accidental death," not a "traffic death," because their annual quota
for traffic deaths has already been filled and their year-end bonuses will
be imperiled if reality does not match state planning. Unfortunately, the
astronomer's family balks at the fiction and insists that a traffic death be
labeled a traffic death. Irritated, the police respond at the beginning of
the next year by hanging a banner outside the Beijing Observatory: STRUG-
GLE HARD TO FILL THIS YEAR'S PLAN FOR THE NUMBER OF TRAFFIC DEATHS!

Fang's tools in lampooning *dangju* are science and logic. Equipped
with these, he fears nothing. He reads Hegel, for example, and informs
us, as if awe for Hegel had never occurred to him, that the philosopher's
pronouncements on physics (he withholds judgment on other areas) are
"pure poppycock and utterly devoid of value for serious physicists." His
confidence holds up just as sturdily on the street as it does in ivory towers. On February 26, 1989, that night when he and Li Shuxian were
stopped on their way to George H. W. Bush's barbecue, they got out and
prepared to walk the remaining distance. Fang writes:

> After only a few steps, however, a bevy of plainclothes police
> surrounded us to block the way. Their leader was a swarthy
> man with a rough manner—the very image of the kind of "hit

man" the police train. He stepped forward, hooked his arm roughly under mine, and said, "I am the special agent in charge of all of security for the Bush visit. The invitation list that the U.S. secret service gave to us does not include your two names, so you cannot go to the banquet."

This told us several things. For one, it showed that the highest priority of the highest-ranking agent in charge of security for the U.S. president was not the security of the U.S. president.

As examples of this kind accumulate—and there are many—the mentality of *dangju* becomes clearer and more subtly explored than it is in any other book I have seen. The China field now includes several biographies of Mao Zedong, Deng Xiaoping, and other top leaders of China's Communist movement; some of these books run to hundreds of pages in length and cover the surfaces exhaustively, but they hardly penetrate the black boxes of *dangju* thinking. Representatives of *dangju* do not give frank interviews, and the wordings of their formal pronouncements are poor reflections, and often conscious dissimulations, of what they are actually thinking. In the end, there is no better way into the black boxes than the one Fang employs: observation of behavior, over many years, in different situations, and logical inference from that behavior. The method sometimes yields extraordinarily penetrating insight, as when, at the end of chapter 4, he likens Communist political theater to a high school drama, or, at the end of chapter 16, when he explains why *dangju* represses suggestions from below even if the suggestions are for things *dangju* itself wants.

I knew Fang Lizhi fairly well and have sought, in my translation, to convey his varying tones and moods accurately. Working with languages as different as Chinese and English, it is impossible to achieve fidelity of this kind through word-by-word matching. I have sought, instead, to use words and phrases that I think Fang himself might have chosen if he had been writing in English for English speakers. This is inevitably a presumptuous enterprise, and I apologize to his departed spirit for presuming to be up to it. But I see no alternative. A more mechanical rendition would be less true to the eloquence and the sprightly wit that the original offers to a reader of Chinese, and I want to be as loyal as I can be to those things. I am grateful to Chin-fei Lee, Ming-tang Chen, Reiko Sato, and Tong Yi for help with technical and colloquial terms, to Li Shuxian and Fang Ke for fact checking (in a very few places I have supplemented the Chinese text with minor facts that Li Shuxian provided to me), to Peter Bernstein for his skills as a literary agent, to Paul Golob for astute editing, and to Ke Chiang Hsieh, who reviewed the whole manuscript for errors and infelicities. Any that remain are, of course, my own.

PERRY LINK
Riverside, California
May 2015

THE MOST WANTED MAN IN CHINA

INTRODUCTION

As I sit down to write these recollections of my personal experiences, some paradoxes occur. I am a fugitive and in peril—but also fairly safe. Some people are hunting me as a criminal, while others are sending me honors.

The Chinese authorities have charged my wife, Li Shuxian, and me with "carrying out counterrevolutionary propaganda and incitement" and have issued warrants for our arrest. Officials in the Communist Party's Department of Propaganda are repeating, a thousandfold at all levels, the official version of us: we were "black hands behind the turmoil" and responsible for the "rioting at Tiananmen."

Meanwhile, we receive a stream of letters from students, scholars, and others—mostly people we don't know, both inside China and in distant lands—and the incessant messages are "We support you!" and "You are not alone!"

In June of this year, two major newspapers in Denmark and Sweden gave me their joint Politiken–Dagens Nyheter Peace Award. In September, in Washington, D.C., I received the Robert F. Kennedy Human Rights Award. In October, in Italy, the University of Rome gave me an honorary doctorate. In November, in Belgium, University Libre Bruxelles will do the same. In December, the New York Academy of Sciences is making me an honorary lifetime member.

Yet, as I write, Li Shuxian and I are concealed in a top secret hideaway inside the U.S. embassy in Beijing. Our rooms, although intended only for "temporary refuge," are comfortable. I have a separate study, and it is quiet. We cannot see trees, the sky, or scenery of any sort, but occasionally we can hear the chirping of birds. The table that I write on was not built to be a desk, but it is large enough, and I also have pen and paper, a lamp, a typewriter, and a computer. If I get tired there are tea and coffee to perk me up. The coffee comes both caffeinated and decaffeinated, and the tea can be either black tea or oolong as I choose.

Still, it would be hard to say we are at ease. The peril always looms. Only a few dozen feet from where I now sit, on the other side of walls that block a person's view, police whose orders are to arrest us are patrolling twenty-four hours a day. They carry rifles. They are unaware that their quarry is actually so near to them. But they do understand what a rifle is for.

It is, therefore, a constant condition of our lives that we do not know when a very abrupt change might occur. Tomorrow? The next day? A few hours from now?

And what, exactly, would the change be? Upward? Downward? Forward? Backward? Success? Failure? Joy? Despair?

The only point on which certainty seems possible is that my life is poised for a major shift of one sort or another. That being so, it seems a good time, whether in order to understand the past or to interpret what will come next, to do a review of where I have been so far.

October 27, 1989
Beijing

1. MY ANCESTORS

I WAS BORN IN BEIJING ON FEBRUARY 12, 1936—OR, ON THE LUNAR
calendar, day twenty of the first month of the year called *bingzi* in the
traditional sixty-year cycle.

The term "place of birth" has been something of a headache for me.
Every time I have applied for a Chinese passport, clerks have filled in the
blank after "birthplace" with the words "Hangzhou, Zhejiang Province."
Clerks do this because Chinese government personnel files do not have a
category called "birthplace." They list only "native place," which is a
fundamentally different concept. A native place is the home area of your
forebears, not necessarily the place where you were born. Somehow,
though, it became standard procedure that the "birthplace" blank on
passport applications was always filled in with whatever showed as "native
place" in personnel files. The error has legs. Today, in a number of reference books around the world, my birthplace is listed as Hangzhou.

Until about a hundred years ago, it was largely true that "birthplace"
and "native place" needed no distinction in China. People did not wander
far from where they were born. The whole life cycle—birth, growth, decline,
death—happened right where you were. For tenant farmers, the earth
they tilled was their entire world; landlords, too, were pretty much
bound to the land. Scholar-officials were the only ones who traveled

much—to other provinces or to the capital of the empire—but they almost always left their families at home when they did so. It was a coveted goal, upon retirement, "to return in glory, clothed in silk, to the native place." Even people who did not achieve such honor wanted to go home to die, like "leaves falling onto roots," as the proverb had it. If for some reason one died far from home, one risked turning into a wandering ghost, never to be at ease in either this world or the next.

The glory of a family could be seen in the geomancy, or *fengshui*, of its ancestral graveyard. "Cleave to the land and be content" was an unwritten ethical principle. Most of the premodern "migrants" (to use a modern term) in fact were criminals, who were punished by banishment to remote places and prohibited from returning home. They were the true, albeit unwilling, pioneers in premodern Chinese society. But in modern times, the idea of remaining contentedly on one's piece of land began to disintegrate. More and more Chinese have taken the "path of criminals" and departed their native places. If you were to take a survey in a major Chinese city today, I think you would find that more than half of the people have a birthplace that is different from their native place.

In 1934-35 the Chinese Communist Party made its famous Long March, in which tens of thousands of people trekked about eight thousand miles from Jiangxi Province to Yan'an in Shaanxi Province. As seen from the viewpoint of traditional Chinese culture, a major consequence of the Long March was that it uprooted a large number of people from their native places. Since the Communists have always glorified the Long March, one might expect them to accept the idea of people departing their native places. This makes it all the stranger that after they came to power, they still chose to identify their subjects by "native place" instead of "birthplace." This shows how strong the Chinese cultural preference is for identification with ancestral lands. Even in modern Communist government files, that's where a person "belongs."

In fact, my own ancestral lands were not really Hangzhou but Huizhou, a place that takes pride in its proximity to the magnificent Huangshan Mountains, one of the most scenic areas in all of China south of the Yangzi River. Huizhou is also home to the highest concentration of Fangs in all of China. Fang is not a particularly common surname, but there are some villages in She County, in Huizhou, where literally every person is named Fang. In 1986, when I was vice president of the University of Science and Technology of China, local Communist Party officials in Huizhou began inviting me to visit and to "look up my relatives." They claimed that they had researched the question and found that I was closely related to the Fangs in their particular area, so it was appropriate—no, it was my *duty*— to pay tribute to my ancestors and to visit my living kin. Their not-so-hidden motive was to use my status as a scholar and university vice president to harvest a bit of glory, even be it empty glory, for their local area. Their plans went awry in January 1987 when I was expelled from the Communist Party, fired as vice president of the university, and demoted to the Beijing Observatory. After that, I wasn't of much use in the quest for glory, and the invitations stopped coming. There is something to the old adage that "the number of one's relatives is not fixed; it rises and falls with one's fortunes."

As it happened, I went to Huizhou three times during 1987 anyway, without any local invitations, because three scholarly conferences related to my work were held there. I knew a bit about my Huizhou ancestors, and these trips allowed me to get reacquainted. My branch of the Fang family had lived in Huizhou until the generation of my paternal grandfather, who left the area in the late nineteenth century. My parents told me that he had set out for the city of Hangzhou all by himself when he was only seven or eight years old. He never returned, and by now I do not have a single verifiable relative living in Huizhou.

She County town, in the heart of Huizhou, had no modern buildings when I visited in 1987. The city gates and the streets looked like antiques, even fossils. The stream that flowed along the city wall was still crystal clear; it showed no sign of the pollution that the modern world had brought elsewhere. A stone bridge about three hundred feet long that spanned the stream had been built more than a hundred years earlier with funds donated by a wealthy widow, and its only sign of modernity was that an automobile occasionally passed over it. Most of the streets were still paved with stone slabs, not asphalt. The most conspicuous structure on the city's main street was a great stone arch, blackened by time, a monument to the eternal glory of a lettered family that had produced a scholar who had once scored highest in the imperial examinations and had entered the emperor's personal secretariat, the revered Hanlin Academy.

The Huizhou region had produced many scholars. Traditional Chinese literati honored "the four essential tools"—paper, writing brushes, ink, and ink stones—and Huizhou or its environs were famous for producing prized varieties of three of the four: Xuan paper, Hui ink, and Hu brushes. I cannot, alas, find any evidence that the Fangs of Huizhou ever produced an outstanding scholar. (My research may be insufficient here; I may be sullying my ancestors.) Anyway, to the extent to which I myself can be called an intellectual, it's probably not because of any genes I inherited from Huizhou Fangs.

"Genetic inheritance," in Chinese thinking, can fall under the heading of "it has always been that way." The general principle is that for any phenomenon whatsoever, if you can find something in the past that resembles it, then you have an airtight explanation for why it exists today. This reasoning cannot explain why I turned out to be an astrophysicist. But, according to some people, it *can* explain why I was expelled from the Communist Party and fired from my job in 1987. It was an example of "it has always been that way."

The specific reference here was to Fang La, probably the most famous of the Fangs of Huizhou, who was executed in the year 1121 after leading a rebellion against the Song Dynasty. The rebellion arose in Huizhou and at its peak spread to parts of Anhui, Jiangsu, Zhejiang, and Jiangxi Provinces; then it lost steam and shrank back to Huizhou, where Fang La was eventually captured and killed. For some of my friends, this story from history became the basis for their "hypothesis" that Fang Lizhi's rebellious streak toward China's ruling regime is an inheritance from his distinguished rebel forebear, Fang La. Accordingly, during one of those 1987 conferences in Huizhou, they decided to "test" their hypothesis by organizing a trip, and inviting me along, to the Qiyun Mountains in Yi County, to the Cavern of Fang La—which was said to have been the rebel's last stronghold.

The cavern itself is not very big and is located on a steep cliff that is difficult to ascend. One can see why it was an ideal place for a last stand—it was hard to attack and easy to defend. Inside the cavern there was no longer any evidence of spear or scimitar, blood or rage; the only faint signs of anything at all were some charred rocks, but who could say whether those were from the fires of Fang La or from more recent visitors?

The only trail to the cavern passes by a stone monument that has been erected to the intrepid rebel. The stone is a homely thing, sturdy and thick, and its inscription is in coarse, unrefined calligraphy. Still, there is no denying that this was the largest monument of any kind to any Fang of Huizhou, and even though it was well known that Fang La had been little more than a big bandit, that "hypothesis" about my being his descendant still lurked in my mind. So I stopped next to the monument and allowed my friends to take a few photos. But the question of whether I was biologically descended from Fang La is something I never seriously looked into. After the visit to Huizhou, my interest in the question dwindled.

My grandfather was neither a Huizhou literatus nor a rebel like Fang La, but a merchant. Huizhou has a long, proud tradition of commerce. This is a strange fact, because the Huizhou area, with its rugged hills and winding roads, is not transportation-friendly. The first railroad line was completed only in 1987—and it ran no express trains. But no matter: for about six centuries, Huizhou commerce was sufficiently dominant in the middle and lower reaches of the Yangzi River that the term "Hui merchants" became standard in historical records.

Commerce is also what led Huizhou people to begin migrating away from their native places. My grandfather, when he moved from Huizhou to Hangzhou, was part of a small tide.

I never met my grandfather; he died several years before I was born. To me he was always a sort of legend. I don't even know exactly what all of his given and assumed names were. What I do know is that I never heard anything but praise for him from my parents or from anyone else in their generation. They all told me how Grandfather, while still very young, left She County to work as an apprentice to a Hui merchant in Hangzhou and how, being smart, hardworking, and ready to help others, he had thrived and prospered until, in his later years, he was owner of several businesses. In terms of class analysis, he was an early-stage capitalist.

This question of his "class background" lingers in my mind for a special reason. When I joined the Communist Party in the early 1950s, my grandfather's class status and history were the grounds on which I gave him some severe posthumous tongue-lashings. Even though he was long gone by the time I grew up, and even though I inherited nothing from him (after his death his wealth dissipated fairly quickly among his relatives and friends), my blood relationship with him still made me the "grandson of a Hui merchant." In Marxism, merchants are exploiters and must be denounced. My grandfather especially needed to be denounced because one of his businesses was a pawnshop, and pawnshops were super-exploitative things that deserved nothing but eradication. (Actually, what Chinese pawnshops did was only a more primitive form of the secured lending that banks do today.) The purpose of my denunciations of my grandfather when I joined the Party was to repudiate the class inheritance that he presumably had passed on to me. In fact, his actual influence on me had been no greater than that of Fang La.

If my impressions of my grandfather are sketchy, this in part is because my father himself was young when he left my grandfather's home in Hangzhou and headed to Beijing. My father, Fang Chengpu (also named Fang Xingsun), was born in 1912, the year after the Qing Dynasty fell and the first year of the Republic of China. China's ancient culture seemed to be falling apart in those years, and my father decided to make a break with his family's traditions in commerce. He chose study, and moreover chose to venture far from Hangzhou and do his studying in Beijing.

I have never been clear on exactly why he did this. I did have plenty of time in which to find out, because, during the forty-seven years between my birth in 1936 and his death in 1983, we were never far apart. But he rarely spoke to us children about his personal history, especially about his thinking during his youth, so I can't even say whether his early attraction to Beijing was to the old Beijing or to the new Beijing. Beijing in the 1920s contained the oldest of China and the newest, the most conservative and the most progressive. It was the repository of the culture that the capital of an empire had accumulated during seven centuries of dynastic rule; but it was also the birthplace of China's modern scholarship and the fount of new trends in thought. Which of these two had attracted my father? Both, perhaps? By the time I was old enough to wonder such things, I could never observe him saying anything that was either especially conservative or particularly radical. His philosophy toward the world, which remained remarkably consistent through all kinds of ups and downs, seemed to be: pay no attention, do not care, don't be moved, don't get involved. But on the other hand, *something* must have caused him to set out for Beijing—alone, and only sixteen years old—to study. His move was not necessarily the boldest the Fang clan had ever seen, but it was highly unusual. Almost all the other offspring of my grandfather's extended family stuck close to the patriarch in Hangzhou.

My mother, Shi Peiji, married into the family and then became one of the ones who stuck close to the patriarch. She lived inside my grandfather's Hangzhou household while my father went to the university in Beijing. Both of my elder brothers, Fang Nianzhi and Fang Fuzhi, were born inside that patriarchal home. But then my grandfather died and his wealth quickly disappeared. My father, who had been relying on my grandfather to finance his studies, could no longer make ends meet and had to quit. He left the university in 1934 and, looking for ways to support himself, eventually found a job with the Ministry of Railways. He brought my mother and brothers to Beijing and set up his own separate little household. I was the first of my siblings to be born in Beijing.

For that reason I never got more than vague impressions of life in a big traditional-style Chinese family. In Beijing we were a small family and didn't even have any relatives living in the vicinity. We children saw none of the comings and goings of kin that are a normal part of Chinese big-family life. It was only when I visited Hangzhou that I got a better sense of my extended family—or, at least, a sense of what it once had been. Even now when I go back to Hangzhou, or even to the general area of Hangzhou, I get the sense of being immersed in a sea of relatives who appear and disappear under various labels—Younger Male Cousin This, Second Maternal Auntie That, and so on. All four of my grandparents lived in Hangzhou, and they seem to have had descendants of every possible kind. To make matters worse, there were all sorts of lateral interconnections. I often felt embarrassed to meet my relatives because I wasn't sure exactly how I was related—and this mattered, because it meant I didn't know the right word in Chinese to use in addressing them. For someone like me, who grew up in a nuclear family, the complex web of family nomenclature was always somewhat mystifying. This also might be why, every time I tried to read the great Chinese novel *Dream of the Red Chamber*, I never got very far. All those family relationships, and the complex network in which they were embedded, seemed alien to me, hard to empathize with—and hence boring.

I don't know how much the ethical values in Chinese tradition have to do with these complex family networks, and I am not sure, either, that they represent the "essence" of Chinese culture. I do know that I am grateful to my parents for the wonderfully simple environment—parents and siblings only—in which I grew up.

Family webs aside, I have always been very fond of Hangzhou. Other than the cities in which I have worked, it is the one with which I am most familiar. In my youth, my siblings and I often traveled from Beijing to Hangzhou to visit my grandparents; later on, we brought our aging mother to visit her relatives there. The Hangzhou rail station became a very familiar place to me. My parents' wedding took place in the Hangzhou rail station hotel.

Their marriage was arranged by their families. This was the norm at the time. But the wedding photos show my mother in a white Western-style gown, not the flowery red dress of Chinese tradition.

My mother, born in 1911, was a year older than my father. Her impulses were different from his, too. She went to high school—a bold move for a woman in her day—and told me that during the Northern Expedition in 1926, she and some female classmates took to the streets chanting slogans like "Down with the foreign powers and out with the warlords!" If the guiding principle of my father's philosophy was "Stay the same no matter what happens around you," my mother's principle was "Watch what happens and make a difference." In the several decades I spent with my father, I could not notice even a slight change in the way he approached life. He never spoke of making any difference; he didn't even express opinions on events in the news. The only thing I ever saw him get exercised about—and this was only rarely—was the need for a drink. By contrast, my mother could, and did, change her life patterns radically as different needs arose. She surprised us. At first she seemed to us only an ordinary mom and housewife, but in the 1950s she suddenly turned into things like

National Model Worker in Childhood Education and Delegate to the All-China Women's Federation. But then later on, just as abruptly, she set activities like those aside and went back to being an ordinary housewife—or house granny, I should say, because she took charge of the third generation, my children and those of my siblings—ten altogether, on her second go-round at parenting, after six of her own. My word "ordinary" of course is not right.

Where my mother got her activist philosophy is a puzzle to me. Her family story is even more convoluted and hard to figure out than my father's. Her father was from Huzhou, famous for its writing brushes. But neither he nor his wife—my grandmother—spoke with a pure Zhejiang accent. My grandmother had a strong Cantonese twang that announced to anyone within earshot that she had grown up somewhere in Guangdong. My mother told me that she herself grew up not in Hangzhou but in Sichuan. Her taste for spicy food, which she passed on to me, is probably a result of her childhood there.

Both of my grandparents on my mother's side must have been from the families of officials, or at least of government clerks or secretaries. This would be the only way to explain why they had lived in different places and had absorbed such different accents. My mother once mentioned to me that her father had told her that his branch of the Shi family included the famous Shi Kefa, who had defended the city of Yangzhou during the fall of the Ming Dynasty in the 1640s. But this might have been just family lore—a way to enhance clan glory or to establish how long the unbroken line of officials was in the Shi family. In any case, my mother said that her father had served in official posts at the county and province levels during the early Republican years, and this must have been right, because she followed him both to Jiangxi and to Sichuan, and that would not have happened unless he had held posts at the county level or higher. My clearest childhood impression of my mother's father, as relayed through my mother, was that he had blue eyes that could strike terror into people when he got angry. Later I met him and saw that, sure enough, he did have gleaming dark-blue eyes.

Even though we often stayed with my grandfather during childhood visits to Hangzhou, I have very few personal recollections of him other than the austere presence that he projected. He had given himself the name Shi Jiulong (Nine Dragons Shi), apparently to reinforce his gravitas. He walked with a slight limp, which was said to be the result of an injury sustained in falling off a train, but to us it only added to his authoritative air. He lived separately from his wife, which I think was the result of his keeping too many mistresses. During his later years, the last of these women moved in to live with him. My mother addressed her as "New Auntie," and we children called her "Little Granny." We knew that she had no children, but knew nothing else about her.

In short, my ancestral family in Hangzhou, in my child's mind, was always hazy and mysterious. I was aware that its members were supposed to be my nearest and dearest, and I knew, too, that my two brothers had been born in the Hangzhou home. But it all seemed extremely distant compared to my Beijing home. The extended family seemed too large, and unfathomable. The buildings that the family inhabited seemed unfathomable, too.

The Hangzhou homes of both sets of my grandparents were near Chengtou Xiang. A bit more than a hundred years ago, Hangzhou was the scene of ferocious battles between the Taiping rebels and the Qing rulers. Most of the structures in the city were burned or demolished. After the devastation, the whole Chengtou Xiang area was rebuilt, and from then on it remained largely intact and unchanged. By the time I visited my grandparents' homes, the neighborhoods were almost a hundred years old. Their wooden door frames, window casings, and gutters were black and decaying, and some of the walls tilted to one side. Once the resplendent homes of officials, they now exuded gloom. The courtyards were small, and the paths and corridors that led to them were sinuous and complicated. To a child like me, who was accustomed to simple rooms in a single house, all of this seemed darkly terrifying. My mother was not superstitious, and in our daily lives in Beijing she never showed any sign of belief in ghosts or spirits; but every time she spoke to us of the family home in Hangzhou, she insisted that she had seen ghosts in it. I do not believe that she really saw ghosts; but I do believe that, growing up inside that dark and dilapidated, deep and unfathomable hundred-year-old mansion, with its crooked corridors and slanting walls, she honestly thought that she had.

I thank my parents for letting me be born in a place free from infestation by ghosts. I was born in Beijing, away from all of those fetters and shadows.

My father died in March 1983, and we deposited his ashes in the mourning hall of a cemetery near Babaoshan on the western outskirts of Beijing. Within a month I began—subconsciously at first—to feel uneasy about this decision. Should his ashes be in a mourning hall in Beijing, physically so far from those of family and friends? I discussed the matter with my mother, who agreed with me, so I insisted that we send the ashes back to Hangzhou. The experience made me realize how deeply the notion that "Hangzhou is home" had sunk into my consciousness, even though I had not grown up there. In May, when Li Shuxian and I were invited to give lectures at Hangzhou University, we took the opportunity to bring my father's ashes along with us, and, bringing my mother, too, we deposited them in his native place, where they belong.

I personally selected my father's final resting place on a slope in the South Mountains, to the southeast of Hangzhou city. The site is in the shade of some pine trees halfway up Yuhuang Mountain. Our stone monument to him is backed by the mountain, on the other side of which lies the famous West Lake. Lying before it is the wide Qiantang River, along whose banks run the tracks of the Zhejiang–Jiangxi rail line. As I stood in the cool mountain breezes that wafted by, gazed at glittering ripples on the river in the distance, and felt the stillness that was broken only by the occasional low rumble of a passing train, my subconscious unease about my father's loneliness melted completely away. He had given me my life in Beijing, and I had now brought his spirit back to his home.

On our lecture trip, Li Shuxian and I did not stay in the old family home. My grandparents had all passed away by then, and we stayed in a modern hotel. As I sensed a new distance from the old family, I also felt, strangely, more intimate toward Hangzhou as a city. Perhaps it was the release from the burdens of family protocol, which had been so constricting during my youth, that finally allowed me to enjoy the beauty of my parents' hometown.

Hangzhou has, of course, always been beautiful. On this trip the feelings came over me that I knew the beauty of the city and that it indeed was my hometown. I remembered times when our mother brought us to the shores of West Lake. It was so much prettier than the lake at the Summer Palace in Beijing, with its presumptuous airs of imperial power. At the West Lake shore, what lay before you were mountains and the glittering lake, crisscrossed with pleasure boats and reflecting the images of pagodas, the whole scene as leisured and pleasant as you could imagine; behind you were rows of shops of every color, offering exquisite local crafts, as fine and brilliant as were to be had. I recalled a time, before I was even ten, coming to West Lake with cousins and going out in a boat to harvest water chestnuts. They were so plentiful at the time, and so easy to harvest! I remember, too, the first time I climbed Chenghuang Mountain to visit its famous temple, of which my deepest impressions as a child were of its two guard-demons outside—terrifying but simultaneously comical, because one was painted a ridiculously white white and the other a ridiculously black black.

Gu Mountain, or "Mount Isolate," which stood at the end of White Dike, had always attracted Hangzhou's literati. I wonder if my father's attitude of transcendence might have originated there, in the Pavilion for Releasing Cranes. He used to bring me to Mount Isolate to visit the famous literati engraving club called the Xileng Seal Society. He liked to go there because he was a collector of seals as well as an engraver himself. It was under his influence that I, too, learned how to carve seals—not to the level of the Xileng Society, of course; but still, if you were to trace things back, I would count as a disciple in that tradition.

There were places in Hangzhou that had been off-limits to me as a child. During our 1983 visit, our hosts at Hangzhou University brought us to see one of them. It was Wangzhuang, formerly one of Mao Zedong's vacation villas. Mao had been dead for several years, but it still remained closed to the public. Our hosts had to use special connections to get us into the mysterious place. It lay on a large plot of sheltered lakeshore and was enveloped by thick bamboo, through the shifting leaves of which the lake was visible. It was said that Mao, on one of his visits, had gotten out of his car and casually commented that "the wind is really brisk here," after which the building was expanded so that, on its next approach, the chairman's vehicle could be driven directly inside it. And in fact, the main building was huge. (The quarters that had been used by Mao's bodyguards were being converted into a hotel for ordinary citizens.) If one peers across the lake from Wangzhuang, one can get a glimpse of Mao's other villa (he had two in Hangzhou); the other one was Liuzhuang, which a few decades earlier had been Chiang Kai-shek's vacation palace.

The breezes on West Lake always carry a gentle bouquet that arises from the combination of the lotus, water chestnut, and floating duckweed that live in the lake. At Wangzhuang, the scent of bamboo added to the pleasant aroma. The mud at the bottom of the lake, on the other hand, was not so pleasant. Lotus and water chestnut plants, no matter how fragrant at the surface, die and rot as all plants do, sink to the bottom, and, if you dig them up, stink. As they lie on the bottom, though, they do no harm to the pleasant scent at the water's surface; indeed they supply the nutrient-rich mud that nourishes the next generation of fragrant lotuses and water chestnuts. Out with the old, in with the new—nature's cycle is so reasonable, so fair. And how could the pleasant fragrance be kept so constant? Can we imagine what the lake would smell like if all the generations of lotus and water chestnut plants refused to sink to the bottom but just stayed, decaying, at the top?

The thought reminds me of China. The country's history is indeed very long. The ancestors are innumerable and their heroic accomplishments are even more uncountable; their accumulated glory cannot be denied. The only trouble is that, having passed away, they are unwilling to sink to the bottom of history's lake. The four-thousand-year-old legacy of China's glorious past still floats on top. We move only from "Confucius says . . ." to "Chairman Mao teaches us . . ." Does this allow growing room for new life? It is time for the masters of Wangzhuang and Liuzhuang (without asking whether it was fragrance or something else that they emitted during their lifetimes) to sink to the bottom of the lake and assist the mud in doing its thing. Just imagine what it would be like, on the day when China's first free election finally arrives, if all of the ancestors and heroes of the past were unwilling to step aside but crowded up to the ballot box to dominate the vote. Wouldn't that be our haunted house again, crowded with its ghosts and demons?

I honor my ancestors. I respect them. But they are too tired. It is time for them to sink to the bottom, be at rest, fertilize. The Leifeng Pagoda near Wangzhuang collapsed a few decades ago—struck by lightning, they say. It is also said that lightning is sly but fair: it tends to target dead trees and limbs, ones that are on the way out anyway, and does the same to the older and more decrepit of the buildings and towers that mankind has built. Nature has it right, I think: we should let collapse things that are ready to collapse, let rot the things that are rotting, and let die things ready to die, no matter how splendid their glory, be it real or false, once was. Even if we oppose the disintegration, we will fail. Eventually it will happen anyway.

I was lucky. I was born into a Beijing family that was a fresh off-shoot of a disintegrating clan from Huizhou and Hangzhou. None of my ancestors—from Fang La in a mountain holdout to the authentic war hero Shi Kefa, down to my paternal grandfather the savvy merchant and my maternal grandfather the triumphant government official—could use the glorious past to suffocate my chances to grow.

2. MY HOME IN BEIJING

From 1936 to 1952—until the age of sixteen—I lived in a family home in Beijing. At first there were five of us: two parents, two older brothers, and me. My eldest brother, Nianzhi, died young, and I have no memories of him. Then came Fuzhi (born 1934), then me. Later three sisters arrived: Yingzhi (born 1939), Yunzhi (born 1941), and Pingzhi (born 1946). This brought us to seven regular family members, but two more, my father's mother and a widowed aunt, also joined temporarily during the early 1940s. Those two ladies both eventually returned to the family home in Hangzhou.

If the value of a home environment were measured in the number of spectacular events it produced, then mine would rank very low. My first sixteen years, at least in my memory, were utterly ordinary—no dramatic ups or downs and nothing that I remember as either especially joyful or painful. Everything was routine: getting up in the morning, eating the breakfast that Mother had made, carrying to school the lunch that she had made, going to classes, and then coming home to eat the dinner she made. Life went on, year after year, like the turning of a dharma wheel: steady, unchanging, monotonous.

In the larger society, though, those sixteen years were anything but. They were filled with turmoil: the War of Resistance (World War II) from

1937 to 1945, the Chinese civil war from 1946 to 1949, and the Korean War that began in 1950. Beijing in those years had three different political authorities: the Japanese occupation government (1937–45), the Nationalists' "Northern Headquarters for the Extermination of Bandits" (1946–48), and, after the Pingjin Campaign in the winter of 1948–49, Communist rule. Hardly any Chinese household could avoid the scourge of war. Many families, especially in the major cities, saw disaster in varying kinds and degrees: interruption of schooling, unemployment, flight, exile. The living were forced apart, while those who died took their leaves forever. Our family, too, struggled to survive, but—call it a small miracle—my own childhood and adolescence somehow escaped major misfortune. For sixteen years I never had to miss a day of school, never had to flee anything, and never saw a dead body. The contrast with my later years, which were free of war but saw me knocked about by calamities of other kinds, makes me wonder about God's mischievousness in planning my life.

How can we explain the odd serenity of my youth? It was as if I were riding in Noah's ark. But who provided the protection? Heaven? Earth? Certain people? Protection in the outside world had something to do with the ancient city of Beijing, I think. The human protection came from my parents.

First, the outside protection. In the uncountable wars and invasions that Beijing has been through in its history, its inner city has almost always been spared. The war with Japan broke out at the Marco Polo Bridge on the southwest edge of Beijing in 1937, but guns and cannon during the following eight years of combat did not reach to the inner city. During the civil war, at one point, artillery was stationed throughout Beijing, but the firing ended after just a few salvos. At no time has the heart of Beijing experienced aerial bombardment or (until June 1989) massacre. Beijing was often the prize over which wars and battles raged, while the city itself, at the center, remained calm. Very few physical scars of war can be found inside Beijing. The most visible relic (which I found fascinating as a boy) was a broken arrow that was lodged in the wooden placard over the Xinhua gate at Zhongnanhai. It was said to have been shot there by the rebel leader Li Zicheng in 1644.

Indeed, Beijing seemed to have a magical deterrent power, something strong enough to deflect approaching disasters large or small. By entering the Forbidden City and standing inside that most expansive of the world's grand imperial palaces, one could sense this power, while appreciating as well one's own smallness and beginning to feel dominated. The ancient city, with its seven-hundred-year tradition as the center of an empire, had an intimidating dignity. This may be why fighters of wars and battles quailed as they approached Beijing, or were diverted to one side or another, bypassing the city's heart. However valorous in battle, invaders seemed reluctant to use Beijing as a battleground.

This strange power of Beijing does much to explain why its residents, especially those born and raised in the city, have such a visceral attachment to it and will do anything to stay there. The special Beijing draw, added to the natural conservatism of northerners in general, makes it no mystery that Beijing people tend to resemble their city itself: self-satisfied, stolid, immovable, and set in patterns that not even war can easily disrupt.

My parents were originally southerners and did not have the stay-put-at-all-costs mentality of Beijing natives. But when war arrived they made the same choice: respond to big change by refusing to change. I cannot say why they decided not to flee when the Japanese invaded Beijing in 1937; I was only one year old at the time. But in 1948, when the civil war was closing in on Beijing, I was twelve, and I can remember that many families were leaving the city. Wealthy families found it relatively easy to pick up and leave, and even not-so-wealthy families, like ours, were heading elsewhere to escape gunfire or, should the city fall under siege, famine. My parents had friends and relatives who lived more or less out of harm's way in parts of Jiangsu and Zhejiang, and we could have fled there if my parents had wished. But in the end they made the same decision as the diehard Beijingers: don't flee and don't move—just cling to your patch of hallowed ground. The result was that my childhood and adolescent years passed inside the eye of some raging storms.

We lived at three different addresses. The first, where I was born, was at Etiquette Alley in the Western City. I have no memory at all of the place. My earliest memories are of the second address, at Messenger Alley, also in the Western City. After the victory in the war with Japan, we moved again, this time to Libo Barracks in the Eastern City, and we did not move after that.

Beijing people paid a lot of attention to addresses. The city had been an imperial capital for seven hundred years, and its physical structure reflected a single purpose: service of the emperor and imperial power. An address said everything about a family's function and standing. Broadly speaking, the city had three regions: the inner city, the outer city, and the area outside the wall. The area outside the wall was for nondescript commoners; it was also the location of the barracks of the capital guards. The outer city was home to lower-ranking Beijing residents and was the bailiwick of street performers and entertainers, peddlers, vendors, and fortune-tellers—all sorts of people. It was also the red-light district and the imperial execution grounds. The inner city—which was a square about three miles on each side—was like a giant suite of offices. Its streets ran straight north and south, and east and west, like a coordinate grid. At the center, the grid's "origin," was the Hall of Great Harmony, the seat of the emperor, in the Forbidden City. An imaginary vertical line through that origin separated the Eastern City from the Western City. A family's address—its coordinates on the grid—said everything about its status within the grand suite of offices. In general, the closer to the origin, the higher the status and the more important the office—although, in general, the Eastern City somewhat outranked the Western City. The names of the various streets and alleys often reflected the ranks and duties of the imperial minions who lived on them.

By the time I grew up, the imperial system had officially been defunct for three decades, but the ethic of "who you are depends on where you live" remained very much alive. Our family's addresses broadly matched our social rank. The first address, Etiquette Alley, likely got its name because imperial servants in charge of ceremonial arrangements lived there. The second, Messenger Alley, was home to *baozi*, the couriers whose special role was to bring people good news—of promotions, success in civil service exams, the bestowal of imperial favors, and the like. In return for their good tidings, these runners expected big tips. One of our neighbors on Messenger Alley, just two doors away, was Cheng Yanqiu, one of the four great Peking Opera stars of the time. And this, too, was fitting:

in the imperial world, performers of Cheng's caliber were also good-news messengers of a kind: it was their duty to sing congratulations on birthdays and other festive occasions.

I can't say for sure what our third address, Libo Barracks, was all about. It may be that a detachment of special police agents was stationed there, because it was right next to Iron Lion Alley, which was hardly an ordinary place. Under Qing rule, Iron Lion Alley was headquarters for the Capital Defense Corps. It was where Sun Yat-sen stayed when he visited Beijing and the place from which the warlord Duan Qirui ruled Beijing in the mid-1920s. The massacre of March 18, 1926, when the Duan government opened fire and killed dozens of protesters, took place there. Later, during the Japanese occupation, it was also where the Japanese stationed their military police. In 1946 it was headquarters for the joint military command of the United States, the Nationalists, and the Communists. There were, in short, plenty of reasons why our street might have been "barracks."

All three of our addresses reflected our social standing within that still-imperial-flavored system. We were a bit below the middle and a bit higher than the bottom. Our financial condition was also roughly in that range. My father held ordinary posts in the Treasury Department of the Ministry of Railways until he eventually reached the level of section head. His salary, which in the 1930s was eighty silver dollars a month (about one fifth of what a university professor got) provided the entirety of our family's support. That left us hardly wealthy, but—at least as far as I can calculate in retrospect—in no dire need, either. The best evidence of "no dire need" is that I am alive today. Let me explain.

The aspect of my childhood that my mother later talked about most was the string of illnesses that I had during the first three years of my life. Whooping cough, dysentery, tuberculosis, water on the lungs—I had them all, and maybe some other things, too. Mother said that I once got so sick that she gave up hope that I could be revived. Infant mortality in China was common at the time, and "unrevivable children" were not unusual. Many families had had the experience, so I was lucky to have pulled through. I find it hard to believe, though, that my mother ever really did, as she said, give up hope, because she also told me that she was constantly taking me for treatment to the famed Peking Union Medical College

(PUMC) hospital. Even when I was going to college, doctors and nurses at PUMC could remember me. They asked my mother how I was doing and commented that they had yet to see another folder as thick as mine. At the time, PUMC was the best public hospital in Beijing, and the most expensive, too. So, obviously, if my parents could send me there—keeping me this side of "unrevivable"—they had to have been at least lower middle class financially. In later years my mother often commented that our family's living standards slipped steadily downward when my hospital treatments began costing so much. This attribution of the family's decline to my illnesses was, I think, my first encounter with unjust accusation. I say this because, beginning from age four, although I was never very strong, I did not get sick anymore. Other children my age were always getting infectious diseases, but I never did. Yet our family's living standards drifted downward anyway—so it's hard to argue a causal relation.

The main reason for our declining living standards was war. The years from 1944 to 1949 (the final years of the war with Japan plus the years of the civil war) were the toughest for us. I remember how every year in autumn, right before school began, my mother had to run around trying to pawn things or to borrow money in order to scrape up our school tuition. Getting past the opening day of school was always a challenge, but we never did, in fact, miss a day of school. At Messenger Alley our whole family—two parents, five children, a grandmother, and an aunt—squeezed into two bedrooms of a total of about 325 square feet, where we lived more or less like war refugees. We children never understood our family finances, because Mother sealed this information from us. She was especially careful not to let any of her money worries leak to us, because she was afraid of distracting us from our studies. Occasionally—when she looked anxious or suddenly went rushing around—we could sense her tension. But we didn't know the reasons, and eventually the tension went away. She drew on her own inner strength in order to carve out and protect a miniature stress-free world for us.

In the fall of 1948 the civil war reached Beijing. The city came under siege and commodity prices shot up, sometimes several times in a day. This caused people to hoard, which made everyone, both hoarders and nonhoarders, very nervous. Mother still tried to protect our separate little world at home, but I was twelve now, and she could no longer keep everything from me. I could see the hazards for myself. Many of my classmates and other children in the neighborhood were helping their families to make money to get through the tough times, even as they continued with their schooling. Some did part-time labor; others peddled goods. This caused me, too, to feel a pressure to bear my share of the family burdens. I came up with the idea of hawking newspapers.

One day in November, around 4:00 p.m., I went to the outlet of the *China Evening News* and bought fifty copies of that day's paper at the wholesale price. Then, imitating paperboys I had seen, I walked north along East Fourth Avenue shouting, "Read the paper! Read the paper!" "Hurry and read the *Evening News*!" "Get all the important war news!" I was naturally gifted with a loud voice, the war news was indeed vital, and people did care about it, so the papers sold quickly. By the time I reached Jiaodaokou I had only one paper left. I decided to take it home and read it myself. In a bit more than two hours I had earned approximately enough money for one meal plus a newspaper. It was the first time in my life I had made any money. I handed the profit to my mother. She, though, was not enthusiastic about my being a paperboy, so that day marked both the beginning and the end of my career in that line. People who knew me were surprised (I myself was a bit surprised) that a scrawny kid like me, who normally did not talk much, all of a sudden found the nerve to go out on the street bellowing "Hurry and read the war news!" This facet of my character seems to have remained dormant for a number of decades. Not until the 1980s, when the government formally charged me with "inciting the public," did it reappear. When the government accusation arrived, it caused me to recall that strangely audacious paperboy. Inciter of the public? Hmm . . .

The problem was that my early home environment contained nothing that remotely resembled "incitement of the public." Father's philosophy was "stay away from every political party." This was not from fear, not from a wish to lie low for self-protection; it was just the way he was. His attitude toward us children was similar: ask nothing, say nothing. He almost never had anything to say about our studies, our character, or our social activities. He was true to his word never to join a political party, but when we showed interest in political organizations he expressed no disapproval, either. We had, in short, no support from him as we made our ways in life—but no opposition, either. His watchword seemed to be "Less is more." His friends called this "transcendence," but my mother thought it was laziness. In fact these two analyses may not be too far apart. The traditional Chinese ideals of "emptying one's will of desires" and "rising above the fray" may, in the end, have much in common with laziness and avoidance of trouble.

Mother's attitude, in contrast, was always to dive in. This difference between my parents had its internal logic. In those troubled times, no family of modest means could have survived if both parents had decided to "rise above it all and take no action." So one might say that it was Mother's bent for involvement that made Father's transcendence possible; or, put the other way, that while Father was transcending, Mother had no choice but to dive in.

Mother was much more skillful at social relations than Father. She was, first of all, a polyglot. To us children she spoke standard Mandarin, but with Father she spoke the Hangzhou dialect. She could speak Shanghainese and Sichuanese, too. She was also the only one in our family who could handle a musical instrument—the accordion. The rest of us were helpless with musical instruments. Mother's social skills made her the family's "foreign minister." She could take the pulse of what was going on around us. When any trendy new term appeared—in daily life, politics, or anything else—she knew it first. In later years, when I began to run into political problems, she could sniff out much of what something was all about even before I began to explain it to her.

Although Mother was very assertive with us children, she was not frightening, because we all could see that her only motive was that we do well, especially in school. She was always happy when we did well on tests, and doing well on tests was never anything that we found especially hard to do.

My siblings and I had different interests and seldom fought over who got what. My three sisters were close in age and usually played together, staying separate from my elder brother and me. My brother was much stronger than I physically and had a broader range of activities and a different group of friends. We went to the same school for ten years but didn't do much together. I was not, in sum, very close with any of my siblings, but we didn't get into each other's way, either. Mother showed no signs of favoritism among us. She very seldom resorted to spankings, and I cannot remember ever getting one myself. My sole memory of serious punishment from her is of one day—I think it was in 1945—when my brother and I went out to see a movie and didn't come home until late at night. Mother was furious, and our punishment was to stand facing a wall without moving. It was not that she disapproved of movies; she was afraid of the danger in our staying out after dark.

She was right that Beijing in those days was not safe at night. Most of the alleys had no streetlights—or just a few, scattered here and there. The nighttime security forces were watchmen who patrolled around banging on bamboo cylinders. We children were warned about kidnappers who abducted children to distant cities for sale. In local slang these kidnappers were called "flower patters," because the way they took control of children, it was said, was to pat them on their heads with a kind of drug that immediately befuddled their minds and caused them to follow the flower patter. Those words—"flower patter"—terrified me when I was little. Whenever I went out alone, I stayed as far as possible from the itinerant junk collectors who wandered the streets. It was said that there were flower patters among them.

One way of avoiding robbery in dark alleys, in those days, was to sing Peking Opera, or some other tune, in a very loud voice as one walked along. Both children and adults used this method. The theory was that if a mugger did his thing, the singing of course would stop—and that would alert neighbors, who could come to the rescue. This method may or may not have worked, but in any case it was common to hear Peking Opera in the alleyways, and love of opera was not the reason for it. It was all about boosting confidence. I did not use this "opera method" myself, because I invented my own, different method. This was to walk—strictly, without exception—close to the walls that lined Beijing alleys on either side. These were the dark areas, in the shadows, where the muggers themselves normally skulked around. My theory was that if I walked there the muggers would think that I was a mugger, too, and, since muggers are usually wary of other muggers, would leave me alone. Even now, whether on foot or on bicycle, I have a habit of sticking close to walls. This must be an unconscious vestige of that youthful "invention."

Other than the occasional hawker's cry or song for mugger deterrence, the streets of Beijing in the 1930s and early 1940s were usually dead quiet both day and night. Daily life for most people, especially in the lower classes, was not much different from rural life. The city's population had grown beyond a million, but living conditions in many ways were primitive. The unpaved alleys, as the locals said, "without wind, were three feet in dust; with rain, were a streetful of mud." Our address at Messenger Alley in the Western City was less than two miles, as the crow flies, from where the throne of the emperor had been—but we had no running water. Our drinking water came from a hawker who arrived every morning with his wooden tanker cart and who collected a fee once a month. Every family kept a large vat for drinking water. The alternative was to visit a nearby well to draw water, just as people in rural areas did. But we had no reason to feel sorry for ourselves, because the imperial palace had no running water, either. Water for the emperors had also been delivered by wooden tanker cart. Imperial water differed only in that it came from a special source—Jade Spring Mountain—that was reserved exclusively for the emperor's clan. When the empire collapsed, the tradition of delivering Jade Spring Mountain water to the highest rulers of the land did not. It persists to this day.

There were no sewers, either. At Messenger Alley we poured wastewater onto the base of a large tree. We took for granted the tree's ability to recycle. In winter, when the ground froze, the recycling function froze with it, and wastewater ice of various colors accumulated, layer upon layer, in one great sheet at the base of the tree. Many years later, when I read in the professional journals that comets are formed of dirty ice, that multicolored slab at Messenger Alley always sprang to mind. Looking at beautiful comet tails in the high heavens, I could not help thinking that they carried a certain stench.

In winter, coal dust was another source of pollution. People burned lumps of coal to heat their homes, and many dumped the ashes onto the streets, where eventually they formed great piles. In some places these mounds rose to a foot or two higher than the foundations of the houses. Coal dust is primarily silicon dioxide, which is extremely fine and light. When vehicles passed by the dust would fly up in the air and take a long time to settle back down again, turning Beijing, one might say, into the original Silicon Valley. My parents had been married in the south, where coal dust was not a problem, and they had chosen white furniture as their nuptial theme. Their tables, chairs, beds—even the little beds for us children—were white, or cream-colored. After its baptism in silicon dioxide, all this lovely furniture turned to a dignified Beijing gray.

In this and other ways we Fangs gradually morphed into Beijing people. Our roots may not have been as deep as those of the Peking Man that had been dug up at nearby Zhoukoudian, but in other ways we became fairly authentic. There was one little way, though, in which we were never the real thing: we traveled. Real Beijing people did not travel. They stayed put, and were happy to do so. Not only did they remain in Beijing; they didn't even move around inside Beijing very much. When we lived in the Western City, we had neighbors who seldom ventured into the Eastern City. Eastern City people didn't come over to the Western side very much, either. This immobility may have been a carryover from imperial times, when there were strict regulations that prohibited servants of the emperor from making informal contact with one another—because such association could become the basis for a rebellion or a coup. The regulations were gone by now, but the habits of life that they had shaped remained. Geographically, the Eastern City and Western City were separated only by the imperial palace and the Forbidden City—a distance of just over a mile. But if a resident of the Western City said, "I'm going to the Eastern City," it sounded about as serious as when someone today says, "I'm going on a journey." When I was in elementary school there were public trolleys connecting the Eastern and Western Cities, but I had classmates who had never been on one. Many residents of the inner city had never been to the outer city, and many outer city residents had never been outside the city walls. The two sides of the city walls were two different worlds.

My parents, though, broke with Beijing custom when it came to travel. My father was averse to motion by nature, but as a point of theory in rearing children he favored the principle that "travel is good." In the war-torn

1940s there was no such thing as a travel industry. War-related disruptions of transportation made people afraid to travel, and less-well-off families couldn't afford it in any case. For them, the only reason to travel was to flee war. Financially speaking, our family was in the class that could not afford travel, but there was a policy that the families of workers in the Ministry of Railways could ride the rails free of charge. My siblings and I took advantage of this rule during our summer recesses from school and (if war conditions permitted) traveled to our ancestral home in Hangzhou. At first our parents went with us, but later they trusted us to go by ourselves. Mother forbade us to walk on the Beijing streets in the dark of night, but she let us journey alone hundreds of miles to the south.

Today, eight hundred miles from Beijing down to Shanghai or Hangzhou seems nothing to speak of. But in the 1940s, with war raging, the trip was a major enterprise, and those journeys left me with impressions deeper than any others from my childhood.

The first trip I can remember was in 1941, when I was five years old and my mother took me to Nanjing, Shanghai, and Hangzhou. The trains stopped at the larger stations long enough for us to get off and buy things to eat. My most vivid impression, though, was not of any food we ate or people we saw. It was the discovery that different places have different odors. Hangzhou smelled like Hangzhou, Suzhou like Suzhou, and the Yangzi River like the Yangzi River. All different. Perhaps the olfactory sense of a child is sharper, more like a dog's, and a child's memory more capable of locking the distinctions in.

The trip from Beijing to Shanghai normally took two days, but it was longer if war intervened. In July 1949, my brother and I headed south on the new Tianjin–Shanghai line that had just opened. War still smoldered in the area, and it took two full days and nights to reach Pukou on the northern bank of the Yangzi River across from Nanjing. There, the whole train got ferried across the river on a barge and then proceeded toward Shanghai. The Nationalists' warplanes were still doing a lot of bombing in the Yangzi delta, and our train, to avoid being targeted, stopped during the daylight hours one day at a small station near Qixia Mountain. July in that area is torrid, and all the more so when one bakes inside a railroad car. Most of the other passengers were traveling on business, either official or commercial, and naturally were curious about my brother and me, two youngsters traveling alone. To be safe we had to disguise the fact that we were traveling for fun, because that sounded unlikely and therefore suspicious. (The civil war was brutal; it was normal for people to be suspicious of one another.) Whenever someone asked why we were traveling I deferred to my brother, who could respond with a fusillade of nonsense. He was better than I at that. I can no longer remember any of the words he used, but we did reach Shanghai safely.

It was when we departed Shanghai that we ran into trouble. After staying in the city for a few days with an aunt, we headed for Hangzhou to see our grandmother. No one saw us off. We went to the Shanghai North rail station alone, saw our train waiting at the platform—and then the world suddenly went haywire. People began running wildly. For a moment we had no idea what was going on, but then we heard someone yell "Strafing!" Next we heard a volley of gunfire. Then we, too, ran for our lives— outside the train station and all the way to a sheltered nook on Baoshan Road. We could still hear gunshots, and some were coming from very close by. After a few more minutes the gunfire stopped and quiet resumed. Later we learned what had happened. We had witnessed a low-flight strafing attack on the Shanghai rail station by Nationalist fighter planes based at the nearby Zhoushan Islands. The gunshots had been return fire from machine guns on the roofs of buildings near the station. After ten years of life during wartime, this was my closest encounter with actual fighting.

When we got back to Beijing, we related our war experience to our mother. It had been much more dangerous than our expedition, one night, to go see a movie. But this time she did not apply the punishment of making us stand and stare at a wall. She felt we had grown up.

3. ELEMENTARY SCHOOL IN OCCUPIED BEIJING

I FIRST WENT TO SCHOOL IN 1941. MY START WAS AT THE ELEMENTARY school attached to Beijing Normal University, where I was a student continuously for five and a half years, the first four and a half of which were during the Japanese occupation of north China.

I began at midyear—in the second term of first grade, when I was about two years younger than most of my classmates. My mother did this not because she thought I was some kind of wunderkind but because two younger sisters had been born and her hands were full enough. She needed to offload me. Nursery school was not an option, because there were no nursery schools in Beijing in those days. Wealthy families hired nannies to care for their small children, while poorer families just let them "graze" in the neighborhood on their own. My parents were in between: they couldn't afford nannies, but they also didn't approve of grazing, so they packed me off to first grade for want of a nursery school. My mother had two other grounds for her reasoning in the matter. One was that I was still weak from my childhood illnesses so wouldn't have enough energy to be seriously naughty at school and cause any embarrassment to her. The other was that the school was right next to where we lived on Messenger Alley. The gate was only about seventy feet away. Mother wasn't really concerned about whether I could catch up with my classmates. If I flunked, it wouldn't matter. Even if I flunked two years, I would still be at grade level for my age.

My progress in first grade mirrored the story of my physical health. From "perhaps unrevivable," my body had somehow pulled through to reach stasis, if not strength; in school, from a condition of "flunking would count as normal," I somehow muddled my way up to middling.

I don't have memories of getting help from my teachers in schoolwork during those years, but I do remember getting help with tying the belt strings of my pants. The toilets were outdoors and had no roofs, and in the frigid winters, my visits to the outhouse could be truly terrifying. My fingers got so cold that no matter how I fumbled I could not tie the belt strings when I was finished. If the school bell rang, calling us back to class, I panicked—which only made the fumbling worse. I would often have to run back to the classroom holding my pants up by hand. Since I was the youngest in the class—the shortest, too—I was assigned to the front row, where my predicament was obvious to all, including the teacher. In second grade I had a teacher named Hua. She was about the same age as my mother and was very kind in noticing my plight and helping with my belt strings. Even today I can picture her voice, face, and smile in vivid detail.

The class work, for children of normal intelligence, wasn't much harder than learning to tie belt strings. The main work in first and second grade was rote memorization of a few hundred, maybe a thousand, Chinese characters. We weren't asked to learn very much about what they meant. This might seem a cruel burden to put on young children—how can you expect them to memorize so many arbitrary line patterns?—but actually it is not. The memory function may be the most primitive element of human intelligence. It doesn't demand any logical processing and generates no great stress in young minds. Very few of my classmates had to stay behind in school because they couldn't memorize characters. I myself slipped through in the first and second grades, and that shows, I think, how hard it was to flunk. In third grade, when I learned how to use a dictionary and could look up characters on my own, my fear of characters went away.

Even though my grades were not great, most of the teachers liked me— at least that was the impression I got. (Teacher Hua, whom I have just mentioned, was one.) This may have been because I was physically small and weak, seemed generally naive and wide-eyed, and did what I was told. There was only one point on which I was disobedient. There are strict rules about the order in which the strokes must be made when one writes Chinese characters by hand. In general, one goes top to bottom and left to right. There are exceptions, but the exceptions are not optional: you still have to follow the prescribed order. Our work was marked wrong if we violated the order. I disobeyed when I wrote my surname Fang 方. I wrote the last two strokes right to left—officially backward. I did this because my father, before I ever went to school, had taught me the "secret" that writing the strokes in this order produces a prettier result. I had tried it myself and found that he was right. So I wrote the character that way and still do today, in the "secret" Fang family tradition.

In third grade my grades began to improve. I was usually around the bottom of the A group or near the top of the B group.

The Japanese occupation did not have much effect on our primary-level education. The closest thing that came to any influence occurred on Saturday mornings when the whole school gathered on an exercise field to listen to the Japanese emperor Hirohito's latest proclamations on the Greater East Asian War and the Pacific War. In fact, though, this was mostly just ceremony. I don't think any of us primary school students, no matter how many times we listened to the pompous but awkward Chinese language in those pronouncements, took anything away from them.

We began Japanese language in third grade. Our school got special attention from the Japanese authorities because it was attached to Beijing Normal University, a national standard-bearer in teacher training. Teachers were sent from Japan to our school both to teach Japanese and to keep an eye on things. I don't remember having any nationalist consciousness at all as a third-grader, still less any clear thoughts about "resisting Japan." But it certainly was true that we third-graders hated studying Japanese. After a full year of study I still had not mastered the fifty *kana* in the Japanese syllabary, and I was by no means the only third-grader in that position. There is something obviously abnormal in the fact that young minds that could memorize several thousand Chinese characters somehow could not soak up a mere fifty *hiragana* or *katakana*—things that in any case had been adapted from parts of those same Chinese characters. Every day at the beginning of Japanese class, we had to stand up and say "Sensei, ohayō gozaimasu!" ("Good morning, teacher!"). Later one of our mischievous classmates came up with "Sunzai, wo hayao geizai yimaoqian," which sounded sufficiently close to the original that the Japanese teachers still thought we were expressing our morning respects, even though to a Chinese ear it meant "I yawn and give you a dime, grand-son!" The phrase spread through the school; we all loved it. This prob-ably counts as my first participation in a political movement—resist Japan!—even though the glaring cowardice of the method is not some-thing I can be proud of.

Another example of our resisting Japan, which I now deeply regret, was to abuse a dog. Not far from our school there lived a low-ranking Japanese military officer who had one small child and one big dog. The animal was as militarist as its master and, to us schoolchildren, several times more intimidating. This led to a decision by a few of our physically larger classmates to beat the dog up. I was too small to be one of the beaters but went along to supply moral support. It turns out that ele-mentary students are more intelligent than dogs, and, in order to avoid detection by the master, we were able to lure the unwitting animal to a secluded corner under a wall, where five or six of my classmates, in a matter of seconds, broke one of its legs. Then we all whooped and fled. We were never discovered, and the dog, now crippled, was much less intimidating than before. This has been my only experience in life of joining a violent action.

Our feat of dog beating did not spring from any lofty principles about national independence; such thoughts were well beyond our understand-ing. Still less had we ever heard of things like principles of nonviolence. Our inspiration to beat the dog sprang more from a desire to imitate the righteous heroes in Chinese kung fu fiction. These are heroes who appear, as if from nowhere, to defend the downtrodden as a matter of principle—in our case, the principle was revenge against a beast that was menacing innocents. I can remember that it was around third grade that we chil-dren were first smitten by kung fu stories. We could read on our own by then, and kung fu books were the easiest to find, so those martial arts masters became the first heroes to occupy our imaginations. Between classes we used to play a game in which we aped them. We would pull our overcoats up onto our heads, half-covering our crowns, and then strut around kicking up fusses and picking make-believe fights in shows of kung fu bravado.

The Japanese occupation forces ruled elementary schools with a relatively gentle hand. Plenty of stories about how the Japanese were oppressing Chinese people circulated privately in those days, among us students as well as in our families at home. My parents often spoke of how one of my uncles had been burned to death by the Japanese. But nothing so fearful ever happened to us elementary school students. That scary dog was about as bad as it got. Only once did I ever come face-to-face with a Japanese soldier. That happened one day on West Fourth Avenue, right after a sudden declaration of martial law, when a detachment of Japanese soldiers—apparently led by a colonel or the like—passed by. Traffic immediately came to a halt while the soldiers formed rigid lines along the two sides of the street, as if preparing for a fierce battle. I was on a street corner waiting to cross when a Japanese soldier, holding a rifle with a bayonet attached, took a stand right in front of me. I could see the mettle of an occupier glinting in his eyes. There were, however, no Japanese soldiers like that at our school. What we heard at school were only things like "Japan and China hand in hand" and "Japan and China warm and close."

In school I was drawn personally into a "Japan-China friendship" activity involving the exchange of calligraphy. Elementary school curricula in Japan stressed the writing of Chinese characters—it was a required course. At one point the Japanese authorities decided to select examples of calligraphy by Chinese students under age ten and send them to Japan to exhibit as models for Japanese children to emulate. They hoped, as a secondary goal, that pen pal relationships between Japanese and Chinese children—"meeting friends through characters"—would naturally follow. I was drawn in because my father had taught me, before I ever went to school, to trace the characters of the master Yan Zhenqing (A.D. 709–785) from stone tablets. As a little boy I had been attracted to the "rhyme within the bones" in Yan's calligraphy, and I imitated it. This led to one of my pieces of calligraphy being selected for export to Japan. I can't remember if I ever heard back from any Japanese person of similar age expressing admiration for my calligraphy in the exalted fashion of Yan. But even if I had, it wouldn't have mattered much, because one of the goals of the Japanese authorities was to encourage Chinese children to read Japanese, which meant that any letter from a Japanese youngster would certainly have been written in Japanese and would therefore have been unreadable by me. My Japanese was well below the level of reading or writing letters. But that, in the end, may also have been for the best. If I had in fact become the pen pal of a Japanese child, then later, when the Cultural Revolution called in 1968 for "purifying class ranks," one more item—"communicating with the enemy"—would no doubt have been added to the list of my criminal activities.

Nearly forty years later, in 1981, I was visiting Kyoto University when a Japanese friend invited me to a performance of the tea ceremony. The hostess of the ceremony was a lover of Chinese calligraphy, and she insisted that I leave a few characters behind to commemorate the occasion. This caused me to remember that childhood exercise sheet that had once floated its way to Japan, and the memory helped me reattach to the particle of skill I had once possessed and to use it to satisfy the sincere request of this hostess.

Toward the end of the war, Japan's control was growing obviously weaker. By the time I was in the fourth and fifth grades, only one Japanese person was still at our school. Maybe the rest had all been drafted. This last Japanese person lived—alone—inside the school. He seemed to have no function in the Japanese system and he showed no trace of the arrogant-occupier attitude. When the Japanese surrendered he quietly disappeared. Only later did we learn that he was an "antiwar element" whom the Japanese authorities didn't trust to be a soldier. They permitted him only to teach Japanese in elementary school.

When I was in fourth grade, the meaning of abstract words like "fairness" and "justice" was just starting to come to me, and I could make only a bit of sense of recondite phrases like "the Imperial Army has turned an advance [won a battle]" or "all fighters became shattered jade [were badly defeated]." I still had no clear social or political awareness. I hadn't begun to mature in these ways, and I lagged far behind most of my classmates in them.

When I was in fourth grade, my brother was in sixth, and we were in the same school. We had parallel nicknames: "Big Square Bean" for him, "Little Square Bean" for me. (*Fang* means "square.") But our peer groups were entirely different. His group were budding activists. They knew how to make their own projection slides, and from time to time they put out their own little hand-copied newspaper. Its content did not reach to the big political and social issues of the day; it was limited, understandably, to the concerns of schoolchildren. But still, compared to the imperial droning we heard every Saturday on the exercise field, this was freedom—the real thing. In later years several of those youngsters in my brother's group rose to high positions. One became a minister of culture. Another was a deputy minister for film and television. Quite a few others reached the level of bureau chief or Party secretary. Their unusual gifts emerged early, one might say. To this day, this group of government ministers, university presidents, and Party secretaries holds elementary school reunions.

I was not part of a group like my brother's, but I used to have two good friends, Bai Daquan and Gu Bei. I say "used to" because, although I have never forgotten their names, I have completely lost touch with them and have no idea where they are. These two, Bai and Gu, were more than just good friends; we were secret sworn brothers.

Swearing brotherhood was nothing too unusual at the time. It was a gang culture that pervaded most of China—although in Beijing, where the imperial authority was strong, it was weaker than elsewhere. Beijing had no Blue Gang or Red Gang as Shanghai had, and no Elder Brother Society like the one in Sichuan. The brothers and sisters of the Boxers did arise briefly in Beijing, it is true; but the Boxers had the support of the imperial authority so were not "secret" in the classic sense. Short of forming gangs, though, the practice of swearing brotherhood or sisterhood was common in Beijing, even in elementary schools. Even the top leader in the country, Generalissimo Chiang Kai-shek, entered a sworn-brother relationship with his deputy commander Feng Yuxiang, and when the Communist Red Army passed through the Yi region on its famous Long March in the 1930s, the front commander Liu Bocheng opened a vein to exchange blood and swear brotherhood with the tribal leader Xiaoyedan. With sworn relationships as conspicuous as this (even between a "slave chieftain" and a

Communist?), it is hardly strange that their allure spread all the way down to us schoolchildren. We wanted to give it a try.

I can remember that afternoon in spring—I think it was in April—when Bai, Gu, and I made a secret visit to an obscure temple in Houhai Park to perform our brotherhood vows. We didn't ask what religion the temple belonged to, because that didn't matter; what mattered was only that a deity with notary power be available to witness our vows. In our ceremony, each of us placed a small paper card, on which we had inscribed the year and month of our birth, on the altar in front of the statue of the god; then we bowed to the god in unison and solemnly pronounced the words, "Not born on the same day, month, and year, but wish to die on the same day, month, and year." That did it; now we were sworn brothers. I can't remember whether we burned incense. I do remember that we began saying we were just like Liu Bei, Guan Yu, and Zhang Fei, the three famous heroes of Three Kingdoms lore, who swore brotherhood in a peach garden. In fourth grade we had yet to open *The Romance of the Three Kingdoms*; the lore came just from hearsay.

Another thing that I picked up from adults as a fourth-grader was newspaper publishing. Unfortunately I produced only one issue. There were no copying machines at the time, but I could use gelatin offset plates, which were what people used in those days to make a few copies of something. The technology was simple: using special ink, you wrote down on a piece of paper what you wanted to print. You then pressed that paper, ink side down, onto a gelatin slab and waited about half an hour for the ink to soak in. That gave you a gelatin master onto which you could press sheets of blank paper to produce copies. It worked for a dozen or so copies before the ink ran out. In my father's work at the Ministry of Railways he had to copy all kinds of charts and reports, and so he could take home a lot of used—but in many cases still usable—gelatin offset plates.

At first I just used the plates as toys. I experimented with different printing techniques, comparing the results. Then it dawned on me: Hey, I could print my own newspaper! It would look better—more official—than the newspaper the sixth-graders were doing, which was hand-copied or, at best, carbon-copied. So I appointed myself editor, copywriter, and publisher of the official newspaper of the fourth-grade class. I named the paper *Universal Truth Will Win* and wrote a lead article titled "Universal Truth Is Sure to Win." The issue also carried some news items about our class and about the school as a whole. It included a copyright page—just like the big, formal newspapers—that listed "Fang Lizhi, Editor," and so on. The spread was two A4 sheets of paper, about 11 by 17 inches. The distribution system consisted of my going to my classmates and handing them copies. But after this most satisfying of launches, the paper ceased publication. It was, like my "ceremony of swearing brotherhood," a one-shot deal.

Both events—swearing a brotherhood and publishing a newspaper—can be seen as a child learning to imitate adult behavior. The model in one case was from the third century A.D., and in the other from the twentieth century, but the impulse to imitate was similar.

When I grew older I came to realize that "universal truth will win" meant something different from what I had originally thought. I had picked up the phrase from my environment, where it was a product of the Japanese invasion. Here's what happened: The main Japanese slogan in China was "Greater East Asian Co-Prosperity Sphere," in which the word "co-prosperity" was a euphemism for the glaring fact of invasion. The cover was threadbare, though, so some of the Chinese who had opted to cooperate with the Japanese invented more palatable phrases, of which "universal truth will win" was one.

As a fourth-grader I had nowhere near the sophistication needed to perceive these subtleties, and I fell for the ploy. Every time we children went to Zhongshan Park I saw those famous words of Dr. Sun Yat-sen, *tianxia wei gong*—FAIRNESS THROUGHOUT THE WORLD—carved into a grand stone monument. The character *gong* (公), for "public" or "fair," was the same that appeared in *gongli zhansheng*, "universal truth will win." That coincidence made it even less likely that a fourth-grader could see the perfidy of the phrase.

"Universal truth will win" is hardly the only example of how the word *gong* has been abused in modern China. In 1958, Mao Zedong said his new communes would be *yi da, er gong*, "first, big; second, public"; and in the 1980s people were told to insist on the *gongyouzhi*, "system of public ownership." *Gong* has popped up all over modern China, deceiving not just fourth-graders but adults of many kinds as well. The word can mean "pub-lic" in words like *gongping* (公平), "fair," and *gongren* (公认), "publicly acknowledged," but it can also mean "lord," with a clear connotation of "male," in words like *wanggong* (王公), "king," or *gonghou* (公侯), "prince." Hence a phrase like *gongli* (公理), "principles that are *gong*," can mean either "principles accepted by all" or "principles of the sovereign." A phrase like *gongyouzhi* (公有制), "system of *gong* ownership," can be understood either as "system of ownership by the public" or "system of ownership by the ruler." So what exactly did Mao's slogans mean? The people who invented them kept this detail under their hats. If the slogans fooled somebody, that was the fault of the fooled. Anyone who had to get by in China, or to understand its society, had to master these subtle ambi-guities. Such mastery is immeasurably more difficult than memorizing a few thousand Chinese characters, which elementary school students do, because this word mastery requires more than memorization and more, even, than rules of rational inference. It requires an exquisite sensitivity to foul odor, trained many times more finely than even that of a hound dog.

This is why, in retrospect, I feel that my mistake in using the phrase "universal truth will win" can be forgiven.

In the end, the Japanese "universal truth" failed. I can remember the scene when news of the war victory reached me. It was on August 15, 1945, about eight o'clock in the evening. School was out for summer recess. I was with a group of boys about my age under a streetlight, playing a game of our own invention, when a shout rang out: "Japan has surrendered!" Someone listening to a radio broadcast of the Japanese emperor's surren-der edict apparently felt an urge to go to the window and yell the news.

I can't remember any spontaneous outpourings of joy over the matter. It may be that there weren't any, because, if there had been, we school-boys, who were always eager for such zest, would have been right there. Yet that shout of "Japan has surrendered!" in fact did not divert us much. It caused us to take a break from our game to get clear on what "surrender" meant, and then we just kept playing. It is worth noting a sharp contrast here with the people who had fled to the interior of China during the war. They often speak of their extreme and unforgettable excitement at the moment of Japan's surrender. I have seen scenes of such public exuberance myself in any number of documentary newsreels. Every time I saw or heard about these scenes I felt deeply embarrassed that my own reaction had been so different. I also felt anger: How could Beijing people be such inert duds? Even in victory they couldn't come out onto the streets and give a few shouts? I had to admit—although I didn't want to—that long-term exposure to occupation had caused Beijingers, at least in part, to accept a slave mentality.

And that was not new. Beijing had long led the country in the proportion of the population with a slave mentality. Even by the time I went to college in 1952, it was easy to find in the city servants and errand runners left over from Qing times. Some imperial eunuchs of various ranks were still around. Beijing slang has a colorful phrase for the insuperable sluggishness of people in this subculture: "Three fists can't pound out a silent fart." And indeed, to extend the hyperbole, one could wonder whether even a Hiroshima or Nagasaki atom bomb could pound out more than something like "It is heaven's will." I remember when Allied aircraft filled the skies in the days after Japan's surrender. Warplanes by the hundreds—P-51 Mustangs and B-29 Superfortresses—whistled and droned overhead, but some Beijingers, as they viewed the spectacle, said only that it reminded them of how crows fill the skies during winters. Now there's a silent fart for you.

It might seem paradoxical that by 1945, Beijing was also famous as a fount of discontent. It was where all of the important social and political movements of the preceding five decades had originated. To those of us who had grown up in Beijing, though, there was no paradox—we knew that there were two different Beijing communities and that they seldom spoke to each other. Beijing activism did not arise from native Beijing culture; it all came from students, scholars, and others who came into Beijing from elsewhere. Beginning with the reforms of Kang Youwei and Liang Qichao and the execution of Tan Sitong in the late 1890s down to the May Fourth movement in 1919 and to the March 18 massacre in 1926, none of the people who were killed, imprisoned, or forced into exile were native Beijingers; they were all from outside. The two groups in the city— the students and scholars, centered at the universities, and the traditional servants and lackeys, centered in the old imperial district—did not interact much. The main reason why the victory over Japan stimulated little excitement in Beijing was that the people in the university culture were still in the interior of China, in Chongqing and elsewhere, where they had fled from the Japanese. I was in Beijing throughout—from primary school to high school to college—and I have a very clear memory of the return of the activist culture after the watershed year of 1945.

In the fall of 1945, I was entering sixth grade. The first new concept we were all taught that fall was that China was now "restored"; we were receiving Restoration Education. During the past five years we had been getting slave education, and Restoration Education was something wholly different. It *was* different, too. The students and scholars who returned from the interior brought with them a new spirit.

My clearest memories of the new spirit are from music class. Until then, music had been my least favorite subject. I had music classes in each of my first five years in school but was always bored. The Fang household didn't have much music at home, either. All my father could do was intone a few poems in crusty old Hangzhou dialect: "I feel the moment, while flowers spill my tears; I grieve to depart, while birds chill my heart," and so on. He oscillated his head slightly to the left and then to the right to mark his rhythm—all very conscientious, but hardly inspiring. Mother knew some new-style songs from the May Fourth era, but it was forbidden to sing them under the Japanese occupation, and we wouldn't have dared to, in any case. Meanwhile the songs we learned in school were all in Japanese style, and I couldn't help feeling that they had something in common with my father's intoning of poetry. They had no melody, and no half-steps—just a recitation of syllables in a regular lilt. Forty years later I found some support for my youthful impression that Japanese singing resembled my father's. I heard Nō drama in Japan and was told that its style of singing, which had originated in the chanting of poetry, had been imported from China during the Tang Dynasty (A.D. 618–907). Singers of Nō, like my father, wagged their heads back and forth as they chanted. The angle of inclination was a bit different from my father's, but that's all. But then I thought, "So what?" After a thousand years, a bit of angle slippage could be pardoned.

According to an ancient Chinese proverb, listening to good music leaves one so smitten that one can no longer appreciate the taste of meat. I had always thought this to be an exaggeration—something, perhaps, thought up by a person who had eaten too much meat. But the music classes we got after Restoration opened my eyes to a whole new world of music. It was not a world that could take the place of meat eating—but neither could meat eating, in whatever amount, take the place of it. Our new music teacher was from Chongqing. He suffered severe sinusitis, which gave him a heavily nasal voice, and he often had to blow his nose during class. But he really sang well. For me, accustomed to the Tang Dynasty style of chanting, to hear his Western-style bel canto voice was to be startled that a human being could make such sounds. He was a strict teacher. To be sure that nobody could hide in the anonymity of the chorus, he made us sing one by one and made us repeat certain notes over and over so that he could pick out our mistakes and correct them. If I can sing at all today I owe it to him; more important, I began at that point to enjoy listening to song. Eventually I developed a bad habit, which many of my fellow astronomers, both Chinese and foreign, are familiar with: I sing in my sleep. The seed of this bad habit was planted by that teacher with the sonorous nose.

But he planted another seed, and this other one was incomparably more important to me. He taught us the song "On the Taihang Mountains," which begins:

> *The sun's red rays emblazon the morning sky,*
> *As the spirit of freedom pours into song.*

These lyrics not only transported my imagination; they also taught me that there was another kind of spirit in the world, a spirit different from the ones that were worshipped in the temples of peach gardens where people take brotherhood oaths. It was the spirit of freedom. This spirit asked for no kowtows from monks or nuns, no offerings of fish or meat.

And just like that, my own spirit was swept away in this dreamlike song.

4. MY PRIME MOVERS

ON THE LAST SUNDAY IN SEPTEMBER 1987, THERE WAS A CELEBRATION of the eightieth anniversary of the founding of my high school, the Beijing Fourth High School. This remarkable school began as an experiment in new-style education after the collapse of China's imperial civil service examinations in 1905. At first it was called Shuntian High School and took students only from the twenty-four counties of Shuntian prefecture. The name change to Fourth High School came with the 1911 revolution, and from then on students had to pass an exam to get in. The school was perennially one of the best in the city, and its eightieth-anniversary celebration made for an extraordinary gathering.

At nine in the morning, a crowd of three or four thousand Fourth High students, as young as current juniors and seniors and as old as alumni in their sixties and seventies, crowded onto the school's athletic field. The sunshine of early autumn was still intense enough to redden faces and draw perspiration from young and old alike, and this solar egalitarianism helped, along with the festive atmosphere, to erase all distinctions of age and occupation. Everyone was a Fourth High student—that was all that mattered.

Some of the liveliest people in the crowd were ones who had been known during their school years as troublemakers, and they were using the occasion to retell incidents of their misbehavior as glorious achievements. Practical jokes were remembered with relish, and the best stories brought rafter-rattling laughter. Spirits soared as alumni recalled what it was like before the fetters of adult life brought an end to an era when it was okay to be naughty. And true enough, I thought—high school indeed is a time when mischief is a sign of budding intelligence. If a reunion doesn't remember the mischief, what, exactly, would be more worth remembering?

My own record of mischief in both junior and senior high school was mediocre. After graduating from elementary school in 1946, I went into an ordinary Beijing junior high school. Standards in the ordinary schools were low, though, so I registered for the test to get into Fourth High. I began at Fourth High at midyear in seventh grade and stayed through twelfth. In 1952, when I graduated, I had been at Fourth High continuously for five and a half years, and this made me a full-fledged Fourth High alumnus—except, I have to admit, by the mischief standard. I had no record there. I was a rule follower.

On that morning in 1987, as I was reminiscing, with a certain regret, on my poor record in practical jokes, I was unaware that a huge one was brewing right under my nose.

It was about 10:30 a.m., and out on the athletic field the formal reunion program was already under way. Representatives of the classes, one by one, were going to the podium to say a few words. Wit of every kind, including political innuendo, was richly on display, and the audience loved it. But the mood changed abruptly when the chair of the event announced that we would hear next from a representative of the parents, Mr. Wang Zhen. The collective gulp was almost audible. This Mr. Wang was famous in intellectual circles—not just because he was about to assume the post of vice chair of the People's Republic of China, but because he had recently called for killing people. During the large political campaign in 1987 to "Oppose Bourgeois Liberalism," this man Wang, who had begun adult life as a bandit and later turned into a "Communist," had openly proposed "killing off a few hundred thousand" as the way to handle the bourgeois liberal intellectuals. And now *this* man, the astonished crowd was asking itself, is our "parental representative"?

If Wang, like the others that day, had chosen to reminisce—if he had shared stories about how he had robbed and pillaged during his bandit years—he might still have attracted an interested audience. But he did not, alas, know his strength, and instead of telling stories he actually tried to assume the pose of "the great parent" and preach to this group of current and former whiz kids. His oration, which floated free from both logic and grammar, served only to certify to his audience that, no, this person would not have gotten into Fourth High as a student. In short, in only a few moments he had made himself the perfect target for Fourth High pranksters. If they let such a golden opportunity slip by, when would there ever be a better one? Go for it!

And so it was, as the portentous Mr. Wang was reaching the zenith of his oration, that I noticed a number of youngish Fourth High graduates suddenly around me, pointing and grinning in my direction. *Uh-oh!* I thought. They're going to make me the star in a prank. That fear occurred to me because just a few months earlier, I had been expelled from the Communist Party for "bourgeois liberalism" and the news had dominated television broadcasts for many days on end; so now, if I was reading correctly what these pranksters were up to, I was headed into the whirlpool of bourgeois liberalism again. And sure enough, more and more young bourgeois liberals stopped paying attention to the great parent at the podium and started sidling over to me to ask for autographs. At first they came in a trickle, then in groups. The activity was distracting, and before long the student monitors who were in charge of keeping order came over, but on learning what it was about, they asked for autographs, too. Then even more people gathered. An entire wing of the audience now was not listening to Wang's speech at all. The two men chairing the event—the Communist Party secretary of Fourth High, who had been my classmate in school, and the vice principal, who had been two grades below me—could see that something was seriously wrong and hurried off stage to try to fix it. Setting aside our relationship as former schoolmates, they grabbed my arms like two policemen, one on the left, one on the right, and escorted me out. Their objective was to end the disturbance by removing the element that was causing it, but their own very conspicuous action only added fuel to the flames. Now a large group of students and alumni was crowding around, and when my escorts and I left the athletic field, this whole crowd went with us. The exodus was large enough that it looked like a planned event. So many people were crowding around me during those moments that I could not get a good look at how Mr. Wang, the killer parent, was doing up on stage. From what people told me later, I gather that the "disturbance" deflated his balloon almost completely.

After the kerfuffle I was stuck in the principal's office at Fourth High, signing autographs, until about 2:00 p.m. When I finally left and walked out of the campus, where so many unforgettable memories of my high school years were rooted, I took a moment to recall that this was the place where I had made two of the most basic choices in my life: physics and Communism. These two forces were the prime movers that determined most of the rest of my life. At first the two had seemed unrelated, but gradually it emerged that they were contradictory in their underlying natures. As their incompatibility became more obvious and intense over the ensuing years, I was turned, step by step, from the rule follower that I had been in my youth to a role player in "disturbances" like the one that had occurred today. This shift had happened because physics, like the other natural sciences, takes skepticism as a virtue, while Communism asks one to adopt unquestioning belief. This generated problems.

During the last three years of the 1940s—which for me were grades seven through nine—belief in Communism swept through China like the circular wind cloud that an atomic blast creates. On the battlefields, the People's Liberation Army seemed able to sweep away the Nationalist troops of the Kuomintang (KMT)—some surrendering, others fleeing— as if they were so much trash. The Communist armies could do this, moreover, without any heavy equipment, whereas the KMT troops had tanks and armored vehicles. The tide turned toward the Communists on the ideological battlefield even before it did on the physical battlefields. Almost all the intellectuals and college students became sympathizers, supporters, or even worshippers of Communism—even without reading any Marx, Engels, Hegel, or Feuerbach. The energy in their sympathies came much less from the discovery of new truth than from a wish to jettison a moribund regime.

The image and prestige of the KMT government and its leader, Chiang

Kai-shek, were fairly good when the war with Japan ended in 1945. At that time even Mao Zedong shouted "Long Live Generalissimo Chiang" in public. Very soon, though, incompetence, corruption, and a dictatorial style brought a nosedive in popular support for the KMT. Inflation was so bad that prices jumped more than once a day. People rushed to get rid of KMT banknotes before their value fell even further, and eventually the "get rid of it" mania extended to the KMT regime itself.

At first I was just a bystander to all this. My first direct experience came on the afternoon of May 22, 1947. It was a typical early-summer day in Beijing—windless, warm, and a great day for softball. After school a few of my friends and I went out to the athletic field (the same one where the "disturbance" I have just described would take place forty years later) to pick up a game. In the second inning, someone came running and shouting, "Police have surrounded the school!" We threw down our bats and ran over to the main building. A gaggle of students, from our school and others, were crowding around the auditorium. The police had already left, but some of the older students whom the police had clubbed were still there. Some heads were smeared with blood.

Asking around, I learned this: two days earlier, on May 20, students had demonstrated at the central government offices in Nanjing and were beaten by police. (This was known as the "May 20th Incident.") Now, on May 22, students from Peking, Tsinghua, Yenching, and Peiyang Universities had come to Fourth High for a rally in support of the Nanjing students and to tell the truth about what had happened on May 20. The Beijing authorities had ordered the police to break up the rally, and they did this by surrounding Fourth High and using ropes to tie down the students who were scheduled to speak. Some students had been wounded by bayonets. I had almost no political consciousness at the time and did not understand the political meaning of what was going on. But seeing the bloodied heads of students turned my sympathies unambiguously in their direction.

This early brush with politics did not pull me in much deeper, though. What consumed me at the time (other than softball) was a little-known book called *Youth Guide to the Manufacture of Electronic Devices*. It was about three hundred pages long and covered everything from how to install doorbells and light fixtures to how to make voltage converters and electric motors. It even told you how to build a radio. Fascinated, I followed every one of its recipes, start to finish. The book also introduced some scientific theory. The foundations of my understanding of electricity came from this book.

One of the first neat ideas that I grasped was that as long as you make extra-sure that a circuit is not complete, there is no danger at all in using your bare hands to touch a wire that can carry 220 volts. I used this knowledge to impress my peers and smaller children. There was a lot of publicity in those days about the dangers of electricity, and people had the idea that only a real expert could know how to handle an electric wire safely. So I devised a little performance, which was to casually (well—not so casually, actually) pick up a wire and let everyone see how unafraid I was. My younger audiences gaped in amazement and admiration. To them this was proof that I could overpower electricity. Even adults were impressed with my electrical credentials. When gadgets broke, they would bring them to me for repair.

The hardest part of building anything electrical, or repairing it, was finding parts. It was prohibitively expensive to buy new ones, so my main supply came from old or broken things that I found at home or in the homes of neighbors. Occasionally I cannibalized from devices that were still in use, and after that my family and neighbors had no choice but to rely on me, because I had changed the circuitry in their equipment and only I understood it. Another source for me was junk dealers who sold used radio parts, most of which were from Japanese or U.S. military equipment. The dealers spread these parts out on the ground, regardless of size or value, and from a distance the stuff looked like rubbish. But if you knew what you were doing there was treasure there. Some large capacitors that I found there were still useful to me even after I graduated from college.

During high school my mother always gave me lunch money, but I sometimes skipped lunch and saved the money to buy parts. My first radio was built from lunch money. My mother didn't know about the meal skipping until she saw the radio, and that brought me a good scolding. What angered her was not my deception, but the loss to my body of all those lunches. Actually, though, I hadn't lost much in total calories, because every time I skipped lunch I gorged myself at dinner—or, if I planned in advance, would fill up on a big breakfast. The pattern had the additional benefit of providing me with a useful ability: even today I can eat a huge meal and then skip one or two with no problem.

The pinnacle of my building electronic devices was a hyper-heterodyne radio receiver. The next natural step would have been a radio transmitter, but that was too dangerous. With the civil war on, any unofficial broadcast—even within the bandwidth designated for amateurs—could be suspected of passing messages for the Communists. This was my first experience of political intrusion upon a completely apolitical interest.

My grades weren't very good during my days of tinkering with radios. They hit bottom in seventh and eighth grade. I did pass, in both language and mathematics, but my grades were always in the low range. In eighth grade my score on the algebra final was only 60, and I almost had to stay back a year because of it. But then for some reason—I can't explain it—a change came over me in the summer between eighth and ninth grade. I was smitten by the elegant logic of plane geometry and spent the whole month and a half of summer recess in the company of a ninth-grade geometry textbook. I scoured every page and did every exercise, and after that my grades jumped dramatically. From ninth grade on, I hardly ever scored less than 100 in math.

Geometry didn't do much for my grades in Chinese, though. I still wasn't reading novels, even though some of my classmates were so deep into kung fu fiction—like *The Seven Knights and Five Braves* and *Swordsmen of the Sichuan Hills*—that they actually thought kung fu heroes existed and headed out into the remote mountains to find them and acquire their magical skills. Other classmates were reading the new fiction of May Fourth, especially Ba Jin's trilogy *Family, Spring,* and *Autumn*; but to me, at age twelve, these books were too much like *Dream of the Red Chamber*: a vast constellation of brothers, sisters, cousins, in-laws, maids, and young masters, most with their romantic entanglements—it was all way too exhausting! The only item I found mildly attractive in Chinese class was ancient poetry. The poems were only a few characters in length, and you could memorize them. Our ninth-grade Chinese teacher came out of the old-school tradition that stressed rote memorization, and he demanded it of us. If you couldn't recite you got a whack on the palm. The whack wasn't hard enough to hurt, but it was embarrassing. I never got whacked because I had mastered the secret of good performance: don't think of the meaning, just spit the syllables out, say them in rhythm, and whatever you do, don't stop—*piao-piao-he-suo-si, tian-di-yi-sha-ou*—until you are done. It always worked.

Once in a while—for other reasons—I did get palm whacks, but from ninth grade on I counted as a "good student."

I first took physics in ninth grade. Our teacher, Ms. Huang, was fresh from the physics department at Jinling College in Nanjing and was too young to keep the lid on a classroom of naughty boys. (Fourth High accepted only boys at the time.) A person needed a stern countenance to subdue such a group, and she didn't have one. One day, for example, she was trying to explain gas pressure. She used the example of a bicycle tire and went to the blackboard to sketch a tire and valve. Her valve, though, looked more like the piston of a steam engine, and for this we boys made huge fun of her behind her back. All of us rode bicycles—very rickety ones, usually—so we all knew about bicycle maintenance, and tires got deflated all the time. Nothing was more familiar to us than tire valves. Maybe our teacher didn't ride bicycles, so was sketching more from imagination than from rich experience like ours. Anyway, we all had great fun asking each other where one could buy a bicycle tire that looked like the one she had drawn. She was my first physics teacher, and I remember her fondly, both when I am repairing bicycles and when I am not.

Near the end of 1948 our school was forced to suspend classes for a month and a half. Beijing was under siege by the People's Liberation Army, and General Fu Zuoyi, the commander of the KMT's Northern Head-quarters for the Extermination of Bandits, expropriated the campus of Fourth High as an artillery base. Soldiers moved into our classrooms and then went to the athletic field (yes, that same athletic field), where they set up a dozen or so 100-millimeter cannons with which to bombard the Com-munist troops in the suburbs. We students were allowed onto the campus so long as we didn't go onto the athletic field. So much for softball.

It was during this extended break that I secretly joined the Federation of Democratic Youth (FDY). This was one of two front organizations (the other was called the Alliance of Democratic Youth) that the Communist Party set up to attract young people and to recruit activists. All Communist activity in the KMT-controlled areas during those years was underground; a Party member, if exposed, went to jail or was executed.

The two student front organizations worked mostly on university campuses. Fourth High was not a university, but it was famous (which is why Mr. Wang Zhen wanted to be a "parent" there), and it was located right next to the Peking University medical school. Fourth High witnessed as many student movements as most university campuses did, and it had underground members of the Communist Party and the FDY as early as anyone else. These groups had been the organizers of the May 22 demonstration.

One day in early 1949 I went to a school outhouse to urinate. The outhouses had no roofs, but other than that they were secluded places. A schoolmate about four or five years older was there, and no one else was, and at one point he turned to me and asked, "Would you like to join an organization?"

"What organization?" I asked.

"A revolutionary organization—one that belongs to us students."

"What would I have to do?" I asked.

"Nothing special, but you might learn something."

"Would I have to leave home? I wouldn't want to do that."

"No, you can stay at home."

We exchanged a few more words and then I said, "Okay, sounds good." The deal was done by the time we left the outhouse.

Two days later this classmate took me to a meeting at the Peking University medical school. A dozen or so Fourth High students, mostly upperclassmen, were already there. This group was FDY's secret branch at Fourth High, and I was introduced: "This is our new comrade, Fang Lizhi, from ninth grade, section D."

I knew very little about the revolutionary principles of the FDY except that it opposed the KMT. I can't remember if it had a charter. I had little sense of whether my actions were dangerous, but I did enjoy the mystique of joining a secret group. In any case, my decision meant, later on, that I had "joined the revolution" at age twelve. According to Chinese

Communist personnel regulations, anyone who had joined a Communist organization before the establishment of the People's Republic of China qualified as a "senior revolutionary cadre." So I was one, in theory. Later I read memoirs by other "senior revolutionary cadres" in which they told how everyone viewed them as boy geniuses and expressed amazement that they could grasp the truth of Communism at the tender age of twelve or thirteen. I was that age when I joined the FDY but (dare I admit this?) was not nearly so precocious. Moreover, I couldn't figure out how the precocious ones, way back then, had managed to get clear on those jargon-laden, German-flavored texts.

After I joined the FDY I found that I liked it, and I indeed did learn new things. The first long novel I ever read cover to cover was one the FDY recommended to me: Nicholas Ostrovsky's *How the Steel Was Tempered.* The author had been a soldier in the Soviet Red Army during the October revolution, and the book recounts his experiences before and after signing up to be a soldier. Everything in it was entirely new to me. The first time I read Marx and Engels's *The Communist Manifesto* was also with the FDY. It was hard to understand, but there was one line I really liked: "The proletarians have nothing to lose but their chains. They have a world to win." I wasn't in any chains yet, but the whole world? I wanted it! Step by step, I was drawn completely in. Before then I had had no political concepts. Communist concepts were my introduction to political thinking.

The siege of Beijing in the civil war ended peacefully on January 31, 1949. General Fu Zuoyi handed over his weapons (it wasn't called "surrender") and the People's Liberation Army entered the city to take over administration. Two or three weeks later, the FDY came up from underground and we all revealed our identities. On May 15, the Chinese New Democratic Youth League was officially established. The two groups that had been underground (the Federation of Democratic Youth and the Alliance of Democratic Youth) were folded into it, and any member of either group automatically became a member of the new League. All of us—a total of about five thousand in the city of Beijing—gathered in the auditorium of the engineering school at Peking University for the inauguration of the League and a collective swearing-in ceremony. The

League's charter stated that a person had to be fourteen to join. I was only thirteen. So at least in this one very small way, the charter was violated right from the start.

July 1, 1949, was the twenty-eighth anniversary of the founding of the Communist Party of China. The total victory of the Communists was imminent, and Mao Zedong himself was on his way to Beijing. On the evening of June 30 a huge celebration was scheduled at the Xiannongtan Stadium. Every Communist Party and Youth League member was invited, and by 7:00 p.m. we were all there. It was raining, and we were in an open-air stadium, but we couldn't have been more excited as we waited for Mao. People were not yet viewing him as a deity, but with the impending victory in the civil war—the sense that we were about to "get the whole world"—he was already a major hero. The rain seemed only to increase the excitement. Eventually we broke into dance—in part to keep warm, in part to express our joy. Finally—it was now past midnight, already the early hours of July 1—Mao Zedong, Liu Shaoqi, Zhou Enlai, and other Party leaders filed into the stadium. By then the rain was getting heavy, so their talks were short and the event ended quickly.

That was the first time I saw Mao and the other top Communist leaders. The next morning the major newspapers all carried Mao's article called "On the People's Democratic Dictatorship." Still aglow from the night before, I read it with special excitement and veneration. In that mood I could never have imagined that less than a decade later, a large number of young people (including me) who had been Mao's dancing followers at the Xiannongtan Stadium would become victims of this same "people's democratic dictatorship." Still less could I have conceived that the same dictatorship, in less than two decades, would bring an appalling death to Liu Shaoqi, the man who had been standing next to Mao and would soon be president of the country.

I was also present on October 1, 1949, at the great celebration of the founding of the People's Republic of China in Tiananmen Square. It is easy to find newsreels of this historic event, so I won't give a detailed description here. All of the major figures in Chinese history, including those whose roles in history were yet to arrive, and excluding only those who had escaped to Taiwan with Chiang Kai-shek, were there, splendidly attired, standing atop the Tiananmen Gate. Down below—although this does not show up very clearly in the newsreels—a crowd of more than a hundred thousand people had gathered. I was one of them. My attire, while not splendid, was trim. The formal program took less than an hour, and Mao Zedong's talk was its high point. Critics have later pointed out that Mao's historic speech drew applause from the high-ranking leaders and the honored guests on top of the Gate but apparently no cheers or jumping up and down from the masses below. To me, as an eyewitness, this is easy to explain. Tiananmen, although well known as a historic site, had never before been used to hold a giant meeting, and its broadcast equipment was far from ideal. It had no high-volume speakers. A lot of the people down in the Square couldn't hear a thing being said up on the podium.

The streets around Tiananmen were narrower than they are today, too, so when the big convocation was over, it took a long time to empty the square. Our group from Fourth High waited about three hours, until nearly 8:00 p.m., to leave. Mao Zedong clearly was in very high spirits, because he, too, lingered after the ceremony. He stood above the Gate watching each group leave, one by one. When our Fourth High contingent finally passed by, he shouted down, "Long Live Fourth High!" That sentence from the podium was the clearest one I heard all day.

My three years of high school following that "Long Live!" were, on the whole, calm. Every year on October 1 we returned to Tiananmen for another big celebration. Mao Zedong was always there, but the amount of time he stayed behind on the Gate got shorter year by year.

In the larger society, though, those three years were hardly calm. Class-struggle campaigns had already begun in the villages, even though the shock waves had not reached as far as urban high schools. Then there was the Korean War. Near the end of 1950 the Chinese People's Volunteer Army went to Korea to do battle with the United States and others, and the "Resist America, Aid Korea" campaign was launched in China. The war had a major impact on international relations and especially on power in East Asia, but it did not actually change life on the ground inside China very much. This may have been because that war, although fierce, was no match in scale for the war with Japan or the civil war. For people who had become accustomed to living through wars, this smaller one came as no particular shock. Moreover, China had been having wars with foreign powers for about a century now: Britain, France, Japan, and so on. So now it was America's turn. It was only natural. Everybody has to take a turn.

The Korean War did exert two effects on my high school life. One was that two dozen or so of my classmates joined the army, mostly to serve as technicians in specialties like artillery or aviation. The other was that we all began to resent English class. The reason was the same as the reason, a few years earlier, for balking at Japanese, the language of the occupiers. Now the Americans were the enemy, and English was their language.

My grades in the last three years of high school, in everything except English, improved steadily. I can't say why. It may have been simply that I matured during those years; but it also had to do with some wonderful teachers.

I started to do better even in Chinese composition, which was the subject that until then I had feared the most. Before my junior year, I had never written a composition longer than five hundred characters—not even enough to fill one page. These minimalist efforts had never earned me a good grade, either. Part of the problem was that I couldn't see why you should have to write more words in order to do well. In plane geometry, my first love, the whole point was to prove things as tersely and elegantly as possible. Why was it different in writing essays? But finally I caught on. I realized why it was, in the old civil service exams in China, that they tested only composition, never mathematics. That was because the point of the exams was to test a person's fitness to be an official, and the one skill an official needs, perhaps above all, is to blow up things from nothing. Math wasn't much help there.

In my junior and senior years I had a composition teacher who no longer asked that we pad our essays and who dismissed the artificial standard of "five hundred characters or more." Thus liberated, my essays actually started breaking through the five-hundred-character level and reached as high as five thousand. I started getting good grades, too. In 1986, a full thirty-four years after graduating from high school, I was still exchanging letters with that Chinese composition teacher. He still seemed able to recall my high school essays. I also tried my hand at poetry during high school, but it didn't work. For young people to write good poetry, some theorists say, there has to be stimulation and inspiration from the opposite sex. Fourth High was all boys. We didn't have any opposite-sex classmates. That must be why my poetry went nowhere.

I always did best in the sciences. My interest in radios waned as I began to get into topics with more theoretical depth. Instead of heading for junkyards after school, I spent a lot of time at the Beijing Library, China's largest at the time, and I found that I had a special liking for physics and mathematics. One day the topic in one of our algebra classes was "solving simultaneous inequalities." The teacher, aware of what I was learning at the library, let me do the explanations. The shame that I had been carrying because of that 60 I had received in eighth-grade algebra was wiped away in one fell swoop.

Even though I was a top student, especially in the sciences, I was never a mover or shaker among my classmates. A group interested in literature and art were the ones who generally called the shots. They were theater buffs, and they were super-active. Some of them later became directors of major Chinese film studios and drama troupes. They drew many of us classmates into helping with their productions, which ranged from simple one-act plays all the way to full-length dramas with several acts and many scenes. They attracted large, cheering audiences—sometimes as many as a thousand people. One of my best friends was the group's leader at one point, so I was naturally drawn in and spent considerable time studying how to "enter the role" according to the great Russian drama theorist Constantin Stanislavski. My conclusion was that you needed a gift in order to do that. I did get up on stage a few times, but no matter how conscientiously I studied Stanislavski's theories, I just couldn't bump myself into that "in the role" state. So my contributions to my classmates' drama projects gradually settled into errand running and logistics. I choreographed music, hid behind the scenery as a prompter, and did special effects. I especially enjoyed the latter, because to me this amounted to applied physics and chemistry. My repertoire of simulations included the light of fires (both near and distant), lightning, smoke, fog, thunder (both near and distant), rasping wind, and croaking frogs.

I was, in short, a "behind-the-scenes manipulator."*

Sometimes our drama troupe managed to cast a spell over an audience. In those moments I would look at my classmates up there on stage, "inside the role," weeping, wailing, and producing tears as required by the structure of the drama; and I would also see, among the theatergoers below, people who were moved by genuine feelings and who were shedding authentic tears. From my vantage point behind the curtain, seeing the contrast between the artifice on stage and the sincerity below, truth and falsity in a mirror, I appreciated how powerful drama could be. No wonder human civilization, from its beginnings, had always had drama, both tragic and comedic. There was no way physics could compete with this.

Still, I preferred physics.

Every high school student who took the college entrance exams in those days was allowed to list three preferences for a postsecondary major. I wrote down: physics, mathematics, astronomy. I was accepted into the physics department at Peking University.

---

*Translator's note: In the spring of 1989, the Chinese state media named Fang a "behind-the-scenes manipulator" of the "turmoil" at Tiananmen Square.

5. ON CAMPUS AT PEKING UNIVERSITY

THE COLLEGES OF PEKING UNIVERSITY ORIGINATED IN DIFFERENT parts of the city—Arts and Sciences at Shatan, Medicine at Xishiku, and Engineering in Chengnan. In 1952 the university was reorganized and the three parts were brought together in the suburbs, on the campus of the recently vacated Yenching University. That location was known as Yan Garden.

My freshman class was the first to go to Yan Garden. I showed up in the fall of 1952 carrying books, supplies, and a few articles of clothing, an eager first-year student in the physics department. The male student dormitory for our class was not yet ready, so we were assigned to the gymnasium next to the Nameless Lake. Several hundred of us crowded together there, on a basketball court. There were no beds; we slept on the floor. There were no tables or chairs, either, so we sat on the floor to read and to do our homework. But these living conditions did not detract in the slightest from the glow I felt inside; Peking University was where I had always dreamed of being.

When you think about it, there is something odd in the fact that Peking University, the oldest and most famous in China, was not even a hundred years old at the time. China's civilization was among the first in the world to emphasize education; more than two thousand years ago Confucius was preaching that "learning benefits all." But universities? Europe's are much older than China's. Even the wilds of Western Australia have a university that is older than the oldest one in China.

The reason, I'm afraid, is that China's rulers in ancient times were (much as they are today) aware that universities could be sources of different views and therefore threats to their rule. In the first century B.C., Emperor Wu of the Han Dynasty founded an imperial academy—something we might think of as China's first "national university." The school grew steadily until, a century later, its students numbered as many as thirty thousand and a number of mature scholars were emerging from it. The students grew more and more independent and offered ever more criticisms of the social order and of the dynasty's rule until the emperor, unready to see ferment that might affect imperial power, repressed the students in what came to be known as the Calamity of the Proscription of Parties. That move brought China's earliest and longest-lived university to an end. No later dynasty ever tried to open another school of its kind. Some of them set up offices that carried similar names, but the vital functions of learning and teaching were absent, so we can't call them universities.

It was not until 1898, thirteen years before the collapse of dynastic rule in China, that the imperial court, now in the throes of final decline, surrendered to modern pressures and established a university. Called the Great Capital School, it was the forerunner of Peking University. Yet the end of dynastic rule did not mean, alas, that subsequent regimes would automatically embrace the academic values of teaching and research. Peking University—like other Chinese universities that came later—was fated to be a source of contention, as the ancient Han Imperial Academy was.

When I went to college I had no idea that I myself would eventually become a focus of such contention. Yan Garden seemed idyllic to me. It stood at a civilized distance from the racket of the city, from the traffic noise and the hawkers' calls, and seemed elevated to its own plane of purity. When I walked through the campus in the cool air at night, past the semi-somnolent Nameless Lake and the Temple of the Flower Goddess that graced its bank, past the majestic water tower that reached toward heaven, and when I heard the bells that tolled occasionally from the clock pavilion, I had the feeling that all these signs were augurs of my future, which, like the scenes themselves, would be peaceful, harmonious, and boundless. A mood of elation welled inside; I felt my feet were set at the starting point of a lifetime project. What could one worry about? Upward and onward!

A spirit like this drove my life for the next few years as I advanced on three fronts: physics, romance, and Communism. At the time the three fit perfectly, like three facets of a gem.

The tide of the Communist victory reached a triumphant crest in 1953. Outside the country, the Korean War had ended—not in overwhelming victory, to be sure, but when the United States, armed with its atomic bombs, was induced to bow its head and hold its tongue—that, yes, was a kind of victory. Inside the country, still less was there any force to rival Communism. The road ahead was shining, and the arrival of the ideal future seemed only a matter of time. My four college years were unusual in that—except for a campaign to "clean up counterrevolutionaries," which did not last long—they contained no dictatorship-of-the-proletariat class struggles. The main goal at the time was economic development. The authorities were saying that the top priority of students who were Party members or Youth League members should no longer be student movements, and need not be class struggle, either, but should be mastery of knowledge that would help to build the economy. Students with poor academic records had no chance of getting into the Party or the Youth League. So at the time, for me, not only was there no conflict between physics and Communism, the two were tight partners.

Almost without exception, the students who were best academically were also the most active politically. I had joined the Communist movement very early, earlier than most of my classmates, but in high school I had never held any formal positions in the Federation of Democratic Youth. Things changed quickly in college. I was named immediately to be a small group leader and a branch member in the Youth League. These were lowly positions but were crucial as indications of the organization's trust. (In Communist culture, "the organization's trust" is a weighty thing; it anchors a person's inner sense of security.) Later I was named to slightly higher-ranking posts, like Youth League representative and member of the Youth League general branch. These small promotions contributed much to the happy marriage between physics and Communism that I felt inside. The two were one.

My belief in Communism was utterly sincere. During my first two years in college I read some of Marx's classic works, including *A Contribution to the Critique of Political Economy* and *The Civil War in France*, with meticulous attention. The books were powerfully persuasive to me. Their immutable, all-encompassing systematicity held great attraction for a young man who had recently set out in pursuit of ultimate truth in the world. Even now, my view of Marx's underlying theories, if you peel off the Hegelian nonsense, is that they are consistent and cogent. Their simple, black-and-white conceptions of capitalism versus socialism and of the proletariat versus the bourgeoisie provide the same kind of theoretical value (as opposed to real-world value) that toy models offer. The works of Lenin and Mao did not give me that same expansive feeling that I found in Marx, but statements from Mao like "Only socialism can save China" and "Without the Communist Party there would be no new China" struck me as truths similar in nature to the laws of physics.

To us students, the Communist Party represented not only truth but moral authority. To get into the Party, a student faced three stringent tests: in political ideology, staunch belief in Communism; in academics, a superior record; and in moral character, not the slightest vulnerability. The admissions process required one to undertake a merciless dissection of every past thought and action that might contain any seed of evil, however minor, and then to take action to wash that seed away. Party admission, if it came, was a marvelous honor. It meant that one had transcended the foul mire of the ordinary world and had turned into a person made of special stuff, rather like a person qualified to vote for God.

The comparison to religion is not far-fetched. The Communist Party in that era, at least to us university students, was more like a realm of rapture than a political party. It was an altar higher than which there was nowhere to reach. All converts standing before it sought the indulgence and acceptance of its exalted authority by constantly applying its precepts while washing dust from their bodies, minds, and souls. And it was a convert's duty, before the altar, to offer up all: one's body, mind, and spirit; one's misfortunes, sufferings, and sorrows; one's joys, one's loves . . .

My own romance grew from this context. Li Shuxian and I were in the same class in the physics department. She was on the organization committee of the Youth League, and I, an ordinary member, was entrusted to her management. On her first foray to exercise that management, she set out for the women's dormitory to look for me. We first-year students had arrived on campus not knowing one another, and it was her duty, as soon as everyone had moved in, to go meet all the Youth League members in our group. She had been given my name orally, and from the sound "Lizhi" had guessed that the characters were *li* (丽) "beautiful" and *zhi* (芝) "mushroom," a lovely and fitting name for this new comrade in the Youth League who—obviously—would be found in the women's dormitory. Eventually she did find the real Fang Lizhi, and I think that that original miscue may have played a role in leaving her with an especially deep impression that Fang Lizhi was, emphatically, male. I, of course, simultaneously made the discovery that my Youth League superior, a person in a position to give me orders, was female. (By the way, we have always called each other by our full names, Li Shuxian and Fang Lizhi, both before marriage and after, which is why I do so in this book.)

Maybe every boy who goes to an all-male high school finds it difficult to accept the idea of taking orders from a girl. Something just doesn't feel right. Although I accepted the authority of my boss Li Shuxian, I did not respect it. I started secretly to monitor her abilities. Could she really manage us? What made things worse is that I had been an ace student in high school and had developed a fierce competitive streak. I would not bow to anything that exceeded me, and still less was going to bow to such a thing if it were female. I had to win! Inaudibly, a serious competition between us was launched.

After the first few rounds I had to admit that my adversary was more than I had bargained for. First, I had to face the unpleasant fact that every time I got a good score on a physics test, she got one, too. I waited for her to stumble—only to find that I myself tended to stumble at the same spots. So in academics it was a draw. Then there was debate class. I had always liked the class, because I had a knack for coming up with fresh perspectives that won approval from my classmates. The trouble was that each time I raked in another little harvest of plaudits, Li Shuxian would stand up with a few words of cool rebuttal and cart away half of the bounty for herself. So there, too, things were a draw. In certain areas I demolished her, though. I could write poetry. On New Year's Day in 1954, the university chose my poem "Raise a Wineglass and Think of the World" for broadcast all across campus. Unfortunately, though, there were other areas in which *she* demolished *me*. Like running. She ran the 800-meter distance on the women's varsity track team.

In the fall of 1954 there was a campuswide competition to select Three-Good Students. Three-Goods were students who stood out in each of three areas: academics, moral behavior (which included, importantly, political performance), and physical ability. The phrase originated with Mao Zedong, responding to a request from another Party official, Hu Yaobang, for a good capsule phrase for such students. Twenty-eight Three-Good Students were selected that year on the Peking University campus, and seven of them were from the junior class in the physics department. Li Shuxian and I were two of the seven. This meant that after two years of head-to-head competition, she and I were still at a draw. My respect for her was born at that Three-Good moment. I didn't come close to showing the fact in public, though.

After the stage of competition came the stage of platonic love. The Three-Good honor caused each of us to view the other as something special, but neither of us dared to use words, and we never tried to meet in private. Whenever chance placed the two of us in the same place at the same time, there was an unspoken understanding that one of us would look for a third classmate to join us. On the weekends there were dances. Li Shu-xian liked them, and she danced well. I almost never went, and never once danced with her. I was no good at twirls or sashays, and I knew it.

But there was one time each day, at the same hour, when we did meet for a few minutes. We both studied in the university's main library in the evenings, although not in the same place. I was usually downstairs, she upstairs, and there were always other classmates around us. At 9:45 a bell rang and the library closed. Everybody got up, donned backpacks, and headed into the night toward the dormitories. Outdoor lights were few, and the crowd in the darkness was like a river of shadows, no one's face distinct. Still, guided by some kind of mysterious intuition, Li Shuxian and I always ended up finding each other. Then we floated with the river, shoulder to shoulder—but always at a safe distance of about six inches. We talked about the day's homework, or something that had happened in class, never anything sentimental. When we reached the dorms there was a routine "good-bye" and separation, but what lingered, unspoken in both of us, was the anticipation of the next day, when amid that same murky stream, another two-way search would open.

We thought (at least I did) that this sort of budding romance should be an offering. Our feelings, our love, should in the first instance—and perhaps entirely—be devoted to our faith and our enterprise, which was Communism. How could we, so soon, let the small matter of love between two people dilute that greater and more devout love? What's more, I was our class president at the time, she was a member of the general branch of the Youth League, and we both wanted to join the Party. This was the time, if ever there was one, to offer our love to the Party.

Near the end of 1954, Li Shuxian's application to join the Party was approved—before mine was. On the evening when I heard the news, I stayed away from the library and did not study physics all night. Instead I wrote her this poem:

> *Every day, the day gets its dawn*
> *But a person gets only one life.*
> *Every year, the year gets a May*
> *But a person gets only one youth.*
> *The dawn in early spring has its allure*
> *And the life of youth glistens yet more*
> *But, I ask: What can rival that special title that now crowns*
> *   your youth?*
> *Would you not say my blood, too, is as pure, as eager,*
> *That my heart, too, is a seed of fire?*

"Special title" meant "member of the Communist Party." For me, romance and Communism had melded into one, just as physics and Communism had.

About six months later we finally walked out of the Platonic world and into the real one. It was May 1, 1955, International Labor Day, an important Communist holiday. In the evening, after participating in the cheering and dancing in Tiananmen Square, we slipped away from our classmates (no longer asking them to accompany) and, like many lovers before us, walked hand in hand to Zhongshan Park.

Wafting tree branches and glittering city lights in the distance lent an unfathomable tenderness to the dim calm. Suddenly, in the high vault of heaven, dazzling fireworks launched from Tiananmen rose, and rose higher still, then fell, one ball of light after another, spreading downward, surrounding us on all sides, wrapping us in a curtain of color. What could possibly be more sweet than this? How could anything exceed our feelings at that moment of support and love for each other?

Inside us, though, we were also carrying the seeds of disaster. These were buried in our other common passion, physics.

I cannot make clear in a few short sentences the many ways in which physics influences human life and society. I should stress, though, that science is much more than lifeless formulae. The spirit and philosophy of physics interact with human life and society in ways that cause some people to fear it, others to love it, and yet others to take abuse for it. You could even say, speaking of the abused, that physics is a new kind of Forbidden Fruit: eating it brings a person wisdom and suffering at the same time.

Skepticism is an indispensable starting point in physics. A person who cannot begin in skepticism, or who lacks the ability to raise questions independently, will never master physics. Physics does not ask you to memorize what is known to be true or false; it teaches you how to find truth for yourself and how to distinguish truth from falsity. Even for the truths handed down from the great masters, when it comes your turn to learn them, if you really want to "get it," you have to start by doubting, by confronting the same questions yourself, and then making your own rediscoveries of the truths. Niels Bohr once pointed out that anyone who is not perplexed when first encountering quantum mechanics cannot possibly understand quantum mechanics.

In our university courses in Marxism, however, the starting point was very different. We were taught that Marxism is a science, indeed the science of all sciences, yet one of our teachers was fond of saying, "The best we can ever do here is to recapitulate Marx with elegance." Something struck me as strange: Science is based in doubt, yet the science of sciences needs only recapitulation? How is that? This was the first little crack in my faith that "physics, romance, and Communism are three in one."

The first time the little crack appeared in public was on February 27, 1955. The occasion was the First Congress of the Youth League of Peking University. Sessions were held in the auditorium of the main administration building. The topic of the congress was the work and responsibilities of the Youth League, and the mode of discussion borrowed a page from Marxism class: elegant recapitulation. In fact, the Party leaders had already determined all of the League's plans, and the objective of the speeches was just to inculcate the messages. The main message was that the Three-Good program is good—more students should compete for the honor.

I was one of the physics department's representatives to the Congress. Li Shuxian was not officially a representative but attended in her role of deputy secretary of the Youth League's general branch. The physics department at the time had more Three-Good students than any other department; fully a third of our delegation were Three-Goods. After day one of the congress, though, we were all bored. We were Three-Goods ourselves, but so what? Did that mean everybody else had to be one, too? We didn't think so. Why homogenize people? Didn't scientific creativity come from trying to be distinctive? We decided to revolt. Out with the boredom! To be sure we got everybody's attention, we plotted to seize the podium the next day.

The chair of the next day's meeting was the secretary of the Peking University branch of the Youth League, Hu Qili. (Hu was eventually promoted to the Central Committee of the Communist Party but was purged after the Tiananmen events of 1989.) The next speaker after Hu was to be Ni Wansun, general branch secretary for the physics department. Our plot was that when Ni was about halfway through his talk, I would jump up on stage, take the microphone, and start ad-libbing. Ni was our coconspirator, so this much of the plan went smoothly. For a few minutes neither Hu Qili nor any of the several hundred delegates in the audience was aware that anything was going awry. Only the physics delegation knew that a coup was under way.

My first ad-libbing point was that the congress so far had been deadly dull and needed a much livelier atmosphere. Next I said that the real question we need to be asking is, "What kind of people does the Youth League want us to become?" Simpleminded, rule-following bookworms—or thinkers with independent minds? Should the Youth League's goal be that everybody gets all the right answers in every subject, or that all young people learn to think for themselves and be distinctive?

I spoke in a voice somewhat louder than normal, and to call my tone "inflammatory" would not have been unfair. After I finished, some physics students from the class below ours, the sophomores, came up on stage and continued in the same vein, adding fuel to the flames. The agenda for the session was by now so thoroughly disrupted that the next scheduled speaker did not know what to do and declined to ascend the podium. A buzz engulfed the audience. Hu Qili, as chair, then came to the microphone to say that the questions the physics students had raised were very good and warranted discussion by the whole group. The afternoon's agenda was changed to small-group discussions of the question, "What kind of people should our education produce?" The Peking University newspaper reported the day's events, with approval.

We had won. And yet, just as our spirits were peaking, a senior in the physics department came over and said, "You people are in for it." He sympathized with us but wanted us to be warned that our view was "incorrect." He told us about a meeting he had attended in 1951 whose purpose had been to criticize "bourgeois tendencies" among professors. "Independent thinking" had been the main item among the incorrect bourgeois tendencies.

At first we thought this student was too nervous and set his warning aside. How could independent thinking really be a mistake? But sure enough, the next day the university Party Committee announced an abrupt end to the "small-group discussions" that had just been born. Then, a week later, another meeting was convened. Every Youth League member who had attended the congress was summoned to the auditorium. This time there was only one speaker—Jiang Longji, the university's Party Secretary. He spoke for five hours without a break. He started with history and moved to the present, then spoke of foreign countries and moved to China, then spoke of old people and moved to the young. He said that the question "What kind of people should our education produce?" needed no further discussion because the Party's policy on education had already answered it with perfect clarity. There was no need for "independent thinking" because Marx, Lenin, Mao, and the Communist Party had already thought so well on behalf of the people that there was no possible way to do any better. Why waste energy on redundant questions?

Ni Wansun, who was a Party member, was officially criticized. So were all the other Party members who had taken part. The university newspaper published a self-criticism. I was spared formal criticism, probably because I was not yet a Party member.

Our little rebellion was quashed but did not bring major disaster upon us. This was, in part, just luck; our caper occurred when no great class struggle was going on. About two years later, Ni Wansun, Li Shuxian, and I participated in another rebellion, which in substance was much milder. That one, though, took place during the fever pitch of a class-struggle campaign, and this made disaster inevitable. Ni paid for it with twenty-two years of his life. (I'll return to this story in the next chapter.)

I joined the Party on June 1, 1955, four months after the skirmish at the Youth League meeting. I found it odd that all through the process of my entering the Party, no one asked me to make a self-criticism about my inflammatory speech. Ni Wansun was one of my sponsors for Party membership.

The general policy of the Party leaders in those years was to trust us students. They saw the Youth League incident as just a bump in the road in their larger project, which was to replace our professors—and other intellectuals of their generation, whom they generally did *not* trust—with us, their new homegrown generation. They thought of us as proletarian intellectuals.

In an authoritarian regime based in class struggle, the "trust" question is ubiquitous. There is no way to stand outside it. Every person, at every moment, belongs to one or another category according to the degree of trust the organization has in the person. The categories, top to bottom, are: can be relied upon, can be used, can be recruited, condition unclear, cannot be trusted, and opponent to be fought against. The way people who live in this kind of authoritarian system watch the risings and fallings of their political value, and the values of the people around them, is not all that different from the way people in a market economy who own stocks monitor the rise and fall of stock prices. In my forty years of living under Chinese Communist Party rule I have spanned the gamut; I have lived in every category, top to bottom, at least once. During my college years, my stock was on the rise.

In the fall of 1955, it rose to an apex when I was chosen to join the top secret academic specialty of nuclear physics. The Chinese authorities had decided to make a move to join the international "nuclear club" by obtaining an atomic bomb, and this led them to inaugurate an elite university major in nuclear physics. My interests at the time were in theoretical physics. I was casting about for a senior thesis topic when, in October, an order suddenly came down that about two dozen Peking University physics students, of whom I was one, were assigned to the nuclear major. Because the topic was so secret, we would be immediately moved off the Yan Garden campus to a sequestered site, not too far away, that also belonged to Peking University. Students from the physics departments of other leading universities were transferred there as well. There were about a hundred of us in all. We were the pioneers in China's nuclear physics research, and many among us became important players in the production of China's atomic weapons. The man who later became commander of China's largest nuclear testing site, in the northwest, was in the group of two dozen or so who were drafted with me from the Peking University physics department.

In the wake of the atomic bombs that fell on Hiroshima and Nagasaki, many Chinese people, after recovering from the initial shock, began viewing physicists with enormous new respect, as if we were some kind of modern-day kung fu heroes, masters of abstruse magical powers. "Nuclear secrets," to them, were parallel to the secret techniques of legendary swordsmen, each absolutely unique to the holder of the secret. It was obvious that the security officer at our special research site held this view. To him, what we were studying was pure kung fu lore. Not a single word of it could leak.

This meant that all our class notebooks were regarded as secret. Each had to be numbered and registered and could not be removed outside a prescribed perimeter. The practice was quite out of tune with the spirit of physics, which pursues universals, not particulars. Nuclear physics as an intellectual field is completely open—it is only certain numbers that relate to weaponry that anyone keeps secret. Ninety-nine percent of what we were writing down in our notebooks could be found in open publications. (The other one percent were doodles, satirical sketches of our professors, or other escapes from occasional boredom.)

The location of our special site was also a top secret. We were instructed to answer the question "Where do you live?" by saying "Postbox 546." I went back to the Yan Garden campus almost every Saturday evening to visit Li Shuxian, and when we said our good-byes I would joke, "Okay, I'm headed back to Postbox 546." Within two months or so my bright classmates in the physics department had ferreted out the truth of where Postbox 546 actually was, but that didn't matter. The name stuck. Everybody still called the place "Postbox 546." All this went over the head of the security officer, however. He kept warning us, austerely, not to let the address leak: "Say you live at Postbox 546!"

Many of our classes in the postbox involved experiments in nuclear physics and nuclear electrodynamics. I had always preferred theory but was fairly good with experiments, too. In my whole college career I made only one serious blunder in a laboratory. It was junior year, and we were creating a vacuum in a McLeod gauge. As the vacuum was intensifying, I opened a wrong valve and air rushed in, shattering the gauge, causing mercury to spill, and polluting the whole lab. Evangelista Torricelli, the great Italian physicist, was right to say that "nature abhors a vacuum." I wonder if he discovered this one day when a glass tube of his own shattered.

With the experiments in electronics, though, I was in my element. Playing with radio parts during high school had prepared me well.

My laboratory partner during the 546 era was Hou Depeng. Like me, Hou preferred theoretical physics but was drafted into 546. He was color-blind, and for that reason he really should not have been doing experimental physics, which can be difficult for a person with this affliction. In our lab, for example, the resistance values of carbon resistors were indicated by three bands of color. A color-blind person, unable to see the differences, could make potentially dangerous mistakes. But an assignment from the Party in those days obviously outweighed such considerations. If the Party asked that you do something, then, well, you were able to do it. It was like God saying "Let there be light" and there was light. It wasn't to be, though. With or without the light of the Party, Hou could not see the band colors and did make a lot of mistakes. Eventually he gave up trying and just watched as I did those parts of the experiments by myself. In the end, though, the light of the Party did come through for Hou. Thirty years later he was promoted to the standing committee of the Party Committee in Guangxi, and this was the highest political position anyone from our class ever reached.

But these little glitches—the Postbox 546 jokes, Hou Depeng's blown experiments, and so on—did nothing to diminish our basic faith in the Communist Party or my enthusiasm for my studies. During my last half year in college, my devotion to physics was manic. At one point I was so taken by the spin matrices of Paul Dirac that I read his *Principles of Quantum Mechanics* almost without stopping.* At other times I got hooked by this or that exercise book on theoretical mechanics or electrodynamics and would work through a thousand or more examples, one by one. In my final month I worked hard shaping sheets of mica that were as thin as locust wings to make beta-counter tubes. For a whole month I hardly emerged from the lab, but the results were good.

The very first slogan that the Communist Party unveiled in 1956 was "Forward March to Science!" So just imagine: Here we were, the first generation in China doing nuclear physics, which was a frontier subfield in physics. Physics as a whole, moreover—whatever its rivals might say—was the queen of the sciences, and "science" was the direction in which the whole society was going to march. Were we not like the mythic Nezha on his magical wheels of wind and fire—the very pinnacle of heaven's selections?

Or, to put it another way, I was in the Communist system's highest category in "trust."

---

*Translator's note: Fang read Dirac's book in English even though his English was so weak that he needed to look up nearly every word. Li Shuxian remembers him telling her that at first it took him a whole morning to read just one page, but later, encouraged by Dirac's elegant illustrations, he could read faster and faster. She could still recall, in 2015, what Fang's copy of Dirac's book looked like. The margins of the first few pages were packed with notes on Chinese equivalents, while later pages bore fewer marks. In a sense he learned English on this book.

6. MY FIRST TRIP TO THE BOTTOM

AFTER MY GRADUATION FROM PEKING UNIVERSITY IN 1956, I WAS assigned to work at the Institute of Modern Physics at the Chinese Academy of Sciences. At the end of August, I found myself with a little more than a week of free time before I needed to report for duty. It occurred to me that my student days were over and that this would be my last summer vacation, so I had better go have some fun while I still could. A classmate and I borrowed fifteen yuan from a professor and set out for the nearby tourist destinations of Shanhaiguan, Qinhuangdao, and Beidaihe. Li Shuxian had already begun her work assignment, so she couldn't come with us. In any case she had already made her own summer trip to Beidaihe.

On a budget of fifteen yuan there was no way we could stay in hotels. At Qinhuangdao we slept one night (with permission) in the classroom of an elementary school. At the Beidaihe beach we sneaked into the men's changing room at closing time and spent the night there. A third night was spent on a train. When we got back to Beijing I was exhausted but ecstatic. This had been my first trip to Shanhaiguan—"the world's first pass," as we call it in Chinese, and "the place where the Great Wall begins." It was also the first time, at age twenty, I had ever seen the sea. At Qinhuangdao, looking out at the ocean waves, so dark they seemed almost purple, I saw little sailboats bobbing up and down, heading out in quest of fish, and thought that my own life, now also in its launch phase, could be compared to them. It made me feel like writing a poem—and I might have, except that another poem, one I had committed to memory during my school days, pushed its way into my consciousness and wouldn't go away:

> Farewell to you, unharnessed Ocean!
> No longer will you roll at me
> Your azure swells in endless motion
> Or gleam in tranquil majesty.*

These are the opening lines of "To the Sea" by the great Russian poet Alexander Pushkin, who wrote it, I think, when he was also in his twenties. The idea of "no longer" did not exactly fit what I was feeling (I would be back to the sea, wouldn't I?), but other than that, I couldn't think of any words better than these, so I stifled my impulse to write my own poem.

Mao Zedong had visited Beidaihe in 1954 and (also perhaps moved by the sea?) had written a poem about it. One of Mao's lines—"beyond Qinhuangdao, some fishing boats are drifting"—makes it clear that he, too, saw fishing boats, and they may have been the very ones we saw, because there were only a few such boats. The main difference in the poems was that the boats did not cause Mao to think of his own lifelong voyage. Still less did he think of Pushkin. What came to Mao's mind was Cao Cao (A.D. 155–220), the ruthless tyrant and master of manipulation at the end of the Han Dynasty. Mao admired him. Another line in Mao's poem— "Emperor Wu of Wei wielding his whip"—shows his wish that he might whip that open sea into shape, as Cao Cao might have.

A few months after my first glimpse of the ocean, Mao's whip of power did come down, and it landed on the independent voices in China. The blow was devastating, and it lent truth, in my case, to Pushkin's line about "no longer" seeing the sea. I did not see it again for twenty-two years.

My assignment at the Institute of Modern Physics was to study nuclear reactors. China's leaders wanted to build their own reactor, and they had

---

*Translator's note: I have borrowed this translation from Russian to English from Babette Deutsch.

us work from an experimental heavy-water reactor that they brought in from the Soviet Union. Their ultimate aim, of course, was to build not just an experimental reactor but one that could produce the plutonium-239 needed to build nuclear weapons. The charge to our research group was to study all the relevant theory; another of our leaders' purposes, clearly, was to hone the skills of people who could later be assigned to work on producing a bomb. There were twelve in our group. One was over thirty years old, but the others were all fresh out of Postbox 546 at Peking University or similar places. Three of us in the group were Party members. I was one of the three, and I was in charge of daily administration.

In the 1940s, Enrico Fermi and others had laid the foundations for the theory of nuclear reactors, and by the mid-1950s that theory had matured. In 1955, at the Geneva Conference on Peaceful Uses of Atomic Energy, the United States and the Soviet Union both decided to make public much that until then had been secret, and after they did this, the theory part of our work became fairly easy. The hard part was computation. There were no computers at the time, or even electronic calculators. Our most modern tools of that sort were calculators that ran on electric motors. But we didn't have many of them, and there were not enough to go around. So our calculating device was often the traditional Chinese abacus, of which there were plenty. When our calculation work reached its peak periods, our whole room buzzed with the clacking of abacus beads. A person approaching might well have guessed it to be the accounting department of a bank or a commercial company. How would anyone guess that the sound of this racket was, in fact, only a prelude to the deafening boom of an atomic explosion?

In the eyes of the Chinese public, nothing was more glorious than working on the atomic bomb. The bomb was a supreme symbol of the nation, both its brains and its strength, and anyone connected with it was automatically a hero. But that's not how many physicists saw it. The core value in physics is creation, not repetition. Whoever shows something for the first time is a hero; a person who confirms the result in a second experiment might also be worthy of note; but from the third time on, the results fall into the category of manufacturing, not physics. Left to their own preferences, physicists would rather find an unglamorous corner in which to do something truly creative than to join in a Great Repetition—which is what the nuclear bomb project essentially was. Moreover, physicists enjoy free and open debate, and the super-tight secrecy that enveloped the bomb project rubbed us deeply the wrong way. Eventually five of the people in our small group, offering this excuse or that, quit. They decided they could do without the tremendous honor of working on the Great Repetition.

I had some of these feelings myself. The study of nuclear reactors never really turned me on intellectually, and I did not find the idea of building nuclear weapons attractive. A number of leading physicists in the world had already announced their opposition to the manufacture and use of nuclear weapons. Agreeing with them, I made a statement of my own: "I don't want to build weapons that kill people." Still, I continued with my work and did not make any transfer requests. I reminded myself that I was a Party member and a member of the Party branch committee. I had weightier responsibilities than to follow my personal preferences.

There was one small area, though, where I could follow my interests— outside the scope of my duties. We were allowed to audit university courses if they could be said to fill a gap in our knowledge or to be necessary to our work. I found a course on heat transfer at Tsinghua University. The design of heat transfer is crucial in building nuclear reactors and is especially important for production reactors and the use of nuclear reactors in generating electricity. It was a major problem in the heat transfer system that caused the 1986 nuclear accident at Chernobyl in the Soviet Union. But the Tsinghua course on heat transfer was dry as chaff and intolerably boring. After listening to two classes I couldn't take it anymore and dropped out. I switched to a course at Peking University on general relativity. This elegant theory in physics, expounded by the great Albert Einstein, was utterly useless to the theory or design of nuclear reactors. I had to admit to myself that a person cannot always be guided solely by duty; what interests you matters, too.

I was drawn to the Peking University campus not only to audit courses but also, on Saturdays, to visit Li Shuxian. She was working in the physics department as the interpreter for a Soviet expert. Under an agreement made in the fall of 1956, the Soviet Union sent groups of specialists to

Peking University to teach and do research. Each was assigned an assistant or two to do written and oral translation. The competence of these guest experts was about the same as Chinese lecturers or assistant professors, but their salaries were far higher than those of Chinese full professors. Their offices were much larger and fancier, too.

So Li Shuxian and I used her expert's office as our meeting place on Saturday nights. We were brimming with enthusiasm and deeply in love, but marriage was out of the question. We both felt we had no right to consider marriage until our careers were launched. We even felt that Saturday sweet talk was not a fully justifiable use of time, so we replaced our romantic trysts with invitations to Ni Wansun and other classmates to come join in serious discussion. Ni was also working as a translator for a Soviet expert. In our meetings we talked about what we had learned from reading or research during the preceding week. We allowed ourselves the adolescent dream that our little Saturday salon might gradually attract more and more people until some day it turned into an influential group of some kind. Starting in the spring of 1957, we convened nearly every weekend for all-out bull sessions on topics that ranged over physics, philosophy, and politics.

I have forgotten most of what we talked about, but one item sticks in my memory. We were discussing an article by Werner Heisenberg about controversies in quantum mechanics. Heisenberg wrote, at one point, that Dmitrii Blokhintsev's "new explanation" of quantum mechanics was nothing more than an attempt to accommodate Lenin's political needs—or words to that effect. Seeing such a disrespectful reference to Lenin shocked us. In China at the time (and now, too), Lenin was a prophet comparable only to Marx. He was one of those four great foreigners—Marx, Engels, Lenin, and Stalin—whose hallowed likenesses were constantly offered to the Chinese public for their adulation. It was unthinkable that Heisenberg's quip could ever appear in a Chinese publication.

Despite the shock, the logic of physics impelled us to push ahead and consider Heisenberg's point. This same Dmitrii Blokhintsev was the author of one of our college textbooks, *A Course in Quantum Mechanics*. The book was published in the 1940s, at the height of the Soviet Union's criticism of "bourgeois science," and its author states up front that his reason for offering a "new explanation" is to criticize and replace "bourgeois quantum mechanics." His new explanation was not bogus science in the way that Trofim Lysenko's far-fetched "agronomy" was. But there was no question that it was an incursion of ideology into an area where it did not belong. It was politics, not physics.

Heisenberg's criticisms of Lenin did not completely undo the place of Lenin in my mind, but they did force me to realize that in the eyes of science, even a saint like Lenin did not have privileged status. His words, like anyone's, were subject to science's rules of logic and evidence. If forced to choose between science and non-science, I would have to choose science, no matter how brightly the halos shone on the non-science side. You can't cheat physics.

In my later career as an educator, Party officials asked me many times why it is that students stray from Communist ideology when they go to college. Where does the "counterrevolutionary" education come from? They tied themselves in knots trying to figure out why students who were carefully selected for "good thinking" when they entered universities turned into "bourgeois intellectuals" once they were there. They took out magnifying glasses to examine every detail of campus life, inside and outside classrooms, and asked school administrators to remove anything that came remotely close to "counterrevolutionary thinking." But it never worked, and can never work, because what they call "counterrevolutionary thinking" is stuck inside science. No course in a physics department is more counterrevolutionary than Physics 1. No one who understands physics can turn around and accept a claim that Marxism-Leninism is special wisdom that trumps everything else.

This is why our weekend salon, even without any outside influences, inevitably led us to follow science and gradually to take leave of Communist orthodoxy. Some historians have held that if Mao Zedong had not launched the 1957 Anti-Rightist Movement, in which he persecuted intellectuals with such a broad brush, later conflicts between the intellectuals and the Communist Party could have been avoided. I don't think this gets it right. The deeper reason why intellectuals left the Party's ideology behind is that science by nature weeds out ignorance. With or without an Anti-Rightist Movement, the split between scientists and the

Party was bound to occur sooner or later. The movement only sped the process up.

In March 1957, the Party Committee of the Academy of Sciences arranged that two of Mao Zedong's recent speeches be read to all Party members in the Academy. I went to listen. Mao proposed to "let a hundred flowers bloom and a hundred schools of thought contend" and encouraged non-Party people to express their criticisms of the Party, whatever these might be. He called for "giving free voice."

In later years, Mao explained that his call to "give free voice" had been an "open plot" (not, as some were saying, a hidden plot) whose purpose was to identify malcontents, lure them into criticizing the Party, and then round them up for a purge. The goal was to "consolidate the Party's dictatorship." This ex post facto explanation implies that Mao had everything figured out in advance—how the backsliders, those enemies of socialism, would all "speak out" on his cue so that he could use the Anti-Rightist Movement to finish them off.

A bit of analysis, though—no more sophisticated than what you can find in a third-rate detective novel—can show that Mao's explanation does not fit what happened. Mao did set a trap, but it did not work as he intended, and what actually happened surprised him. This can be seen from the fact that on May 15 he published an article titled "Things Are Beginning to Change" in which he describes his movement as transitioning from the "speaking out" phase to the repression stage. So, if we accept his claim that "I saw it all in advance," then we have to say that by May 15 most of the people for whom he had set his trap had already fallen into it. In fact, though, it was only *after* May 15 that the first protest posters went up at Peking University and on other campuses. What later came to be known as "the great speaking out" by students and young intellectuals—the high tide of criticism of the Party by "rightists," as Mao later called them—all happened after May 15. It could not be clearer that Mao did not anticipate that high tide.

Mao apparently calculated that Marxism-Leninism, with Maoism added, had by 1957 achieved such a remarkable victory in China that even if things weren't perfect, people would find them almost so, and that if he invited people to speak out, he would get only minor criticisms that would do more to help than to harm. He could appear magnanimous without sacrificing any actual power. In particular he could count on it that the "new intellectuals" whom the Communist Party had cultivated in the universities since 1949 would be his staunch supporters.

It is important to recognize that Mao's assessment was not entirely wrong. Among the young people I knew at the time (and this includes me), it was hard to find anyone who, when it came to politics, was not a supporter of Mao and the Communist Party. Not everyone was a fanatic, but the support was solid.

My nuclear reactor group was very busy with calculations in the spring of 1957 and was not involved in the rising ferment. We were preoccupied with the march toward science—where was there time for "speaking out"? For scientists, moreover, the slogan "Let a hundred flowers bloom and a hundred schools of thought contend" was unexciting. It was trivially obvious. The idea that free competition of viewpoints is necessary for scholarly progress was not something that we needed a four-hour speech from Mao Zedong in order to understand. Galileo had made the point more than three hundred years earlier. So we just kept working, our abaci buzzing.

March, April, and the first half of May passed in this way. We had no sense of any plot, whether hidden or otherwise. On Saturday, May 18, I went to Peking University as I usually did on Saturdays, and, as usual, met with Li Shuxian and others at the Soviet expert's office for a big discussion of all things discussable. The campus was its normal quiet self.

But two days later, on May 20, Pandora's box opened. An eye-catching poster appeared on the east wall of the main dining hall, which was one of the students' favorite gathering places. The poster bore a poem (again we see that poems start things) whose title was "It's Time":

> *Sing, young people, open your throats and sing*
> *Let's put both our suffering and our love into words*
> *Don't feel alone in your pain, your indignation, your depression*
> *Lay it all out—the bitter and sweet, the pungent and foul—in the*
>   *light of day*

The poets were two juniors in the Chinese Department. Their poster brought a torrent of response from seemingly every corner of the formerly quiet campus. In a matter of days the wall was blanketed in posters of all kinds. "Speaking out" was truly under way.

I did not meet the authors of "It's Time" in 1957, but I did meet one of them, Shen Zeyi, thirty-two years later, in the spring of 1989. He had paid for his poem with more than twenty years of his life—he had been banished to China's northwest—and in 1989 his head was mottled with gray. But his eyes still gleamed when he spoke of his poem. When he recited it for me, it was as if nothing had changed for him during the thirty-two years since he wrote it. And he was right to be proud of the poem. It was the opening salvo in the first major conflict between Chinese intellectuals (especially young intellectuals) and the Communist Party.

The posters that mushroomed in the dining hall area were aimed not at "mistakes" the Communist Party had made, but at the fundaments of its ideology. Mao, in encouraging people to speak out, had acknowledged that the Party's "work style" had shortcomings of three kinds— subjectivism, bureaucratism, and factionalism. He called these "the three evils." His real purpose in naming specifically three things was to define the scope within which popular criticism would be welcome. But the student posters, right from the start, leaped past those bounds and raised questions that, however obvious they may have been, Mao had not guessed anyone would raise. The central question, which took several forms, was: "If three evils have appeared, what caused them?"

But this was forbidden. Communist governance could not allow that question to be asked. To probe it would lead to an evaluation of the pros and cons of the system as a whole, and such an inquiry was off-limits because the superiority of socialism was beyond doubt. It would not matter what criteria one used or how one did the measurements in any evaluation of the system, because one began—had to begin—with the conclusion: socialism is wonderful.

When the question of the "origins of the three evils" was raised, the students who had written the posters that began the ferment were thrust into a terrible and unanticipated predicament. None of the students who had followed them had meant to put them there. Most students generally approved of what the Communist Party had been doing from 1949 to 1957 and were not surprised, or especially irritated, that things like "the three evils" had popped up. They had inquired into "origins" mainly because they had been trained to seek the causes of things. Why should the "three evils" be an exception? The science students among them had learned, moreover, that there are no such things as propositions that cannot be questioned. Their support for the Communist Party and socialism could not outweigh this training. This is why I wrote, above, that the conflict between young scientists and the Communist Party arose from principle.

But there was another factor that added to the problem. A year earlier, Nikita Khrushchev had delivered his "secret speech" at the Twentieth Congress of the Soviet Communist Party, denouncing the "cult of personality" that had developed around Stalin and recounting the late Soviet leader's abuses of power. The speech was strictly banned in China, but you could find it at Peking University in the Soviet newspaper *Pravda* as well as in Western news accounts. Many people had heard about the speech in greater or lesser detail, and translations in several versions circulated among the students. Until then, Stalin had been one of our demigods; when he died in 1953 some of my classmates shed tears. Were we now to believe that he had slaughtered innocent people in the name of class struggle? Even if we didn't want to believe it, after Khrushchev's speech we had to take the idea seriously. It was another principle of science that you don't follow precursors blindly, no matter how godlike they seem. But this questioning, too, did not sit well with the Party.

And so the peaceful coexistence of "speaking out" and the "whip of power" (that whip that Mao admired in Cao Cao) came to an end. A clash was inevitable.

When the news that "Peking University is in trouble" reached us at the Institute of Modern Physics, we listened in silence and kept working. But the news kept coming and got more and more startling every day. I wanted to go see for myself but adhered to my pattern of waiting until Saturday to do so. I went on Saturday, May 25, for my regular discussion with Li Shuxian and Ni Wansun.

Our topic that day was the student posters. All three of us were members of the Communist Party and, during our student days, had been officers of the Communist Youth League. In theory, therefore, the people the students were complaining about included us, however we might sympathize with them. We felt no impulse to write posters ourselves, but the ones that were already up caused us to think hard. The "three evils" did indeed exist in the university, as the students claimed; and they had indeed hurt people, including some of our classmates. As Party members, should we accept some responsibility?

Our answer was yes. A cardinal rule for Youth League officers was "to be the Party's loyal assistants." There had been no vicious class-struggle campaigns during our tenure, but still, as we thought about it, our "assistant" work had indeed harmed some of our classmates. For example, in 1955, when Ho Chi Minh, the chairman of the Communist Party of Vietnam, came to China, students at Peking University were asked to form a welcoming party at the airport. This seemed a simple matter at first, but when we learned that Mao Zedong, Zhou Enlai, and all the top leaders of the Chinese Communist Party were going to be there, too, the task turned into a "crucial political responsibility." The organization asked us to use class-struggle criteria to select students for the welcoming party. Classmates with "backward thinking" were for that reason "unreliable" and should not be included. In retrospect, now, we could imagine what this likely did to the self-respect of those classmates. And we had probably been even more thoughtless during the "Movement to Eliminate Counterrevolutionaries." None of our classmates was officially a "counterrevolutionary element" (one could not have gotten into college as such), but there were some who had "backward thinking." During the month-long campaign, those classmates endured fierce and unreasoning invective at "denunciation meetings." The three of us had helped to organize and convene those meetings.

We felt guilty, and we felt a strong urge to do something to change the work style of the Youth League so that this kind of abuse could not happen again. Ni Wansun suggested that we write a joint letter to the Central Committee of the Party with our own suggestions for improving the work of both the Party and the Youth League. Li Shuxian and I agreed. In some way that was hard to pinpoint, Khrushchev had influenced us. He seemed to have given new energy and life to a Soviet Communism that had grown stale. We hoped that our own Communist movement could get some new life, too.

On Sunday, June 2, when I went again to Peking University, I learned that Ni Wansun had finished a long outline for our contemplated letter. It covered the gamut of the Communist Party's shortcomings and errors, but, to match Mao's guidelines, he had organized it as "dogmatism" in the realm of theory, "subjectivism" in the realm of thinking, and "factionalism" in the realm of work style. We spent an afternoon discussing and revising the outline, and then made writing assignments: Ni would do the main part and Li would do the section on the Youth League. I wanted to write, too, but my workload at the reactor was just too heavy; I couldn't spare the time.

By the time of my next trip to the campus, on Saturday, June 8, the sky had changed color. The *People's Daily* published an editorial that day titled "What Is This For?" and Mao Zedong issued a document for Party members called "Organize Forces to Counterattack Against the Savage Attacks by Rightist Elements." This marked the onset of a political campaign whose name, straight from Mao, was "Counterattack Against Rightist Elements."

Over the past few decades the Communist Party of China has rolled out a number of class-struggle campaigns, and they have hardly differed in their methods. A single general formula can encompass them. I have no doubt that in today's world, with its savvy computers, any human being with an intelligence level at or above that of Wang Zhen could easily use this formula to direct the sort of class-struggle campaign that the great Communist Party of China directs. The formula includes these steps:

1. **Identify the target of the struggle.** By definition, the enemies in a class struggle are "a small handful," which means they should not exceed 5 percent of the people concerned. Accordingly, it is the duty of the struggle leader to home in on this percentage. The smaller the deviation from it, the better. The reason Li Shuxian was labeled a rightist and I was not had everything to do with this formula.

There was room to accommodate her at Peking University, but not room for me at the Academy of Sciences.

2. **Fabricate charges.** By definition, XXX elements ("rightist" elements in our case, but the formula works for anything) are anti-Party and antisocialist. Accordingly, it is the duty of the struggle leader to find evidence until it reaches this level. For example, one of the student posters at Peking University had complained about shoddy service at the university barber shop. It said people emerged looking as if the haircuts had been done by nipping dogs. Well, that poster was enough to make its author a rightist. Dogs bite off hair in socialist barber shops? How reactionary can you get!

3. **Ferret out the hidden cliques.** By definition, XXX elements organize small anti-Party cliques. Each has a program and has plans for pursuing it. Accordingly, it is the duty of the struggle leader to denounce each small anti-Party clique organized by XXX elements. It doesn't matter if clique members have never met one another.

4. **Organize "criticism struggle sessions" of various sizes.** These, too, follow a standard formula. No matter how contrite and forthcoming a victim might be, people in the crowd have to shout out "Phony! Come clean!" Then, at the end, they raise their hands in unison—just as you can see representatives to the National People's Congress doing on television—to cast votes.

In any case, it was as easy as that. Thousands, even tens of thousands, of naive and innocent students and young intellectuals were trapped in the class-struggle machine and branded as rightists. Quite a few of them, unable to handle the insult to their self-respect, committed suicide.

The authorities knew that Ni Wansun, Li Shuxian, and I had planned to send a letter to Party Central. When the shock of June 8 arrived we hadn't yet mailed the letter, and now we decided not to. We assumed we were safe. After all, the Party charter permits members to write letters to Party Central. Moreover, none of what we wrote in the letter had appeared anywhere else, like in a wall poster. Since our visible actions had not crossed any line, we should still, we thought, be seen as free of any "mistakes." And indeed, all through August, nothing happened to us.

In September, the attacks on the rightists were petering out, and the cries of "Phony!" were heard less often. It seemed the campaign was about to end.

But life is never completely free from chance. It was also in September that Deng Xiaoping, director of the office of the Anti-Rightist Movement for Party Central, and Peng Zhen, the Party Secretary for Beijing, came to visit Peking University in person. They were startled to see the protest posters that school authorities had confiscated, and Deng commented, "This school really produces some high-quality rightists!" They decided on the spot to make an exception for Peking University and to raise the number of rightists to be ferreted out on this campus a few points higher than the 5 percent that was normal elsewhere.

So the campaign at Peking University mushroomed toward a second high point. A new search for people who fit the rightist formula was launched, and that search uncovered our plan to write a letter to Party Central. Our case fit the class-struggle formula perfectly. The letter had been addressed to Party Central, so clearly it was "anti-Party"; we had first made an outline, so obviously we had a "program"; we had been meeting every week since May, so we plainly had "plans"; and there were three of us—plural!—so obviously there was an "organization." Our case became a model for the campus purge. Our letter outline was printed and distributed, with sharp denunciation attached. Ni Wansun and Li Shuxian were both labeled rightists.

I was denounced, too, and also had to listen to some catcalls of "Phony!" but I was never officially labeled a rightist. This was only because Peking University was no longer my "work unit." I was under the Chinese Academy of Sciences. Deng Xiaoping had not visited the Academy, so he had not honored it with extra percentage points in its quota for rightists. The Academy's original 5 percent had already been filled up. All the "rightist hats" had been distributed to others, and there was none left for me.

Still, it was a splendid success: in a single blow an entire gang that had planned one whole letter that had never been mailed was completely annihilated. Ni Wansun was fired from the university and sent to do labor reform. He returned to his post twenty-two years later. Li Shuxian was kept at the university as a "teacher by negative example"—a euphemism for a political pariah. In December I was expelled from the reactor research team and assigned to a farming village to do labor.

News of other great annihilations came in one by one. That classmate of mine at Fourth High who liked to play leading roles on stage had entered the Chinese Department at Peking University, and then, after graduation, had gone to work at the Central Academy of Drama. From time to time he sent me theater tickets, for everything from the Western opera *La Traviata* to a Sichuan opera version of *The Dough-Kneading Jug*. Then suddenly the tickets stopped coming. He had been made a rightist. Hou Depeng, the color-blind physicist, went to work at the Party's Central Propaganda Department after emerging from Postbox 546. He and his colleagues started a discussion salon there, which I attended a couple of times. Then it suddenly stopped. Hou's name appeared in the *People's Daily* in the first group of rightists to be named. People who have studied the question say that about a third of the one hundred members of the class of 1956 of the Peking University physics department ended up labeled as rightists. The "degree of trust" for our cohort had plummeted.

This was also the point at which the stock of the Communist Party of China itself reached an apex and began a slide toward its low point.

7. LIFE IN THE FIELDS

In the early 1980s, during a trip to Europe, I was chatting with some physicist colleagues about where we had been in life and commented that I had worked several times in the fields. One of them was puzzled, wondering why I had used the plural for "field."

"You mean *field*, right? *Field* theory."

It made me think that English has a defect here. How can a single word be used for such different concepts as "field" in physics and the places where farmers work? Maybe the confusion never arises for my English-speaking colleagues because, for them, it is so unlikely to have worked in both kinds of field. But for us Chinese physicists it was fairly common. From the 1950s through the 1970s I was sent from physics study to farms four different times.

My first trip—from December 1957 to August 1958—was simultaneously a very serious matter and a relaxing break.

Near the end of the Anti-Rightist Movement, the Great Leader announced that "cadres should go to the countryside for manual labor." I was named to go, and for me history seemed to be repeating itself. I had been in the first cohort to join the Communist Youth League and now I was in another first group. And there was more to the parallel: just as I had been, according to the rules, too young to join the League, now my status as "cadre" also fell short of proper standards. In Communist terminology, "cadre" and "masses" are correlative terms: a "cadre" means an administrator and "masses" means people who are administered. The phrase "cadres go to the countryside for labor" means, in theory, that officials go down among the people whom they rule, joining in their labors and savoring their pains and pleasures. On the face of it this is a good thing to do, and at first it seemed an honor. For a low-ranking science intern like me to be viewed as a "sent-down cadre" was a major and unexpected boost.

As it turned out, the high-ranking Communist cadres selflessly allowed all of the honor to go to us low-ranking types. Not one among the high-ranking saw fit to join. Most of the several dozen who went from our Institute of Modern Physics were young. The two other honorees from my own research group were a research intern (like me) and a laboratory worker. The post of lab worker was as low-ranking as one could get, yet this man was viewed as a "cadre" who could be sent down. Later it became apparent that all of the people who received the special honor were ones who had "had problems"—meaning political problems—during the recent Anti-Rightist Movement. From day one, in other words, it was clear that being sent down was in fact a form of punishment—wrapped in "honor," but a punishment in fact.

In mid-December we gathered at the Qianmen Railway Station in Beijing, loaded down with our luggage, ready to head for villages to the south. There were plenty of higher-ranking cadres in attendance—but only to see us off. They pinned on each of us a big red flower of the kind that, in imperial times, were for scholars who had passed the civil service exams or for grooms at weddings. Their words of congratulation, encouragement, and best wishes gushed and swirled, generating a most lively atmosphere. It truly seemed that we were receiving a high honor, as if we were the first group of passengers headed for paradise. Later, in reading history, I learned that "honor-plus-punishment" was not an invention of the Communist Party of China but a standard technique of earlier Chinese authoritarians. In the fourteenth century, Zhu Yuanzhang, the first Ming emperor, while executing his chief marshal, Xu Da, at the same time erected a monument in honor of Xu. This huge lonely monument still stands on the outskirts of Nanjing.

Li Shuxian was among the people who saw me off at the rail station. She didn't say anything in our last poignant moments together, but it was profoundly comforting to me that she was there.

The village to which I was assigned was in Nanxingguo Township in Zanhuang County, Hebei Province. Zanhuang County spans the eastern foothills of the Taihang Mountains; its western half is in the mountains, its eastern half on the adjacent plains. Nanxingguo is in the east. The closest rail station, about five hours south of Beijing on the Hankou line, is a little stop called Yuanshi. From there to Nanxingguo one went by horse cart. If you were lucky enough to find one of the two-horse carts that had rubber tires, it was a bit more than a hour away.

It was dusk by the time the cart carrying the three of us reached the village. No one seemed to be there. No dogs, either. Not even a whisper of green was on the earth—just grayish black. Very few trees. On the flat, dull-looking fields, a few branches that looked as if they had survived some kind of disaster were sticking up here and there. There were no lights in the village. In the distance loomed the dim silhouette of what looked like a giant rock, crouched on the plain like something that prehistory had left behind. Could *this* be what the foothills of the Taihang Mountains, in that song "On the Taihang Mountains," which had so moved me in grade school, really looked like? The beautiful feeling that the song had planted inside me suddenly evaporated.

Too desolate, too destitute—that is the only memory I have of my first impression of the place. In my youth the idea of material hardship had never really bothered me; I had even entertained romantic daydreams about living in rough and risky conditions. But what now lay before me was not riskiness or roughness but only dull, sluggish poverty. It was a life that demanded nothing of intelligence or courage, a life any dullard could keep passing through, mechanically, without disaster but without anything else of note, either. It had been this way for a thousand years— perhaps two thousand. The place got the name Zanhuang, which means "praise the emperor," when an emperor happened to pass through a few centuries ago. After that the wheel of life kept turning without change. The glorious visit had all but decreed that there be no change.

The three of us moved into a vacant room in the home of the village head. It had no electricity—just like the rest of the village. We slept on an earthen platform bed, which, because it was of one piece with the exterior ground, had to be thoroughly heated every night. We immediately fell ill with colds if we didn't do this. Even people who can swim in January cannot tolerate the cold that seeps through the ground during Hebei winters.

Platform beds are warmed by lighting fires in a cavity beneath their surfaces. The main fuel in our village was wheat stalks, and it was very hard to get them to burn if they got damp. Matches were in short supply, so flint stones were the usual way to light the stalks, and we learned how to use them. First you lay a little roll of fluffy paper on the ground, then knock a small iron block against a flint stone to produce sparks that fall onto it. If you do it right, the sparks will bring the paper up to the combustion point, and it will begin to smolder flamelessly. You then blow gently on the paper to lure flameless combustion into flamed combustion. Then you apply your little flame to dry straw, let it grow, and use it to light the wheat stalks, which then produce a larger flame. You have to keep blowing—now softer, now harder—at every stage of the process. It takes considerable lung power to keep the fire going. (It may be that the reason why eagles had to keep coming to eat Prometheus's liver was to reduce his ability to blow and to steal fire for humanity.)

Water technology in the village was only slightly ahead of fire technology. The only water supply was from a well that was about thirty feet deep. A windlass at the top of the well was used to draw buckets of water from below. It worked on human power exclusively, but it worked well enough that human power sufficed. The hard part was to be sure that the empty bucket, when lowered into the well, landed on the water's surface upside down so that it would sink into the water and fill completely. If that maneuver failed, the bucket might fill only halfway, or might even float on the surface without filling at all. It is by no means easy to control the orientation of an object thirty feet down when one's only connection to it is a soft rope. It took me more than two weeks of practice to master the necessary remote control techniques. During those days, as I toiled at the wellhead, experimenting with water buckets as Isaac Newton once had, I thought: How many other physicists have had this kind of connection with Newton's buckets?

Because it lay on the flat land in the eastern part of Zanhuang County, Nanxingguo was materially better off than neighboring places. I had a high school classmate who had been working at the Institute of Philosophy in Beijing when he was sent down to the hills in the western part of Zanhuang County. Where he was, there were not even wells. Rain was the only water source. The villagers dug deep pits to hold runoff, and the resulting ponds provided water for drinking as well as every other use. In winters, when the rains stopped, the ponds ran low and the use of water for any purpose except drinking was strictly prohibited. My philosopher classmate went four months without washing his face or rinsing his mouth. Maybe this fit him as a philosopher, I thought. In high school we gave him the nickname of "the thinker" because he liked to imitate the pose of Rodin's famous sculpture. He often seemed lost in thought, in a world all his own. It may have been that life in the remote mountains, without face washing or mouth rinsing, brought him closer to the rarefied terrain that philosophers explore.

Some of the non-philosophers in our sent-down group decided they couldn't take it anymore and absconded. The laboratory worker who was sent down with me headed back to Beijing on his own after a month and never returned. But most of the sent-down, including me, stuck it out and gradually adapted because we really did believe that tempering ourselves in desolate and primitive conditions was the only way to make our souls more saintly.

We all knew that the reason we had been sent down was that our thinking needed reform. Those who had been criticized in the Anti-Rightist Movement were especially vulnerable to guilt feelings. They often felt that only heavy and bitter physical labor could help them to redeem their errors and begin life again. It is important to realize that this guilt mentality was sincere; it was not feigned. Many people set to work feverishly as soon as they arrived. *The toughest job? The dirtiest? I'll do it!* They seemed to feel there was a direct correlation between how hard they worked and how much error they were redeeming.

Still, for many, the question "Am I really wrong? Really guilty?" recurred from time to time. The problem was that two principles, each irreproachable in its own right, and seemingly as irrefutable as Kant's categorical imperative, were in conflict. Principle one was logic. When the Party called for annihilation of the "three evils" (bureaucratism, dogmatism, and subjectivism), the students who dared to ask what produced the three evils were automatically labeled "rightists." But what was wrong with asking the question? Were we to believe that phenomena exist without causes? Principle two was Mao and the Party. Whatever happened, there could be no doubt that Mao and the Party were correct. It was faith. Mao had personally launched the Anti-Rightist Movement, so the rightist views he was criticizing had to have something wrong with them.

Fatigue and exhaustion from labor might have worked on me as a sort of narcotic, helping me temporarily to set aside this nettlesome dilemma, but that did nothing to help resolve it.

Then another shock arrived, and this one was harder to absorb. On January 2, 1958, I received a letter from Li Shuxian in which she wrote that she had been formally expelled from the Communist Party at the end of 1957. We had seen this coming, because Deng Xiaoping had already said in his reports on the Anti-Rightist Movement that all "rightist elements" within the Party would be purged.

One problem was that I was still a Party member. According to the principles of class struggle, there was not the slightest question about what I should do—I should sever ties with Li Shuxian. A member of the Communist Party could not be in love with a class enemy, and rightists, by definition, were class enemies. The rule was merciless. How many loving couples were forced by the Anti-Rightist Movement to separate abruptly and become nothing more than passersby on the street? No one knows. All the tender feelings they had had were of no use. Among my colleagues and friends who faced this terrible dilemma, not one escaped. All were forced to make public shows of "clean breaks" with their romantic partners.

Now it was our turn to face the question. On January 4, 1958, I left Nanxingguo and returned to Beijing.* I went to Peking University, where

---

*Translator's note: Fang was allowed the return trip, at his own risk, because officially he had "volunteered" to go to the countryside.

the Yan Garden campus lay under a deathly pall. The alternatives for Li Shuxian and me were stark: be true to our political faith and separate, or be true to our feelings and stay together. Fate awaited and time was short. I can no longer remember how much we said to each other during the forty-eight sleepless hours that ensued. (Perhaps she can recall more than I, and perhaps will leave a fuller account in memoirs of her own.) But I do recall that the stare of grim reality somehow made us more clear-eyed and rational. In the end it was not completely our political faith, and not completely our feelings of love, but more the guidance of reason that led us to our decision: we would "freeze" our love. What did "freeze" mean? Even now we cannot put it into precise terms, but the word did allow us to find a path across the complexly interconnected landscape of the disaster we found ourselves in. Eventually the tactic did allow us to reconnect, safely and happily.

During the "freeze" we stopped writing letters and cut off all connection in space and time. The connection between our hearts was somewhere else, outside space and time.

When I went back to Nanxingguo I understood things more deeply, and my mood was calm. I threw myself into labor. It was the coldest time of the year, and the village was digging a well. Daytime temperatures peaked around 25 degrees, and a wind blew from the north. The ground was frozen, and we followed the tradition in Chinese well digging of doing it all by hand. Two dozen or so of the strongest men in the village did the basic labor, while another two dozen or so people, some of whom were women, worked in assisting roles.

The first step in building a well the Nanxingguo way is to dig a pit about thirty-five feet deep and nearly twenty-five feet in diameter. At some time more than three hundred million years ago, the foothills of the Taihang Mountains had been a sea beach. This explains why, when we reached a depth of six or seven feet, we began finding pebbles that had been carried from the mountains by rivers that had flowed into the sea. The deeper we dug, the larger the stones were, until, beyond twenty feet down, they were a foot or more in diameter and very hard to remove. Even the strongest workers among us could not keep at it for more than an hour at a time, so we organized ourselves into teams of five and took turns going to the bottom of the shaft in one-hour shifts. This was the most efficient method of energy allocation.

At a depth of twenty-five to thirty feet the roundish stones were fewer and we encountered sand. This was the ancient sand of that original beach. The great scholar of the Song period Shen Kuo (1031–1095) had dug seashells in this area, but we had no inclination to follow him in this amusement because our work was already getting too dangerous. The walls of the pit were beginning to cave, and stones of various sizes often tumbled down. The safety gear for a worker at the bottom of the pit was a stiff hat woven from strips of willow.

At depths beyond thirty feet, water began seeping into the well bottom, and that created the difficult task of scooping out wet sand. If any sand remained at the bottom, seepage into the well would be slow, and it is precisely the rate of seepage—the amount of water that enters a well per unit time—that defines a well's quality.

I joined in the sand scooping. At the beginning of this well project, we "sent-down cadres" had been assigned—along with the women, the old, and the feeble—to do assistant work. The farmers couldn't trust our mettle, so they gave us the lighter work. To me, though, descending the well seemed a romantic challenge. I thought I could do it, persisted in saying so, and eventually was included on one of the heavy-work teams that did sand scooping.

This was the routine: before going down the well, we each took a gulp or two of a local liquor that was about 60 percent alcohol. Then, in the chilly wind, we removed all of our clothing and grabbed a rope to aid in the descent. The water at the bottom was knee-deep. We scooped sand with our two hands, so arms and legs were both always wet. We filled baskets with sand and then attached them to the rope for elevation to the surface. As the baskets ascended they dripped water continually, so we, at the bottom, were constantly soaked. After a while the heat from the local liquor wore off and a severe chill set in. The only defense against the chill was to generate body heat by scooping ever more feverishly. When it became clear that most of us could maintain such a pace for only half an hour, we reduced the shifts from an hour to twenty-five minutes. After ascending, in the still-frigid air, we had to dry off and put our clothes back on immediately. Then we took another swig of the local liquor, rested, and waited for the next call to service. For some of the farmers, if truth be told, the only reason for joining the work teams was to get those two swigs of liquor.

But there was another perk: people who went down the well could eat white-flour pancakes. The normal staples for farmers in the area were sweet potatoes and corn. Food made from white flour was available only during a two-month period in summer after the wheat harvest. So white-flour pancakes in winter were a special treat indeed, a symbol of the honor that was attached to work at the bottom of the well. It came at a price, though. People who descended wells too much could contract "cold legs syndrome," a recurrent and incurable condition in which the knees are sore and numb. All of this—for water.

For me, the greatest reward for going down the well was neither liquor nor pancakes but camaraderie with the farmers. Our shared toil at the well bottom led them to accept me. My "thought reform," in this sense, had succeeded, and my remaining days in the village passed more and more easily. It is worth reflecting on why this was so.

The original concept of the people who designed the policy of sending intellectuals to the countryside was that farmers would reform the intellectuals and make them more loyal to the Communist Party. The theory of class struggle held that poor farmers and other villagers, as archetypal supporters of Communist rule, would condemn and correct the "erroneous" thinking of intellectuals. Moreover, since intellectuals would be an isolated minority in the villages, the pressure to change would be much stronger than in the cities, so thought reform would be more fast and efficient.

What actually happened shows how artificial the theory was. It is true that farmers, especially the "poor farmers," were big supporters of the Communist Party, but this was because the revolution had given them land, not because they shared the ideology of Communism. They did not behave in the way the theory of class struggle predicted.

Chinese villagers respect many kinds of local gods and spirits but generally do not live under concepts of transcendent religion. Things like religious wars are unknown, and worries about "ultimate concerns" are rare. Overarching visions of Jehovah, Allah, Communism, or whatever have little relevance to their daily life. The whole county of Zanhuang did not have a single presentable Buddhist temple; there were a few small Christian churches, but not many believers. When we sent-down intellectuals suddenly appeared, the farmers could not have cared less about our overall worldviews or ultimate concerns. It didn't even occur to them to ask about such things, let alone offer "criticism" or "struggle."

Viewed from the villages, the Anti-Rightist Movement's strong emphasis on ideology stood at an extreme. A gaping mismatch separated Party goals in the cities and life in the villages, and there was no way the farmers could do what the Communists wanted them to do. For us "sent-down cadres," life in the countryside, far from bringing more pressure on our "thought," brought less.

The main standard that the farmers used in judging newcomers was how well a person worked. If your work was good, they accepted you and the distinction between you and them melted away. When I worked on the well with them, I became part of their community. They trusted my ability to work, and I felt a new self-confidence. There was no sense at all that anyone was "being reformed."

When spring came I did what all the other young men in the village did. I plowed the land, carried water on shoulder poles, raised pigs, drove horse carts, and more. Finally I just moved in with one of them. He was single, two years older than I, and we shared everything—house, food, and work. The only thing that separated us was that he smoked and I didn't. He often urged me to try, and once in a while, because I couldn't find a way to resist his generous enthusiasm, I did take a few puffs. Those are the only times in my life I have ever smoked.

Then came the heat of the summer, when, like all the other men in the village, I went naked from the waist up. It was cooler that way, and it saved on laundry. (Customs like this have roots in poverty.) The women of the village, old and young alike, found nothing objectionable when we sent-down males observed the pattern. The only occasions that made us put our shirts back on were meetings at which sent-down females were present. That made us revert to urban custom. Photos from those years show us with bare chests, deep tans, and firm muscles. From surface appearances (i.e., without going into our "thoughts"), we looked like completely authentic farmers.

Mao Zedong wrote a famous article in which he says that intellectuals are short on intellect because they can't plant crops or slaughter pigs. Chinese newspapers liked to reprint this article every time a campaign to criticize intellectuals came along. After the summer of 1958, though, we sent-down cadres lost our vulnerability to taking those silly claims seriously. We learned that those skills that Mao had claimed to be even more difficult than the ones it had taken us twenty years of laborious study to acquire were, in fact, things we could pick up very easily and were now doing every day. At the pace we were learning, a year might be enough—two, at most—to learn all of them. Sometimes we could actually make improvements, because we had the advantage of modern knowledge.

Let's look at Mao's example of pig slaughter. What Mao took to be some kind of great skill in fact is not hard at all, because, at the point when Chinese farmers kill a pig, it has already been tied up and cannot move. The killing is easy. The hard part is to go out into a field and catch the pig. Pigs don't behave like sheep. Sheep move in groups and are easy to tend, but pigs fight over food and run around in all directions. When they scatter, the person tending them has to chase them down and bring them back together. Chasing pigs is hard work. Don't be fooled by their fat bodies and short legs—they can really move. My top speed in the hundred-meter dash (with wind at my back) was 12.5 seconds, but I couldn't catch a pig that was running in high gear.

In short, it is beyond question that catching pigs is harder than killing pigs. Mao Zedong's august pronouncements about pig slaughter only show, I'm afraid, that he had no experience as a pig farmer. (Many of Mao's edicts are less awe-inspiring after you have the chance to test them in the real world.)

By summer, when we "sent-down cadres" had pretty much been accepted by the farmers, some of us started getting love letters or other amorous approaches from local young women. I got a letter myself. None of these initiatives, it turned out, produced anything to write a novel about, but it was another sign that the local people viewed us sent-down types not as targets for "reform" but the opposite, as targets of pursuit.

The phenomenon isn't hard to explain, either. In general, when two different cultures are peacefully juxtaposed, the relatively more advanced of the two will influence the relatively less advanced, and this happens regardless of whether the more advanced side is a minority or a majority.

Chinese villages at the time were sorely in need of the import of something more advanced. What they got next, unfortunately—and it came by force—was the import of something more like a runaway pig. It was Mao's "Great Leap Forward."

In June we took in the wheat harvest. Zanhuang County had a bumper crop of more than 1.5 tons per acre, and the farmers were elated. But then an article appeared in the *People's Daily*, the authoritative national newspaper, that a certain place had made a great leap and produced eight tons per acre, more than five times as much as we had! Most farmers didn't read newspapers, however authoritative. But I believed the newspapers, and I reported to the farmers what I had read. None of them believed it. They just said, "The scales there are wrong." It was true that measuring standards in China were hardly uniform, and differences from place to place could be considerable. But it was hard to explain a fivefold discrepancy that way.

I didn't press the point with my farmer friends. Then, a few days later, that authoritative newspaper reported that in some other place the wheat harvest had broken the forty-tons-per-acre level—more than twenty-five times better than ours! This time I didn't relay the news to the farmers, but they heard about it anyway, and now they stopped saying that they didn't believe it. The spirit of the Great Leap Forward was pushing through the land, descending level by level through the Communist bureaucracy, demanding that each locale begin its Leap by producing twice as much grain, then five times as much, then ten. The farmers, who were not in the habit of opposing what the Communist Party said, did their best to obey. (I can't say, of course, whether they might have privately had the thought that the Leap would work if we just adjusted the scales.)

When the Leap started, I was assigned to write slogans, and for two weeks I wrote them on every conspicuous wall in the village. My characters were big, about two meters square. The instructions said that the bigger the characters were, the bolder readers would be and the greater the Leap would be. The two slogans that I wrote the most were:

More, faster, better, cheaper!
Struggle upstream with all you've got!

And:

One year is enough
For a ten-year plan!

The first of these was a headline that appeared in that same authoritative newspaper almost every day, and the latter was a slogan I had seen on many other walls. I never did know what "ten-year plan" meant, and it seemed no one else did, either.

As the hottest part of the summer arrived, the temperature of the air and the craziness of the politics ascended in direct proportion. The authoritative newspaper had a report of a place that again had increased grain production by an order of magnitude, to two hundred tons per acre. Meanwhile a new directive descended through the levels of the bureaucracy: "do deep-plowing." Researchers at Communist Party Central had discovered that when seeds are sown after deep-plowing, harvests are much larger. Word came down that in places where plowing was as deep as half a meter, harvests increased fivefold. The spirit of the message was that the formula could be extrapolated: if you plowed one meter deep, the increase would be tenfold.

With that our village began a nighttime campaign (it was cooler at night) to deep-plow. I was in good health but still could not match many of the farmers in arm strength. So I resorted to "invention" and found a way to deep-plow faster than people with stronger arms could. The term in Chinese for "deep-plowing" was *shenfan*, literally "deep turnover," and it asked only that the soil be inverted, not that it be broken into small pieces. I calculated that it would take less energy just to cut the soil into large squares and then invert them. By this method most of the work was in only two dimensions, not three. "Deep turnover" could be achieved more quickly.

Next, the spirit of the Leap leaped all the way to the heavens. As the ever-deeper plowing continued, the whole village galloped into Communism faster than an insane pig. The next month was the only one in my life spent in pure Communism. Every household in the village closed its kitchen and people ate in a communal mess hall. There was no charge for the food—currency had been abolished—and everyone took what he or she needed. During the day the commune members slept or studied the news of the Great Leap Forward, and when evening came they formed work brigades to go out into the fields, carrying oil lamps, to do deep-plowing. A canopy of stars above and an array of bobbing lights below illuminated the murky working fields, whose eerie silence was broken only by the occasional barking of a dog. Dig deep, dig deep, dig deep deep deep! Dig for the ideals of Karl Marx, right here, right now!

I should admit that, at the time, I did not adequately perceive the falsity and lunacy of the Great Leap. The reports of cabbages weighing 550 pounds and sweet-potato harvests of four thousand tons per acre did not, at the time, arouse my doubt—I guess because I felt that agronomy was not my field of expertise. Maybe there were indeed "different scales" at work—or something I did not understand.

What did trigger my skepticism was a paper on "physics" that appeared in the *People's Daily* during the time we were doing deep-plowing. The author was Qian Xuesen, a professor who had recently returned from the United States and whom Mao Zedong had praised to the skies. Qian's argument, which still sticks in my mind, was that, based on the principle of conservation of energy, and using the solar constant (i.e., the rate at which solar radiation arrives on the earth's surface), one can calculate the maximum number of calories that can be produced per unit of land. Qian showed that this upper limit was far higher than even the amazing numbers in the Great Leap reports. He wanted to give the Great Leap the credibility of physics, and his point was that the Leap so far was by no means "Great" enough. There was room for even bolder leaping.

But, to repeat, you can't cheat physics. Even setting aside the question of whether Qian was using "science" to flatter political power, the science itself was just plain wrong. His calculation was based on conservation of energy as described in the first law of thermodynamics. But by 1958 it was already well known that this law does not hold for systems of plant growth. What plants "consume" is not energy in this sense but negative entropy. The flow of negative entropy from the sun to the earth is what would determine the upper limit of plant production. To use conservation of energy to calculate crop maximums is fundamentally mistaken. (And even if we were talking about energy, the amount of energy the sun sends to the earth is about the same as the amount the earth radiates back out to space.) The only thing the article really proves is that its author had no understanding of what was already known in the field of nonequilibrium thermodynamics. (I should apologize for using technical jargon in a memoir, but in this case I see no other way to say exactly what I feel a need to say.)

Freedom is vital to science; science dies without it. When Qian's ridiculous article came out, Chinese physicists could see it for what it was, but no one had the freedom to say so. Not even purely scientific criticisms were possible, because this author was a favorite of Mao Zedong and this article's conclusions supported the Great Leap Forward. But the even more baleful fact is that the dictator of a mammoth political party could be so benighted and reckless as to use obsequious "science" to make policies that affected nearly a billion people. How can a country that imprisons science expect anything but disaster?

On the eve of the catastrophic collapse of the Great Leap, I left the village to go to the University of Science and Technology of China to teach physics.

8. INTO THE UNIVERSITY OF SCIENCE AND TECHNOLOGY

I WORKED AT THE UNIVERSITY OF SCIENCE AND TECHNOLOGY OF CHINA (USTC) for twenty-eight years and four months, from the end of August 1958 until January 1987. My entry and my exit, separated by nearly three decades, shared an interesting point in common: both coincided with an expulsion from the Communist Party of China. The two expulsions were, moreover, done in the same way.

The charter of the Communist Party of China sets out the procedure for expelling a member. First, there is to be a meeting of all members in the concerned member's branch. The concerned member has the right to attend and to present a self-defense. After full discussion, the question is put to a vote. If the vote passes, the matter goes to the Party Committee at the next highest level and, if approved there, becomes official. Plainly, it would be a lot of trouble to expel a Party member in this way. But the Party Charter also provides that in emergency situations, higher levels in the Party can expel a member without going through a meeting of the local Party branch or giving the person in question an opportunity for self-defense. Expulsion of this latter sort has immediate effect.

The term "emergency situations" normally refers to warfare or to events like fires or earthquakes. At such times, much can happen in the blink of an eye and there may be no time to hold a meeting—and that is when the expedited-expulsion provision in the Party Charter can take effect. On the two occasions when I was expelled from the Party, we were not on a battlefield, and I didn't notice any earthquakes. We were holding classes at a university. Still, the provision was invoked and I was expelled immediately, without a meeting or a chance to defend myself.

The underlying reason for emergency treatment of my case, in both instances, was not really that the case was special (although it was, both times, not a common case); the more fundamental fact was that the authorities viewed universities as a kind of battlefield. Mao had said, "We [Communists] have no university professors; they all belong to the Kuomintang, and they're the ones running [the universities]." He also said, "the real power in the worlds of scholarship and education lies in the hands of the bourgeois intellectuals, who in fact are Kuomintang people." In short, universities continued to be viewed as KMT zones. The KMT armies had been defeated, but the universities remained battlefields on which the KMT intellectuals had not yet surrendered. This was the underlying cause of my two "emergency expulsions," and it reveals how the Party has viewed universities for decades.

USTC was founded in 1958. When I reported for duty it consisted of only a hundred or so people doing preparatory work. My initial position was Teaching Assistant in Physics, but there were no students yet. The university's initial charge was to create a teaching institution in science and technology using the intellectual resources of the Chinese Academy of Sciences. There were three additional, more concrete goals: atomic bombs, guided missiles, and satellites—or "two bombs and a star," as our catchphrase put it. Plans for these were just getting under way.

The Chinese Academy of Sciences, modeled on the Soviet Academy of Sciences, offered no courses and accepted very few graduate students. It was a good idea, therefore, to launch a university like USTC where the assemblage of talented scholars could also be teachers. The first group of professors at USTC were all from the Academy of Sciences, and many were China's best scholars in their fields. Compared with China's economy, which was stalled at the time, USTC's growth was remarkably fast. In 1980, when China opened to the world, Peking University sent the largest number of physics graduate students to the United States for advanced study, but USTC was right behind with the second-largest number.

USTC was born in the wake of the Anti-Rightist Movement, and the Communist Party, still leery of the intellectuals, laid down some extra-strict guidelines: education was to serve the proletariat and was to be combined with productive labor. The key lines in the school anthem were:

> *Greet the eternal east wind and raise the red flag high!*
> *Be red, be expert, in factory as on farm!*

It could have been the anthem of a Communist Party training ground. In September 1958, a high military official who came to speak at our opening exercises put it plainly: USTC should adopt the model of the Resist-Japan Military and Political University, an army school at the Communists' prerevolutionary base at Yan'an in Shaanxi Province. USTC's campus had, in fact, once been the campus of the International Party School, whose mission was to train activists from around the world—mostly from countries where the Communists were not yet in power—in how to carry out Communist revolution.

Guo Moruo, president of the Academy of Sciences in 1958, served ex officio as the first president of USTC. Guo was a famous poet during the New Culture Movement of the late 1910s, but no trace of his interest in poetry rubbed from him onto USTC. By that time, too, his own "poetry" was embarrassing. I remember this example:

> *Old Guo, not so old,*
> *Many poems, not so good.*
> *Everybody, work together*
> *Learn from Chairman Mao!*

On one point he was right: you could not make a mistake if you took everything from Chairman Mao. There was a time in 1961, for example, when new instructions on education were passed down from Mao through the bureaucracy, and one of the important points was that students could use crib notes. In appreciation, students began openly copying at exams—and citing Mao. Faculty monitors had to pretend they didn't see.

Still, I was happy to be at USTC. Whatever the irritations, I was back to physics research and out of the nuclear reactor game. I could work on things that interested me again. Life is short, and one of its pleasures is to pursue one's real interests. That line about "in factory as on farm" didn't bother me at all. I could dig wells and catch pigs. Big deal. In the fall of 1959, the teaching assistants at USTC were organized for the "on farm" part of the school's mission; we were sent to the mountains outside Beijing to plant trees. At noon that day, I ate nine standard-sized steamed buns, which was tops in our group and also stands to this day as my record intake for a meal. I had not forgotten village life. Hard work and eating were still easy for me.

I was, of course, not as naked—in either my upper body or my innocence—as I had been at Zanhuang. Throughout my eight months in the village, I had always clung to the belief that if I labored hard I could return to my former political status of "trusted person." But my expulsion from the Party had shown me that in matters of politics, sincere effort, in no matter what quantity, might mean nothing.

It was clear that my plan to write a letter to Party Central in 1957 had brought a change in nature, not just degree, in my trust ranking. I was in an "other folder" now. In a feudal social system, a person's status, once fixed, is extremely hard to change, and the same is true in a class-struggle society. Once you are in an "other folder" (even if they don't print this on your ID card) it is nearly impossible for you to rise again. No effort of yours will be recognized. Realizing this point freed me from the illusion that "more reform" would restore me to trust. The naïveté and sincerity with which I viewed the Communist Party during my youth was now dead and gone.

I still clung to one part of the illusion, though. I thought the Party would at least observe that bedrock value of Chinese farmers and find a place for someone who did hard and honest work. If I just stuck conscientiously to my work, there would still be growing room for me in the system. So I threw myself into teaching, and I really enjoyed it.

My teaching began in 1959, USTC's second year. I taught a bit of almost everything—from first-year general physics to advanced-level modern physics, and from basic laboratory to theory of several kinds. In 1960 a professor from the Institute of Modern Physics was teaching a course on quantum mechanics when, for some reason, he had to withdraw halfway through. I was assigned to take over, and the students didn't seem to mind that a mere teaching assistant had replaced their professor. This boosted my confidence.

It was also around that time that I began my own research work. I chose particle physics, but the working conditions were difficult. We could read Soviet academic journals, but there was a six-month lag for access to Western journals, and preprints were not available at all. There were a few others at the university interested in particle physics, but they were younger scholars with little research experience, and our discussions were not very fruitful. Isolation and closed doors are two great enemies of physics research. Despite the difficulties, though, I was doing what I wanted to do, and my interest remained strong.

In the spring of 1960, I began submitting articles for publication. One of them, called "Calculation of Nucleon Electric Radius by Corrected Propagation Function," was accepted in the fall by *Acta Physica Sinica*. The executive editor of that journal, Professor Qian Linzhao, was teaching at USTC at the time. One afternoon, in a stairwell where no one else was present, he stopped me. His face somehow expressed joy and gloom simultaneously. He told me, with elation, that my paper was about to go to press; then, with difficulty, he said, "But we can't use your real name. Can you change the name?"

It was obvious that he was not expressing his own view. Nor was he relaying a decision by the board of *Acta Physica Sinica*. Nowhere in the world do physicists write under pseudonyms.

I understood. My activity (publishing papers, in this case) had exceeded the bounds that were allowed to citizens in the "other folder" and had to be blocked. Forbidding me to publish under my own name also served as a warning: "Don't forget your status!" There was no room for resistance; I could only comply. The name that sprang to my mind was Fang Zhi, because I had used it once before, in junior high school, when my brother and I (he more than I) had written an article and published it in a newspaper. But Professor Qian couldn't accept that name, because it resembled the original name too closely. I had great respect for Professor Qian as an elder in my field, so I backed off from choosing the pseudonym and asked him to choose one for me. He agreed.

My paper appeared in *Acta Physica Sinica*, no. 1, 1961, under the name Wang Yunran. When I saw the name, my respect for Professor Qian shot even higher. He had used this name to send a signal to the world that in order to publish a physics paper in China one needed not only to pass muster with peers but to receive a nod from the king. "Wang" means "king," and "Yunran" is "wills it so." Qian was, moreover, prophetic. The principle of "the king wills it" soon appeared as a formal regulation: any manuscript submitted to *Acta Physica Sinica* had to undergo political inspection at the author's home institution. Without such approval, it could not go to press. After the Wang Yunran piece, the next few articles I sent to *Acta Physica Sinica* were all sent back because they had failed this political approval. Those rejected papers did achieve something, though. They became a bridge between me and Professor Qian, and the two of us, despite our age difference, became close friends.

If, for a moment, we put ourselves in the shoes of the authorities, it is easy to see why, among academic fields, physics is so frustrating. First, you have to have it; you can't just sweep it away, as you can, for example, psychology. (Actually, psychology is useful, too, but never mind.) Second, none of the great proletarian teachers can figure out the class nature of what physicists talk about—electromagnetic radii and such. (For the field of psychology, the determination is easy: psychology is bourgeois.) How can one apply proletarian dictatorship to the field of physics? These were tough problems. Not sufficiently tough, though, to spare physics from the long arm of proletarian dictatorship.

The authors of papers in *Acta Physica Sinica* in those days were listed as Nuclear Physics Group 401, Theory Group 918, Cosmic Ray Group 515, and so on. In some of the papers it was impossible to see the name of a single Chinese person anywhere in the whole article—except, of course, the name Mao Zedong. Just as Dmitrii Blokhintsev in the 1940s Soviet Union had to refer to Lenin as his guide in quantum mechanics, so, in the 1960s, Chinese physicists had to cite Mao as the supreme helmsman in their work. In an effort to assuage China's high-level intellectuals, many of whom had been frightened out of their wits by "class struggle," Chen Yi, who was regarded as the most open-minded among the top Communists, came out one day in the early 1960s to say (this is my summary, not verbatim), "Don't be afraid, just keep rowing your own boats; with the Communist Party at the helm, you all can relax." Chen's words, which were later contracted to the rhythmic slogan "you row the boat, we'll hold the rudder," spread widely. Intellectuals wanted to believe them. Some were even moved to tears: the supreme proletarian authority was reserving a safe place for intellectuals! On the great ship of Communism, they could be oar station number 401, number 918, or number 515—inert tools, but safe.

My mention of the "tool" metaphor here is no exaggeration. In the early 1960s, the *People's Daily* repeatedly exhorted the Chinese people to imitate the model soldier Lei Feng and become the obedient "tools" of the Party. The most that I, as resident of one of the "other folders," could aspire to was the role of a tool that didn't even have a number.

Li Shuxian's standing in the system was even lower than mine. She wasn't allowed a pen name. She worked on several translations of physics papers by Soviet experts, but when they were published, her name appeared in no form at all, with or without disguise, either on the cover or in the acknowledgments. Officially, she didn't exist. Hers was a "nonperson folder."

When I was expelled from the Party the reason for the "freeze" in my relationship with Li Shuxian went away, so we got back in touch. She, like me—only a bit later—had been "sent down" to the countryside, in her case to Mentougou on the outskirts of Beijing. In the fall of 1959, when Mao Zedong announced an amnesty to celebrate the tenth anniversary of the founding of the People's Republic of China, she was among the pardoned. She was transferred back to Peking University and her rightist hat was removed.

In fairness to future readers, I should add a note here. A few decades from now people may not know that "hat" does not refer to headgear. "Her rightist hat was removed" means something different. A hat was a category, not a material object. To say someone wore this or that hat was to identify his or her position in the sociopolitical hierarchy, and to "remove a hat" was to vacate that status. Hatted positions were almost always tainted positions, the result of one or another kind of repression by the proletarian dictatorship. How the repression happened is a large and complicated question that is beyond my scope here. The question merits study, though, and I predict that historians of the future, looking back at this period, will inaugurate a subfield called "hatology."

Li Shuxian's hat was off, which was a formal upgrade of status, but in fact there was little change in her condition. She was now a "dehatted rightist." (My apologies again to readers unfamiliar with these technical terms. You might find them tiresome, but I see no way around them.) She was sent back to the university to work but was not allowed to teach, let alone do research. She was assigned to work at the school's factory.

For nearly two years between 1959 and 1961, Li Shuxian and I lived basically as we had before the Anti-Rightist Movement. I went to the Peking University campus on Saturdays and we spent the weekend together; the rest of the time we were apart, at the university and at USTC, struggling along in parallel. We wanted to stick with our original plan of getting our careers on track before tying the knot.

But by the summer of 1961 we couldn't hold out any longer and decided to get married. I had published only one paper—that "king-wills-it" paper—and she had no publications in her name at all. This was well short of what we had first had in mind under the principle of "establishing careers before getting married." We had failed. But we both felt there was really no choice about the marriage question. In our current positions we felt boxed in, with no space of our own. Only by setting up a household, we thought, could we have our own little bailiwick.

Beginning in 1961 the ambiance for teaching and research in the universities dissipated as politics intruded more and more. There were fewer academic seminars at USTC, and one day per week was devoted to "political study." The atmosphere got tighter still after Mao unveiled his directive to "do class struggle every year, every month, every day." People in the universities started informing on one another. At one point a lecturer at USTC was able to lay hands on the transcript of an informer's report on a few people who had been talking, in a dormitory for lecturers, about a corruption case that they had read about in the newspapers. The report contained passages like this one:

> A: How can stuff like this happen right before the eyelids of the emperor?!
> B: (*pointing at A*) Are you running a fever?
> F: Who's got aspirin for him?
> C: (*chuckles to himself*)

In those days informers did not have tape recorders or video cameras, but their transcripts were no less detailed than if they had. The key elements in the snippet above are that A used "emperor" to refer to the highest authority and that the others had responded with mirth. This proved that everyone present was disloyal to the highest authority. Today, as I write, A is in the physics department at Zhejiang University, B is in the math department at Hong Kong Polytechnic, and C is at the Harbin Institute of Technology. F is me. Use of the word "emperor" to refer to the man at the top was pretty standard in those days, so this particular passage was not enough to result in any punishment for us. But we learned something from the episode. We learned how closely we were being watched, even in casual contexts. How, after that, could we just relax and do research?

This was a major reason why Li Shuxian and I decided to marry. We knew the regime was still not wealthy enough to install bugs in every private home. So, if we had our own, we would have a little island of security.

The early 1960s were also an era of man-made famine. After "deep-plowing," Chinese villages fell before the God of Death. Within three years, twenty million people (some say forty million) died of starvation. Something in me resists recall of those years, and especially of the people whom the famine robbed of their human dignity. For just a bite of food, a person facing death by starvation will trade all morality, all custom, all reason. Such a person becomes no longer human, but an animal—indeed less than many animals, who stop short, no matter how hungry, of eating their own kind. And what was the word for this? Tragic? Brutish? Disgusting? Pitiable? No, this was "socialism saving China." In the most chilling cases, every person in a village starved to death—there was no village—and yet the slogans painted large on the ghost-village walls still grandly announced that "Communism is heaven, socialism the bridge." Just like that, among those favored citizens of socialism, a few tens of millions were granted prior-emigration passes to the Communist heaven.

Universities were assigned a "research question": What cooking methods make people feel more full on the same amount of grain? This challenge led to the discovery of the "double-steaming method" for cooking rice. Steamed twice, rice becomes soggy and unpalatable. When food is hard to stomach, people feel there is "more" of it. Other researchers discovered the "cold food" theory: the human stomach senses the presence of cold things better than warm things, so if people eat cold things they will feel full sooner. But others disagreed, arguing that hot food makes more sense, because hot food by definition contains more calories. In short, "fullology" was all the rage.

This context, too, inclined us toward marriage. Having our own home could provide some warmth even as the world outside edged toward doomsday. We married on October 6, 1961. The ceremony took place in a meeting room in the physics department at Peking University. It was a simple occasion, but many friends came, in defiance of the fact that we were both "other folder" citizens. Some of our teachers came, too. There were still a lot of good people in the world. Everything went smoothly and happily except for the minor infelicity that we could offer only pears as refreshments. During the famine, pears were the only fruit one could buy, but in China it was taboo to serve them at weddings because *li* (梨) meaning "pear" is a perfect homophone for *li* (离) meaning "separate." And the pear-predicted separation did indeed come about: between 1969 and 1987, for eighteen years, Li Shuxian and I would be forced to live apart, one in the north and one in the south.

Our marital home was a 120-square-foot apartment in Building 16 at Peking University. Does fate do recycling as a way to tease? Building 16 was where Li Shuxian lived in 1952 when we were freshmen at the university. It is also the building closest to the dining hall and to "the triangle," the most politically sensitive spot on campus. Its east wall is where that 1957 poem "It's Time" was posted. The Li Shuxian and Fang Lizhi of 1961 were already a far cry from what they had been in 1957, to say nothing of 1952. Such are the perversities of fate. Who could have guessed in 1952 where we would now be? Our shining ideals of the early 1950s were gone forever, but we still weren't ready to give up. We were only twenty-five!

Our daily routine reverted to what it had been during our student days. We ate in the student dining halls and hit the books right afterward. The difference was that now we didn't have to go to the main library and sit separately, one upstairs and one down. We could sit in our own home next to each other. The desks we worked at were the same little student-model desks.

My first joint project with Li Shuxian was to translate *Quantum Mechanics* by Leonard I. Schiff. In 1962, when I was teaching quantum mechanics, Professor Huang Wuhan handed me a draft translation of Schiff's book and asked me to check it before publication. I found the translation so bad that I decided to do a new one. Li Shuxian's political status at the time did not allow her the right to publish translations, but she joined the work anyway, because this book was one that both of us really liked. She was pregnant at the time, and some people were counseling us that the mother's translating would be good for the fetus.

By the time we had finished the book, class struggle had grown so intense that not only Li Shuxian but I, too, was barred from publishing. Our translation of Schiff's book was banned before it could appear. I recalled the way the farmers of Zanhuang had measured value: by honest labor. That standard was the opposite of the one the Communist Party was now using.

Somehow, largely by luck, that Schiff translation survived the tumultuous Cultural Revolution years and we finally published it in 1980, eighteen years after we had begun work on it. A whole generation had passed in the interim: the fetus that had benefited from its mother's translating was now a freshman in the department of applied physics at Peking University and at that very time, by chance, was studying quantum mechanics. Professor Huang Wuhan, who had originally suggested the translation, was not so lucky; he had been unable to withstand the political persecution and had committed suicide.

Our first son, Fang Ke—the translation beneficiary—was born on Valentine's Day in 1963, and that happy event seemed to bring a lucky bonus with it: Professor Qian Linzhao recommended me to Professor Li Yinyuan of the Physics Research Institute (PRI) in the Academy of Sciences. Li directed the research section on the theory of solid state physics and invited me to join his group. It was a great opportunity for two reasons. First, the research environment at PRI, China's oldest institution for physics research, was much better than that at USTC. Second, any paper on which I collaborated at PRI could avoid political censorship by being submitted for publication through PRI, where it fell between the cracks. Political monitors at USTC would not see it, because it was not a USTC paper. Monitors at PRI would see it, but they had no control over me because my work unit was USTC. Quite a number of my papers slipped through this loophole, and I have felt grateful ever since to Professors Qian and Li, who discovered this "dislocation gap" and allowed it to work for me. (One of Professor Qian's special fields, as it happened, was "dislocation" in solids.)

My move to PRI meant that my research shifted to solid state physics. I worked on the effects of impurities in solids. Physicists already understood that the slightest impurity in an ideal crystal could cause major changes in its properties. The entire quality of a crystal is determined by its extremely tiny impurities. But this was not a cutting-edge field. After one year and two papers, I shifted to laser physics.

The first operating laser in the world was built in 1960, and China's first one was built at PRI in 1963. Laser physics was a brand-new field, just opened to exploration, and a whole range of topics awaited study. I chose two: laser coherence, which meant studying laser line width, and nonlinear optical effects, which focused on the two-photon effect. Except for going to classes and to political study sessions at USTC, I threw all my energies into this research, and 1964 became my most productive year since 1957: I completed six papers, of which four were immediately published in *Acta Physica Sinica*. Only one other person that year had as many articles in the journal as I had. Every time Professor Qian Linzhao saw me he gave me a kind smile. I knew he was proud of me.

But once again, the two of us were wrong. Even though our tiny sliver of satisfaction came entirely from physics and had nothing to do with the great proletarian dictatorship, and even though my papers discussed only the brilliance of laser beams and cast not even the tiniest of shadows across the brilliance of Mao Zedong Thought, still, a few days into the new year of 1965, I was punished again—sent again to do rural labor.

The mayor of Beijing at the time was Peng Zhen, number 9 in the Communist hierarchy. Perhaps he, too, had studied impurities in crystals, because he joined with the minister of public security, Luo Ruiqing, to come up with a new term: "crystal city." A crystal city was a city whose residents included not one single class enemy; it was a purest-of-the-pure proletarian city. The plan was to make Beijing into one. Every present or former target of the proletarian dictatorship, any hat wearer of any kind, was accordingly ordered out. I had no official hat but of course was an "impurity," so I was ordered out, too.

About one hundred people in USTC received removal orders. Most of us were only impurities, not hat wearers. Our first temporary station was the Changyang farm to the southwest of Beijing. The work there was roughly the same as at Zanhuang. The differences between the two experiences were, first, that China's villages had lost the naturalness and sincerity that they had had before the Great Leap famine, and second, that the people sent down had nothing of the naive idealism they had brought with them in the 1950s. In addition to labor we had to engage in political study that forced every person, every day, to violate conscience by lying, exaggerating, performing loyalty pledges, and displaying fake smiles. People's true feelings were hidden deep beneath wretched masks. Everyone was aware that no matter how hard you worked, or how sincere you tried to be, nothing could expunge the marks of impurity that you bore. You were like Jean Valjean in *Les Misérables*, for whom no amount of effort could either wipe away the crime of stealing a loaf of bread or spare him from being hunted for the rest of his life. The people sent to Changyang harbored no hope; all they could do was await the orders that would send them even farther from Beijing.

My orders of this kind came in April 1965. I was to report to an electronics factory in the city of Yingkou in Liaoning Province. The banishment from Beijing—from my family, and from physics—would be permanent. One by one, the others in my sent-down group faced their fates and departed. I got ready to leave, too. It was virtually unthinkable to disobey orders. The entire country was "proletarian." Where would one go?

It was almost a miracle that in the end, I did not have to follow the orders. The matter was forestalled because Yan Jici, the vice president of USTC and the most senior living Chinese physicist, had taken my published papers to Liu Da, the Party Secretary at USTC, and expressed his puzzlement. Why would we be sending away a young man who had just begun to show this kind of promise? Just like that, Liu Da canceled the order.

This counts as a near miracle not only because it was so extremely uncommon but because it depended on the coincidence of *two* extraordinarily unusual events. First, even though Yan was vice president of the university, he had no authority over its affairs because he was not a Party member. All of the administrative power in a university lay with its Party Committee. For a non-Party vice president to address a Party committee about the transfer order of a teaching assistant was almost unheard of. Personnel questions were out of bounds for non-Party members. Second, a Party Secretary had accepted a request to keep at school a person with a record of "impurities." This, too, was immensely unusual. There were several later occasions on which this same Party Secretary, Liu Da, looked out for me. In 1987, after my second expulsion from the Communist Party, he came to see me even though he had been retired several years.

"The Communist Party does not like you!" he said.

I said nothing. A few seconds later, he added, as if talking to himself:

"The Communist Party doesn't like me, either."

This might explain why he had accepted Yan's suggestion in 1965. In any case, two near miracles had occurred, and it was a third that they had coincided.

When I left Changyang in 1965, fall classes at USTC had already begun, and I immediately resumed teaching, this time a course in quantum electronics. I was promoted from teaching assistant to lecturer. Despite this turn for the better, I was still aware, of course, that the authorities didn't like me. *If you don't like me, then so be it,* I thought; a person cannot live only to have others like him. If I'm an "impurity," then fine; I will live with my basic nature. Perhaps, in a sense, a society is like one of those crystals: its attributes are determined by its rare impurities. If this is so, an atom of impurity will be much more powerful than an atom of conformity. Romain Rolland said that "we are not just small, insignificant wheels on this war chariot as it rumbles forward."

Yes, I thought, *no matter how tiny we are, we must be more than little wheels.* If I can just hold on to my own rudder, I can still play my small part in shaping the way things are.

9. DAYS UNDER THE DYNASTY

Life returned to something more like normal when I returned to USTC after the stint at the Changyang farm. I spent most days on teaching or research, and although I didn't achieve any big breakthroughs, my papers did keep getting published, which was satisfying. Pretty soon career paper number thirteen came out, and right when I reached that unlucky number, China's Great Proletarian Cultural Revolution broke out as well.

In one respect the Cultural Revolution differed from all the previous campaigns the Party had run. All the earlier ones had had named targets—the Eradicate Counterrevolutionaries Movement in 1950 was aimed at "counterrevolutionary elements" who were trying to duck and hide after the revolution; the Anti-Rightist Movement of 1957 aimed at "rightist elements"; and so on. But in the Cultural Revolution, it was never easy to say exactly who was and who was not going to be "revolutioned," as the neologism put it. Even now people have different answers to the question of what was going on during the wild years from 1966 to 1976.

My own analysis is that those were the years when Mao Zedong announced himself as emperor. He did not name his dynasty or reign period, but in every other way, in both form and substance, it is easy to show that he had become emperor. I noted in the previous chapter that university lecturers in the early 1960s were already using "emperor" in a facetious sense to refer to Mr. Top Leader. Mao's image was in transition from national hero to imperial monarch. He liked to draw public comparisons between himself and Cao Cao and the First Emperor of Qin, two of the cruelest potentates in Chinese history.

Then, during the Cultural Revolution, Mao went on to adopt the forms and accoutrements of an emperor. On every document that the Communist Party sent out and at every meeting that it convened, wherever and whenever the name Mao Zedong appeared, the words *wansui! wansui! wanwansui!* appeared as well. *Wansui*, literally "[may he live] ten thousand years," is glossed in the *Dictionary of Modern Chinese*, the Communist Party's officially approved dictionary, as "a term used in feudal times for address of the emperor by courtiers and commoners." That's it. There is no second definition, none that says "also used by the citizens of People's Republics to address their leaders."

In the late 1970s, after the end of the Cultural Revolution, the son of one of my colleagues was preparing for college entrance exams. As he was struggling to memorize the names of all the dynasties through more than two thousand years of Chinese history, he suddenly felt that one was missing.

"What dynasty is it today, Dad?" he asked his father.

The father, helpless either to laugh or cry, said nothing for a moment, then, in an angry burst, stammered, "What dynasty?! The Mao dynasty! The Mao dynasty! The Deng dynasty! The Deng dynasty!"

That son was no dolt. He got into Peking University and later went to a university in Philadelphia for a Ph.D. in physics. The father was my color-blind college lab partner Hou Depeng. At the time, in the late 1970s, Hou was president of Guangxi University.

This dialogue between father and son was not as absurd as it may seem. In theory, China's imperial system ended once and for all with the 1911 revolution, but the history of the ensuing decades shows that the "once and for all" part was not true. In 1915 Yuan Shikai pronounced himself emperor and held on to the position for eighty-one days. From 1932 to 1945, Pu Yi, who had been Qing emperor from 1908 to 1912, "restored" himself as emperor of Manchuria—even though he was a puppet of the invading Japanese. These are the two most famous gambits toward being a post-1911 emperor, but neither amounted to much compared to the ten years of Mao's emperor-like rule.

On June 1, 1966, the first day of the Great Proletarian Cultural Revolution, all classes at USTC and other universities were canceled. Libraries and laboratories were closed as well. All faculty and students threw themselves into the new political movement. Some of the students organized themselves as Red Guards and started picking out and denouncing the "black elements" they found around them. A titanic struggle between red and black was now under way.

I was not in the first batch to be picked out and "struggled." For a while I was still one of the "revolutionary masses." The first group to be struggled, called the Black Gang, were Liu Shaoqi, president of the People's Republic of China, a few others of Mao's associates at the top, and bureaucrats at all levels who were aligned with them. Quite a few intellectuals were struggled, too, but most of them were the "old authorities" whose names had appeared in the newspapers many times. It's a good thing the Red Guards didn't read *Acta Physica Sinica* or my recent productivity might have put me in that first batch.

Since someone like me was neither fit nor willing to be on the other side—the attacking side—my place at the public "struggle sessions" was with the bystanders, the neither red nor black, the people who just stood and shouted *wansui! wanwansui!* from time to time. Eventually I could even do a bit of research after I got home. I was working on nonlinear Raman scattering in those days, but there was nowhere I could send my papers, because *Acta Physica Sinica* and all the other journals had closed.

The library at the Academy of Sciences had cut back its hours but still stayed open, so I sometimes went there to read. I remember that it was in an issue of *Physics Today* that I learned about the discovery of cosmic microwave background radiation and its implications for hot cosmology. Modern cosmology was infatuating me quickly. But the library soon closed entirely, and my new love for this field, like my love for Li Shuxian a few years earlier, had to be "frozen" for a while.

If one area was being frozen, another was turning red hot. This was

Red Guard activity. It is not widely understood that one reason, indeed the main reason, why so many young people threw themselves so passionately into the worship of Mao Zedong in the fall of 1966 was something that had little to do with Mao Zedong Thought. It was that, beginning in August, under the policy of "great revolutionary link-ups," they could ride the railways free of charge. So long as you said you were a Red Guard, were on a mission to "stir up revolution," and shouted *wanwansui!* a few times, you could hop on any train and go anywhere in China you liked. No ticket or credential was necessary. It was only natural that the number of young Mao fans skyrocketed. Later, beginning in October, no person of any age needed a ticket. All one needed was to say that one was "making revolution."

A group of my colleagues, including the ones I called A and B in the previous chapter, got caught up in this excitement and went on revolutionary link-ups. Their revolutionary destination was the revolutionary Kham grazing area in eastern Tibet, formerly known as Xikang. Announcing their intention to "stir up revolution," they set out to see yaks and Tibetan herdsmen. In short, they were part of a great tide of free tourism, the only one that has ever existed in Chinese history. The only thing one might compare it with was the great tide of free eating that happened during the Great Leap Forward in 1958.

By November I myself couldn't hold out against the temptation of free travel. Five colleagues and I packed a few things and set out from the Beijing rail station on a revolutionary link-up. We felt a bit nervous about it, because, among the six of us, three and a half were "impurities." One had been expelled from the Party (that was me), two had been punished by the Youth League, and one was an overseas Chinese from Indonesia. (Overseas Chinese in those days were semi-impure by definition.) So we always had to be afraid that Red Guards might discover who we were and direct some denunciation and struggle at us. But once we melded into the river of all the other link-up travelers, our fears subsided. There were Red Guards all around us, but they were so eager to get on trains and go make revolution that it apparently didn't occur to them that some of the people they should be focusing on were right under their noses. Just in case, we had made some preparations. I had carved a large round seal that read COMBAT BRIGADE 71, UNIVERSITY OF SCIENCE AND TECHNOL-OGY OF CHINA. In those "revolutionary" times, any group could call itself a "brigade"; you didn't have to register with the police. So, if needed, we could always use this chop to show that we were members of a combat brigade.

There was one sense in which it was indeed true that you needed a spirit of combat in order to do revolutionary link-up (or call it revolutionary tourism). Getting on or off a train was always a battle. With every door and every window open to anyone's use on any basis, the scenes were pretty much what you might imagine them to be. I was a university lecturer, but I would have been sunk if I had tried to maintain decorum appropriate to that status. I wrestled my way through the windows just like everybody else. Luckily, my thirty-year-old body was still in good enough shape to hold its own with the younger Red Guards. Unluckily, our first wrestling bout landed us on the wrong train.

That train was bound for Nanjing, a place I had already been and didn't really feel like going to again. I wanted to go someplace farther away. But by the time we realized what train we were on, getting off was hopeless. The crush of people behind us had made it unthinkable. So: ahoy, Nanjing!

After the train left the station, most of the riders, exhausted from the boarding struggle, one by one fell asleep. But entry into somnolence did nothing to reduce the pressure that everyone exerted on everyone else. Push-back was still requisite.

Suddenly, in the middle of the night, we all were woken by a frenzied voice.

"No air! No air!"

The cries were coming from under a seat. The people who had gotten spaces under seats originally had felt privileged. Those were little protected spaces, where the pilings of the crowd could not reach. No one anticipated, though, that the crowd would get so thick that even air was sealed out of those cubbyholes. The people in them were gasping—and now shouting—for air. People on top, realizing what was at stake, started shouting, "Carry forward revolutionary humanism! Give the people some air!"

Then, in rhythm with our shouting, we heaved our bodies in unison to allow a wedge to open so that air could flow down beneath the seat.

Our trip took us to Nanjing, Suzhou, Hangzhou, and Shanghai. I had been to all of these places before, so nothing felt very new. For me the only new leg in the trip was a steamboat ride from Suzhou to Hangzhou. Like the trains, the boat was free of charge, and this was my first trip ever on China's famous Grand Canal, which had been built in the seventh century A.D. Emperors had used it for pleasure excursions. Two hundred years ago, when the Qianlong emperor made a famous trip to the Yangzi region, he traveled the very same route from Suzhou to Hangzhou that we were now traveling. It was said that when Qianlong's magnificent fleet passed by, ordinary people crowded the banks of the canal shouting *"wansui! wanwansui!"* On our trip, the noise of the steamship engines was too loud for us to hear if there were any *wansui*s coming from the banks. But we could smell foul odors that rose, from time to time, from the surface of the gray-black water of the canal.

Hangzhou was my family's old stomping grounds, so when we arrived there I served as guide for Combat Brigade 71. A misty rain was falling when we visited West Lake, so all of the gorgeous scenes of the lake and the mountains in the background were foggy at best. The combat brigade was acutely disappointed. I kept reminding them of the popular Hangzhou saying:

> *With bright lake and glittering surface, clear days are the best*
> *With murky hills and drifting mists, rain has its charm as well*

I added that when you can't see clearly, you have the advantage that more space is left to be filled by beauty that your imagination can supply. But it didn't work. Challenged in the imagination department, the brigade remained in a funk.

Spirits had recovered by the time we left Hangzhou. When we got to the rail station, though, the crowds were even worse than they had been elsewhere. (As a rule, the prettier a place was, the more revolutionaries came to visit.) How could anyone get on a train? For better or worse, the railway staff invented an ingenious technique. Instead of announcing which platform a train would arrive on, they kept that information secret and announced that anyone who wanted to board should follow a designated staff member. The staff member set out walking, then walked faster and faster, then broke into a run, and ran faster and faster, looping around, until the followers thinned out into a more or less single-file line. This assured that when they finally reached the train they could board without pushing. (Slow runners couldn't get on.) When Combat Brigade 71 joined this melee, its revolutionary solidarity was destroyed. We couldn't find one another and eventually ended up on different trains. Three of us got on a boxcar built for livestock or prisoners. There were no seats, only very small windows, and an open toilet in the center. I later learned by watching films that this was the same kind of car Hitler had used for transporting Jews in Europe. I sat at a distance from the toilet, and a night on the train passed quickly.

We got our room and board from universities or other organizations. Room was free on link-ups, and board very inexpensive. In fact it didn't matter if a person had no money at all; you could just write a note, or intone, "Chairman Mao beckons us to the future," or the like, and the food went onto Mao's tab (i.e., the local people's tab). The custom was rather like the itinerant monks in the old days, traveling from temple to temple without paying, knowing that if they chanted "*a-mi-tuo Buddha*," the Finance Ministry in Heaven would provide.

Our revolutionary link-up ended in December. Every member of our scattered combat brigade found his way back to Beijing by the end of 1966. People might wonder how a movement like the Cultural Revolution, so utterly steeped in politics, could have contained such bubbles of free tourism. But it did. I would wager that at least 90 percent of the people doing link-ups either were in it purely for tourism or, if they did have "revolution" in mind, had not the slightest notion of what their revolution was for or whom it was against. The point of the ferment was, in fact, not revolution—it was for someone to proclaim himself emperor.

I should acknowledge that this insight about Mao's self-proclamation as emperor came to me only later. In 1966 I was still a half-believer. The all-out worship of Mao that I felt in 1949 while waiting for him in the rain at Xiannongtan was, to be sure, long gone by 1966. Many things, not least the Great Leap famine, had shown me that Mao's policies were wrong. But I still felt that he might have meant well despite terribly messing things up. Maybe his Great Leap policies had come only from a wish that China become rich and powerful a bit more quickly. Similarly, my faith in the Communist Party, which was so complete when I was young, had been much deflated. Yet I still felt that the Communist Party was basically different from the Kuomintang or other political parties. The only real hope for China's progress, I thought, was that the Party itself might make progress. As for Marxism, it was still basically my political faith when the Cultural Revolution began. Nothing had replaced it in the sphere that it occupied. In 1965 Xu Jialuan, a colleague a dozen or so years older than I, told me that he really wanted to study abroad and that his first choice was the United States. I told him that if I could go abroad my first choice would be the Soviet Union. My ideal at the time was still Soviet-style socialism. The fact that the Soviet Union's exploration of space was ahead of America's at that time reinforced my faith in socialism.

In my youth a powerful idealism had brought me to Communism, and at one level, the embers of that idealism were still warm. I had taken many shocks and setbacks in the intervening years, but the *ideals*, anyway, were not dead. That is why, when the Cultural Revolution began, and Mao proposed that the Communist Party revolutionize itself from within, my interest once again was captured. I wanted to believe that Mao and the Party finally had seen the error of their ways and now would move forward more reasonably. At a minimum, I thought, they would follow the Soviets and make China into a place where science and technology were strong.

But this hope, like my earlier ones, was quick to collapse. As we went through 1967 and 1968, the universities still held no classes and recruited no students. The laboratories and libraries remained closed. There was no new call for science or technology—nothing at all but politics. You couldn't even get away from politics by studying at home, because the Cultural Revolution had turned into armed combat. University campuses resembled the European Middle Ages, with mobs patrolling around in helmets and wielding clubs, always on the verge of battle. Our home on the Peking University campus was right in a place where two factions were constantly battling, making quiet study impossible. For Li Shuxian and me, living in a combat zone was all the worse because we had to worry about a five-year-old boy. Finally we decided we couldn't take it anymore and abandoned our little home of six years in favor of living with my parents at the Libo Barracks.

During those years, 1967 and 1968, a number of credible stories leaked out about the people at the top of the regime, and just as Khrushchev's secret speech on Stalin had caused me to reevaluate Stalin, these leaked stories caused my mental images of the top Communists in China to shrink drastically. Despite the great respect I had once had for them, when I saw their moral and political qualities in the light of these accounts, there was no way I could identify with them any longer.

The fundamental difference between them and me was that their working concerns were all about factions and power networks, whereas I was worried about scientific method and principles. Marx had held that his theories were "scientific" in the sense that even if the topic were factionalism, the approach to it should be scientific. There should be no parting of the ways between "Party nature" and science. This had been one of Communism's main attractions for me. Short of accepting a split personality, a person who embraces science cannot easily leave it behind.

Many facts made it clear to me that the so-called "two-line struggle" at the top of the Chinese Communist Party was nothing but a great catfight for power, in principle no different at all from the palace warfare under the dynasties that involved the emperor, high officials, and powerful families. To me, the victors (Mao Zedong and his group) deserved no veneration, and the losers (Liu Shaoqi and his group) deserved no sympathy, because neither side was speaking for the idealism and the scientific spirit that I cared about.

Oddly, though, I began to feel that the catfight was liberating me. It allowed me to set aside the naive illusions of my youth as well as all the pain and trouble to which my sincere pursuit of them had led. There was relief in this. I had turned thirty—the age, as Confucius put it, of "establishing oneself" in the world. I could see that the future would be tough, but I felt ready for it.

In the summer of 1968 it became my turn to be a target in the Cultural Revolution. Universities began "cleansing class ranks," a phrase that meant struggling against the "impurities," the new label for which was "ox ghosts and snake spirits." The term formally included landlords, rich farmers, counterrevolutionaries, bad elements, rightists, traitors, spies, and power holders who were taking the capitalist road. Ox ghosts and snake spirits were incarcerated on campuses and could not go home.

I was detained in June, just before the birth of my second son, Fang Zhe. My official category was "rightist who slipped through the net." This meant a person who should have been declared a rightist in 1957 but somehow wasn't. On the day I was detained, our home was raided. The intruders didn't take away any property (despite our official status as the "small propertied class," we didn't have any property to speak of), but we did suffer a significant loss. Hoping to forestall further trouble, we hurriedly burned more than a hundred letters that Li Shuxian and I had exchanged during our separation in 1958 and 1959.

I was held in a dormitory that had been converted into a makeshift prison, where Red Guards monitored the ox ghosts and snake spirits. I had three roommates, all, like me, lecturers in physics. Three were rightists (or net-slipped rightists) and the fourth was a counterrevolutionary: in his high school days, he had joined the Three People's Principles Youth League, the KMT's counterpart of the Communist Federation of Democratic Youth that I had joined. The four of us could still talk physics, so daily life wasn't entirely terrible.

The Red Guards checked on us twice a day. They demanded that we write a daily confession and use the rest of our time to study the famous "little red book" (miniature in height and width but 256 pages thick) entitled *Quotations from Chairman Mao*. This work wasn't hard. Our confessions, which were about a thousand characters each, took about a half hour to write. We copied Mao's *Quotations* for about a third of them, copied political exhortations from the previous day's newspaper for another third, and filled the final third with our own "reflections," which meant expressions like "I have profoundly come to realize that . . ." Later we figured out that no one was actually reading the confessions. The guards were merely noting down whether we handed them in or not.

After that, I made a practice of copying my confessions more than once. If I used characters of somewhat different sizes, I could hand in the same thing, a few days later, and no one noticed. This mass-production method not only saved time, it also meant that I always had a pile of confessions all set to go.

Perhaps because we never fell behind on confessions, the guards gave us favored treatment. They let us go outside for labor every afternoon. This gave us sunshine and exercise, which felt like small blessings wrapped inside the larger disaster we were undergoing. Our labor was making mud paste. The paste for sticking up political posters had always been made of flour, but the posters got so numerous that people ran out of paste and had no more flour rations, so somebody came up with the bright idea of making paste from mud. The invention does much to explain why so many posters could keep going up for all of ten years. That is not a joke; I think it is true.

Struggle intensified during the winter of 1968–69. The authorities sent two groups, the Workers Mao Zedong Thought Propaganda Team ("Work Prop Team" for short) and the Liberation Army Mao Zedong Thought Propaganda Team ("Lib Prop Team" for short) to run our campus. By then we detainees totaled more than four hundred. We had to line up before every meal and walk into the dining hall single file. Later, in the early 1980s, I was a visitor at Cambridge University and sometimes attended formal dinners at High Table in King's College. There, too, people lined up to enter the dining room single file. The most exalted and most lowly human processions bore a resemblance, I realized.

The expanded struggle netted Professor Qian Linzhao, whose category was "suspected spy." This was because he had been acting director of the Academia Sinica in 1949 when that esteemed national-level research body moved to Taiwan. He went to Taiwan himself for a while and then returned to mainland China. Aha! There was the rub: Why did he come back? His motive was unclear, so he was a "suspected spy."

During one spell, Professor Qian and I were roommates, with four others. When the guards were not around, he would tell us about his student years in the 1930s in London. Storytelling like this of course had to be sealed from the ears of the guards. If discovered, it could count as "pining for the old world" and be punishable by at least a scolding and at worst a formal denunciation. We were lucky that Professor Qian, although more than sixty years old at the time, was still quick-witted. One day he was telling us how he had gone to Cambridge to visit some friends and go biking. Cambridge is hilly, and once, while he was coasting downhill, his brakes failed. His bike flew forward, out of control, he panicked, and . . . *Rawk!* A guard suddenly pushed our door open. He may have heard our cheerful banter from out in the hall. In any case, as soon as the door swung open, Professor Qian stopped—on a dime. We all reverted immediately to somber-looking faces and planted our noses in *Quotations from Chairman Mao*. After the guard left, Professor Qian did not resume his story. To this day I do not know how he got off that bicycle.

But let me not give the impression that those days were all comedy and farce. A lecturer in chemistry named Cai, two years younger than I, had a background that paralleled my own: a Peking University graduate, a teacher at USTC, and now a "rightist who slipped through the net." The ox ghosts and snake spirits of the chemistry department were our next-door neighbors, and we saw them every day at meals. One day we couldn't find Cai. He had waited until others went to eat and then thrown himself to his death from a fourth-story window.

A colleague in physics, a lecturer named Ji Weizhi, had not been detained but seemed destined for that fate in the next phase of the campaign. One day he disappeared, too. His body was found in a laboratory, already stiff, bound in coils of electrical wires whose ends had been plugged into a socket. His field had been electrodynamics.

A teaching assistant at USTC who had graduated in physics from Peking University three years after me was not an "impurity" of any kind. But one day someone found her body on the roof of a building, dead from poison. She had never been struggled, but from her friends we learned that the daily ordeal of seeing abuse heaped on others had finally been too much for her, and she had decided to take leave of this world.

On average, the struggle sessions at USTC were not as frightening as they were elsewhere. There were ten suicides that winter at USTC, and this was below average.

We noticed that suicide rates were higher among people who were *about* to be struggled or who felt they were next in line for detention. People who had already been struggled or detained had lower rates. This apparently shows that *impending* disaster—the stage at which ruin looms and creeps ever nearer—is the most frightening. Once it hits, there is less room for terror. The traditional Chinese technique of public decapitations utilized this same psychology. Normally, the people watching decapitations were more terrified than the people being decapitated. Mao Zedong borrowed this ancient principle when he invented the tactic of "holding hat in hand," that is, holding the threat of a political label over your head and letting you know that it might descend at any moment. "Hat in hand" terror led to many suicides. Those of us who were already hatted were, in general, more relaxed. We could even enjoy stories about runaway bicycles in Cambridge.

In any case, the first high tide of suicides ended in early 1969, and in March of that year the government sent everyone at USTC to go build a railroad. Railway construction was one activity that did not stop during the Cultural Revolution, and we were sent to work on a line that connected Beijing with Yuanping, in Shanxi Province. This line had an extremely important function. It linked to the Beijing subway system to form a single route that reached the heart of the city where the top leaders lived. The point was to give the leaders a quick underground escape route in case of emergency. On the eve of the June 4 massacre in 1989, troops suddenly appeared at Tiananmen Square who had not arrived through the streets. They had come by that same Yuanping–Beijing rail line that we had worked on.

The main workforce in railway construction was the Railway Militia, which was run like an army, and we transplanted intellectuals were their adjuncts. We, too, were organized into squads, platoons, and companies. We slept one platoon per tent, and it was very crowded. A person's sleeping space was about three and a half feet wide. I slept next to my platoon leader, Cheng Fuzhen, who later became an important collaborator with me in astrophysics research. The militaristic standardization to which we were subjected had a fortuitous side effect in my case. On campus I had been a "target of the proletarian dictatorship"—very low in the caste system—but at the railroad worksite all intellectuals had the same label: "objects for reeducation." For me, relative to others, this was actually a boost.

We were assigned to build the Lianggezhuang railroad station near Zhoukoudian. The rail line had been designed with many tunnels (perhaps because it was an important escape route?) and our work site was between two of them. One was 260 feet long, and the other, which was still being dug, would be longer. The work inside the tunnels was assigned entirely to the Railway Militia. Our job was to blast the mountainside and move loose rock to construct a flat area between two hills.

We were divided into five work details that did six-hour shifts around the clock. We worked six hours, rested twenty-four, again worked six, and so on. The six hours of work were intense and dangerous. The final task in each work shift was to blast the mountain to knock loose rocks for the next shift to work on. So each time we set out to work we had to negotiate piles of loose rock. It was easy to slip and fall, and falls were unusually hazardous because newly blasted rock is sharp. The first skill we had to learn was how to maintain our balance on sharp, unstable rock.

The actual work brought even more peril. Our job was to go to the top edge of the blasted area and push rocks downhill. We did this while people were working down below. So long as the rocks bounced down singly, the danger was still not too great. But sometimes, because the rocks were loose, pushing one would trigger a general rockslide. You can imagine the dangers for the people below. It was worse at night, when the people below could only hear, not see, the cascading rock. As they worked with their hands, their ears had to stay super-sharp. The slightest sound of a rockslide sent them scurrying for cover. Gradually, we up top learned which rock patterns were most likely to trigger rockslides and could shout advance warnings to the people below. That helped a lot.

The fallen rocks were loaded onto trolleys that ran on a temporary rail line into a valley below, where the rocks were dumped. A trolley loaded with rocks could be pushed by a single person, and that was actually fun, because when you reached the beginning of the downward slope you could hop on and coast down. Sometimes, though—maybe because the rider found it so much fun that he forgot to apply the brakes, or maybe just because the brakes failed—the cart went too fast, jumped the rails, and tumbled into the ravine.

We were lucky there were no fatalities, but there were some permanent injuries. A colleague who later worked with me in an astrophysics group had the forefinger on his right hand squashed and never could straighten it out again. That is only a minor example, of course. It is an uncanny fact that among all the injuries, not one, at least in our group, happened to any of the ox ghosts and snake spirits. I personally came through without a scratch. It was as if the Creator was shielding the pariahs of the empire.

After I got used to the work, I didn't mind doing the night shift from midnight to six a.m. In fact I preferred it to the others. Our work was near the mountaintop, where, about four a.m., one could observe a subtle brightening at the horizon. Then it would grow, and in that limbo between seeming-bright-but-not-yet-bright, the vault of heaven announced its gentle promise of fathomless hope and yearning. Some people, when they watch sunrises, pay attention only to the moment when the sun breaks the horizon. But actually it is the black sky, when it first shows a pregnancy with light, that is most moving. Fundamentally this is the same psychological principle that makes political hats most frightening when they are impending, not when they are actually put in place.

Our railroad work ended in May. Before it was over, Li Shuxian and our elder son, Fang Ke, came to visit me. We went to visit nearby Zhoukoudian, where "Peking Man" had been discovered and where an anthropological museum had been built. Political turmoil had closed the museum, but the walls around it were low enough that even six-year-old Fang Ke could climb over them. So we visited. The sites where Peking Man's bones had been discovered, and the caves that had been his home five hundred thousand years ago, showed no signs of revolutionary molestation. Peking Man may have been the only resident of China not to be assigned a class status.

Some people like to call the Chinese "descendants of the Yan and Huang emperors," but in fact most Chinese are not that. Yan and Huang were two ancient areas in the Yellow River basin that conquered their neighbors and were home to the original Chinese people. But the people in the conquered populations, as well as all the "barbarians" who got mixed in later, were not "descendants of Yan and Huang." My ancestors in Huizhou, all the way back to Fang La, cannot be called Yan-Huang descendants.

Genetically speaking, the Chinese descendants of Peking Man probably far outnumber the descendants of Yan and Huang. So perhaps we should change our cliché to call ourselves the "descendants of Peking Man." My visit to Zhoukoudian caused me to reflect that talk about "descendants of" has nothing to do with anthropological science and much to do with politics. The phrase "descendants of Yan and Huang" was likely invented by Yan and Huang themselves, or their heirs, in order to make clear that their dominion over other human beings was anchored in bloodline. Chinese emperors in the dynasties often referred to their subjects as their "children." But if calling the people whom one rules one's "children" makes one an emperor, what, I asked myself, does that make today's Communist Party of China, which openly asks that "everyone be the good sons of the Party"? The first precept for children in all the elementary schools was "Be Chairman Mao's good child!"

I resolved to tell my own son this: "You are not Mao Zedong's child. You are yourself."

10. REEDUCATION AT BAGONG MOUNTAIN

THE THREE MONTHS FROM MAY TO AUGUST 1969 WERE VERY ORDI-
nary ones for our little family. In the context of the times, though, "very
ordinary" counted as highly unusual.

There were four of us: our sons Fang Ke and Fang Zhe had joined
Li Shuxian and me. I reflect now that during the more than twenty years
since our marriage, years when the boys were born, grew up, and went
off to college, China was not involved in any foreign wars. (There were,
to be sure, some border skirmishes, but they did not amount to much.)
You might think that a small family living during an extended period
of peacetime would, whether or not it prospered, at least not be forcibly
knocked apart.

But no. For our family, those three months in 1969 were the only ones
we spent together in a normal way during twenty-plus years. We were
divided sometimes between two locations and sometimes among three,
but we were never, save those three months, together. And we were not
unusual. Many people in our generation, especially intellectuals, had the
same problem. It was a hallmark of Mao's China. In our case, the silver
lining was that we were merely separated—not, as others were, driven to
destruction or death.

When I returned to Beijing after my work assignment at the

Lianggezhuang rail station, it was the first time I had been allowed to go home in nearly a year. June 3, 1968, was the day the Red Guards had come to arrest me and other USTC ox ghosts. Our second son, Fang Zhe, was born nine days later, on June 12. So he was nearly a year old before I saw him for the first time in May 1969.

Then began our three months of ordinary life. I remained "hatted"—a target of the proletarian dictatorship—but could at least go home to sleep every night. On Sundays I could even take my boys out to Jingshan Park or Zhongshan Park and be a proper dad for a day. But those three months turned out to be a calm between two storms, rather like a little Lianggezhuang rail station set between two tunnels.

Even though the days were calm, I couldn't do physics. Some of my books had been lost, and with Red Guard house raids all around us, others were hidden away; in both cases, they were inaccessible. The libraries remained closed. My spare time and energy, such as they were, went to printing photographs. I built my own photo enlarger, and it actually worked! It brought back memories of my junior high school years, when I had tried to build a pinhole camera and had failed; now, twenty years later, this homemade enlarger was my revenge. It was easy to build a darkroom then, because the nights were already very dark, and I printed a lot of photos, sometimes deep into the night. This caused no problem of sleep deficit, because my daytime hours were filled with political study sessions in which most people were half asleep anyway. I could catch up then.

The new political storm cycle began at the end of the summer of 1969, when the government issued a formal command (the so-called Lin Biao Order No. 1). It said that the Soviet Union was about to invade and war was imminent. All universities were ordered to leave Beijing as soon as possible. Peking University announced that the entire school would move eleven hundred miles south to Liyuzhou in Jiangxi Province, and other universities rushed to make their own evacuation plans. The only other time Peking University had left Beijing was in 1937, when it and other schools moved to the southwest to flee the Japanese invasion of north China. Now, thirty-two years later, there was another great migration of the universities, but the reason—the real reason—was not an imminent Soviet invasion. It was the idea, hatched at the top of the Communist Party, that peace makes people revisionist and that only struggle and war can preserve revolutionary Marxism.

Li Shuxian was in the first group to be shipped out to Jiangxi. Before she left, she, Fang Ke, and I went for one last visit to the Summer Palace. The park there is world-famous, and tourists often gape in admiration. For Li Shuxian and me the charisma had long worn off, because, in our student days, we used to go there almost every day in summer to swim, and now it was just an ordinary place. On that last day, though, we looked for pretty spots and took photos. Li Shuxian left for Jiangxi on August 29, 1969, and that day marked the end of our life as a family of four. Ke, Zhe, and I stayed in Beijing at my parents' home.

USTC was also under orders to leave Beijing, but it was hard for school authorities to find a destination. The claim that a possible Soviet invasion was the reason for moving the universities logically implied that the universities were things to be treasured and protected, but the reality, in those politically fevered days, was the opposite. Nobody dared to receive a politically dubious thing like a university. USTC sent messengers to Sichuan, Henan, Shandong, and elsewhere looking for a temporary home—and came up empty. After three months, the only place that said yes was Nanyang City in Henan, home of Zhuge Liang, the strategy wizard famed in *The Romance of the Three Kingdoms*. Still clinging to a shred of its tradition of respect for learning, Nanyang offered USTC to move into Zhuge Liang's very own thatched hut. A thatched hut couldn't hold a university, though, so that didn't work.

Other universities had the same problem. No one wanted them. They were, in effect, hanging a sign in the marketplace that said NATION'S PRECIOUS PROPERTY, FREE FOR THE TAKING, and there were no takers. But who could blame the non-takers? Mao had just summed up the universities as "shallow ponds, full of turtles"—where "turtle" was the word *wangba*, similar in sense to "bastard" in English. Turtle schools, full of bastards? Who would dare to want them now?

In the end, Anhui Province accepted USTC and allowed it to move to the capital city of Hefei. I'm not sure if this had anything to do with the fact that Anhui is famous for turtles. Eighty percent of the foreign currency that China was earning from the export of edible turtles was earned in Anhui. In this province, anyway, the creature's reputation was not one hundred percent bad.

So our whole school headed for Anhui. The evacuation process was rushed and a bit ragged—almost as if a foreign invasion really were the reason for it. We later calculated that about half of the university's equipment was destroyed in the move. Who needed an invader? We had wrecked half our luggage all by ourselves.

My own departure took place in January 1970, right after the Chinese New Year. Leaving Ke and Zhe with my parents, I headed for Anhui with some colleagues and students from USTC's physics department. Li Shuxian would be transferred back to Peking University in 1971, and although I applied many times for a transfer back to Beijing, it was never approved, so our family life from this point forward was limited to short visits during vacations.

It turned out that Anhui's willingness to take USTC was not part of any plan to strengthen education in Anhui. Local universities had suspended classes four years earlier, and there were no plans to resume them. The place of professors in the province was not to educate but to receive proletarian reeducation. The train that took us to Anhui did not even stop in Hefei. It brought us straight to the mining region in southern Anhui to receive reeducation from coal miners.

The coal mines were near Bagong Mountain—"mountain of the eight lords." This was where, in the fourth century A.D., Emperor Fu Jian of the Former Qin Dynasty led an invasion of the Eastern Jin. When he reached the city of Shouyang he ascended the city wall to survey the enemy troops. There were no telescopes then, but Fu Jian, peering out, could descry a fearsome gathering of Jin soldiers in the distance. Behind them, arrayed on the mountainsides, he thought he could make out support troops, extending apparently without limit, swaying in readiness. Fu Jian was shocked, ordered a retreat, and later was defeated in what became known in history as the great Battle of the Fei River.

It later turned out that his defeat had to do with poor eyesight. There had been no Jin fighters on those hills. The swaying things were grasses and trees, not people. This is the story behind the Chinese idiom "every leaf and limb a soldier," used for satirizing paranoia, and Fu Jian has been a laughingstock for centuries. But wait. Didn't he have excellent company in today's world? Hadn't the Great Commander of today—even with the advantage of telescopes—ordered a massive retreat without ever laying eyes on an actual enemy soldier?

When we got to Bagong Mountain it was bare. There was no sign of any swaying grasses or trees. Collapsed mines had caused cave-ins here and there, leaving the surface a patchwork of unsightly undulations, like a mangy bald head. It was hard to imagine the famed ancient battle site. But the walls of Shouyang city, higher than most, were still intact, and it was still possible to imagine Fu Jian standing atop them, peering out at the mountain.

We were assigned to the Xiesan mine, which had been built in the 1950s using Soviet technology and was one of the most productive in southern Anhui. Most of its daily output of two to three thousand tons of high-quality coal was shipped to Shanghai.

Lesson one in our reeducation was to descend the mines and dig coal. Men over fifty-five and women were exempted, but for others it was compulsory.

My first descent remains the clearest in my memory. We changed into full miners' gear, including headlamps, then got into cable cars that descended vertically into the mountain. There were two mining levels at Xiesan, one a bit more than three hundred feet down, and the other about a thousand. We went to the higher level first.

A miner met us there and led us to the active digging area. The main tunnel was about fifty feet wide and was equipped with lights. It looked rather like a subway tunnel. The branch tunnels, though, had no lights except for the headlamps of miners, and the narrow paths could be negotiated only single file. We followed one another in the dark, paying especially close attention to the swaying beam of light cast by the person in front. This was the only sign of where to go, and any deviation could be costly. The web of tunnels was complex, and if you were not careful you could get lost, and that—if you wandered into an area filled with gas—could cost you your life. Where the tunnels curved, the person in front of you might momentarily disappear, leaving you in total darkness except for your own lamp. It was important not to panic when that happened.

The closer we got to the digging area, the tougher the going was. Eventually there was no path, just tunnels of various sizes, some so small that only one person could crawl through at a time. The digging area itself was more expansive. It was a space about seven feet high, twenty feet wide, and more than a hundred feet long. Tightly packed columns of steel rods held it in place. At intervals along that hundred-foot stretch—called a "palm," in mining argot—miners were digging coal.

I discovered that coal digging in some ways resembles rock digging for railway construction. First, chunks of coal are blasted loose. Then miners use shovels to toss the loose lumps onto a conveyor belt—called a "slipper"—that runs the length of the palm. Coal is less heavy than rock, so this digging was easier labor. The drawback in the mines is that you can't enjoy the scene of a torrent of rock cascading down a mountainside. Inside the pitch blackness, you can't see anything but the coal under your feet and the moving slipper. You can barely even see the miner next to you, which probably explains why there is very little conversation. Normally there are no sounds except those of shovels hitting coal and the grinding of the conveyor belt.

I remember an incident when the eerie silence was broken. One of the intellectuals being reeducated accidentally stepped onto the conveyor belt, stumbled, and got carried along with the coal. He might have suffered the same fate as the coal itself if other people, farther down the line, had not heard his cries and pulled him off. But the utter blackness that had endangered his life had also, thankfully, saved his pride, because there could of course be no eyewitnesses to the ridiculous spectacle of a man riding a conveyor belt on a pile of coal. When it was over, everybody went back to silent digging.

"Mealtime!" Whenever this word rang out, everyone stopped, sat down on the palm, and waited for a cloth bag containing flatbreads to be passed down the line. Each man took one. That was lunch. Then a jug of water was passed along. Everyone took a swig or two. That was drink. We didn't wash our hands before eating. There was, first of all, no place to wash, but somehow we also did not feel a need to wash. Everything was black in any case; we could hardly even see those hands that might need washing. The environment somehow caused a psychological suspension of ordinary rules.

Only when we came out of the mine at the end of the day did we know how blackened our bodies had become. If you'd offered me a flatbread then, I wouldn't have dared touch it with my hands. The water in the miners' bathing pool itself was black and had bits of coal suspended in it. But no matter. After rinsing in it we were much cleaner than before.

After I'd been down the shaft a few times, I got used to it. I joined a "tunneling team," whose job it was to open tunnels, cut into coal beds, and prepare palms for coal collection. This work was harder than shoveling. There was no ventilation, and coal dust hung in the air. Heat from deep in the earth, sealed there for hundreds of millions of years, radiated from below, leaving us so hot that everyone worked naked. Psychologically, digging tunnels through coal beds is significantly different from digging a tunnel through a hill. In a hill, you can sustain yourself on the faith of getting through to the other side, to light. But tunneling in a coal mine, you dig from one blackness to the next. In the diminutive light of your helmet lamp, all you can make out are a few naked bodies in front of you, wriggling forward in the blackness toward somewhere deeper, somewhere even blacker.

Is hell black? Could it be blacker than this?

Many people, Karl Marx included, like to quote the famous words from the "Inferno" section of Dante's *Divine Comedy*: "It is written at the gates of hell, 'Abandon all hope, ye who enter here.'" My own feeling, as I ascended, with naked body, from a thousand feet deep in the mine, was that the great poet had hung his sign over the wrong door. He should have hung it at the doors of those countries that were pursuing the invention that Dr. Marx called "proletarian dictatorship." It turned out that lesson one of my reeducation—the actual lesson, not the intended one—was this: I began to doubt Marxism itself.

In Marxist theory, no worker is more proletarian, more solid a base for Marxism, than a miner. I was now surrounded by miners, but I got no sense at all of what Marx had claimed: that these classic proletarians were on their way to exercising a dictatorship. The Communist Party of China held that workers, peasants, and soldiers were the bulwarks of the "people's democratic dictatorship" that the Party was leading. As of the spring of 1970, I had lived among all three bulwarks and never got the slightest impression that any of them were interested in the Party dictatorship. They did not ask, and obviously could not have cared less, what my label "rightist who slipped through the net" was all about.

Quite the contrary, I had made friends among them. That young farmer in Zanhuang with whom I had shared everything—house, food, work—stayed in touch with me until the early 1960s. Then his messages stopped coming, and I had to wonder if he had died in the Great Famine. After two months of working in the mine I also got to know some of the miners. Dictatorship over class enemies like me? Nothing could have been further from their thinking. They just wanted to make friends. So I had to think: Why did theory and reality diverge so? This question had occurred to me at Zanhuang, and now it came back at the mine.

Then something happened that made everything clear. One day, great red banners appeared at the mouth of the mine, courtesy of local propaganda officials:

Work in a craze for thirty days
Push tonnage to a higher phase!

and

For Labor Day, here's a must:
Ten thousand tons or bust!

and so on. I noticed that the slogans were not, in fact, very political. Their goal was just to fire up the miners to work harder and produce more coal. I knew from working inside the mine that if the miners wanted to, it would be easy for them to produce more coal. Of the eight hours a miner spent on one shift, only about three, on average, were spent at work. The rest of the time was used in other ways, including, near the end of the shift, just sitting in the dark and waiting for the shift to end. If this empty time were converted back to work, production would go up 10 percent or more for each reconverted hour.

The miners, the "proletarian masters of the country," paid no attention at all to the banners that appeared at the mine entrance. Down below, they still worked their three hours and then sat down to wait for quitting time. Every person—the whole team—did this. The dictatorship of the proletariat was a formidable thing on the earth's surface, but a thousand feet underground it lost some of its punch. As I sat there in the darkness with the miners, musing on all of this, one of them said quietly, "Sixty cents of pay buys sixty cents of work."

Eureka. That comment helped unlock my puzzle. There in the blackness, I could suddenly see that the miners were not "masters of the dictatorship" but the opposite. They, like me, were on its receiving end. The only difference was that the control mechanisms were different. For me it was the label "rightist who slipped through the net"; for them it was their fixed sixty-cent wage. My subordination showed in my inability to remove my label, theirs in their inability to get a fair wage. In both cases, the dictatorship forced us to accept what it dealt us. That verbiage about "masters of the country" was fluff. To the miners, it mattered not a whit who won the power struggles in Beijing; they couldn't have cared less about either faction.

My new understanding soon got corroboration. In May, the authorities ordered us to go to Wabao Lake, just south of Shouyang, for a session on "recalling the bitter past to savor the sweet present." This was to be part of our reeducation, but in fact we already knew the script well: Farmers would stand up to say how awful life used to be and how pleasant it is today. They would say that in the old society they were serfs (how bitter, how bitter!), but after the Communists came they were masters of their own fate (how blessed, how blessed!). But even though I expected to learn nothing, I wanted to go. It was a chance to get out for a little trip and breathe a bit of different air.

What I did not imagine was that the Wabao farmers might turn out to be poorly trained in ideology. They started off fairly well: "the Communist Party liberated us," and so on. But when it came time to "recall bitterness," they all said that the bitterest times were during the Great Famine of 1959–62. They went on to recount all sorts of scenes of people starving to death. This presented me and the others who were being reeducated with a dilemma. To nod our heads would be political anathema; to shake them was a moral impossibility. Could we laugh? That would be worst from both points of view. All we could do was seal up our writhing inner feelings and allow nothing to show on the surface. The official in charge of the session evinced obvious discomfort. But he, too, was trapped. The farmers' words were grossly "incorrect," but he was in no position to cut them off because only moments earlier, he had been at the podium announcing that he himself was eagerly awaiting the chance to "learn diligently from his brothers in the peasant class."

In his summary comments, he tried to salvage a correct interpretation of what had been said. "The Great Leap Forward years were different from the years before Liberation," he intoned. "After Liberation, peasants were their own masters." I found this astounding. He was distinguishing between two ways of starving to death: when you starve as a "serf" it is bitter; when you starve as a "master" it falls into the category of sweet. A remarkable invention indeed: the doctrine of "sweet starvation." But at least one thing was now clear about the more than three million people (in a total population of about forty million) who had starved to death in Anhui: they had had sweet deaths.

The experience deepened my insight into the political position of the farmers, another of those "three bulwarks" of the people's democratic dictatorship. They, like the miners and the intellectuals, were on the receiving end of the dictatorship.

In short, it became clear to me that Marx's ideal of a "proletarian dictatorship" was an empty abstraction that was not going to happen. How could proletarians really be the dictators? Whoever did the dictating would be, you could be sure, no proletarian. The followers of Marx had taken this empty abstraction and pushed it to the point of hypocrisy and cruelty.

In the summer of 1970 a new campaign arrived, and with it the struggle and the cruelty intensified. The name of the new campaign was "Arrest 516 Elements." And who were these "elements"? I doubt that any reference book has, or ever will have, a clear definition. All we knew was that it was a new "hat" in the arsenal of the proletarian dictatorship. Perhaps the regime's hats had become so similar and so numerous that, like the streets in New York City, numbers had become the most reasonable way to name them: it was now time to go after group number 516. (I shivered on my first visit to New York when I learned that a suburb had a telephone area code numbered 516.)

Whatever the definition, the actual 516 victims were students, for the most part, especially ones who had been Red Guards in the early stages of the Cultural Revolution. The high tide of the campaign to arrest them came in June, July, and August, the last three months of my stay at the Xiesan mine. My status as a hat wearer meant I had no right to participate in politics (too bad! I could not go out hunting 516 elements!)—but it also disqualified me as quarry, since a hat was already on my head and there was no obvious room for another one. This was just fine with me. After four years of nonstop denunciation and struggle, people were so sick of political movements that many felt going down into a mine was preferable. But unless you were an already-hatted person like me, you had no choice. You had to join the campaign. If you didn't attack others, that fact turned you yourself into a target for attack. So you had to choose which role to play—attacker or attacked—and this is why people like me, banished to terrain outside this cruel dilemma, felt oddly privileged. I was still subject to the dictatorship, to be sure, but my freedom from the 516 campaign actually brought me a wisp of elation.

I continued to get labor assignments. Some were in the mine, some on the surface. Eventually I was assigned to pull flatbed carts. These little vehicles were the most common means of moving cargo in Anhui. Made of wood, they were like horse carts, but smaller. Their beds were about three feet wide and eight feet long, and their pulling poles stuck out about four and a half feet. They had two rubber tires. They were usually pulled by humans but could be fitted for donkeys as well. Rivers of small flatbeds flowed everywhere in Anhui (and predominate even now, as I write in 1990). For a little more than a month, I was part of the flow.

Pulling a cart was a pleasant sort of labor. It was summer, so I could strip to the waist, like the other cart pullers, and enjoy the open sunshine without fear that police would say anything. Anhui is hilly. Its roads go up and down, and pulling uphill could be tough going; but then there was the coasting down, cart and puller as one. The work had an oscillation—now hard, now relaxed—that made for good exercise. When I got tired I could take a break in the shade of a tree and cool off. When thirsty, I could buy a slice of watermelon. It was cheap, and sellers were everywhere. In theory it was against the rules for a hatted person like me to buy food on the streets without advance permission from supervisors. Yet I could feel completely confident that no supervisor would come along asking to see my permission slip to buy watermelon, because they were all too busy chasing 516s. So there I was—no supervision, no politics, a body bathed in sweat, a road bathed in sunlight, watermelon stands lining the way—pulling, coasting, flowing within the river of the flatbeds. It felt great. Only temporary, perhaps? Yes, but which escapes from the burdens of life are anything but temporary? In any case, my body, out in the air and sun, was the big winner during that interval of cart pulling.

When I came back from my sun-filled days on the road, body bronzer than usual, I thought I noticed some envy in the expressions of my colleagues who had no hats and therefore no rights to go out pulling carts in semi-freedom. They had to spend their days pursuing 516s, and their faces were pale, even sickly. Then it turned out that some of them really were sick. In July, when the mosquitoes came out, malaria followed. For several days my cart and I were pulling nothing but malaria victims. There was no public transportation between the Xiesan mine and the local hospital, so patients had to go by flatbed. The load was grim, but, from a cart puller's point of view, optimal in size. A cart loaded down with heavy things was of course hard to pull; an empty cart was also irritating, because it would bounce around on the uneven roads. A human body of about 150 pounds was just right—neither too heavy nor too light.

I remembered my mother taking me, more than once, to ride on human-pulled rickshaws in Beijing and Shanghai. If that was inhumane, and a sin, then those days in Anhui when I spent day and night ferrying sick people to the hospital by rickshaw may have been my atonement. Even though I made many hospital runs, and was bitten by plenty of mosquitoes, and never had a preventive injection, I did not get malaria. Was this reward for the atonement?

The breakout of infectious disease did nothing to slow the campaign against 516 elements. Even though I took no part in the campaign, its progress was as obvious to me as to anyone else. As it picked up speed, students disappeared one by one. The 516 suspects were separated out and detained, similarly to the way in which I had been detained and held during the "cleansing of class ranks" at USTC. Some of the 516 elements were held in miners' housing at Xiesan, but "serious" cases were shipped to Hefei and incarcerated there. One Red Guard who had been charged with supervising us hatted people stopped showing up in July. It turned out that he had his own hat now, a 516 hat.

Then began a new round of suicides. One student who had been a very active Red Guard at the beginning of the Cultural Revolution was among the "serious" cases sent to Hefei. A few days later we got word that he had jumped to his death from the fourth floor of a building. This was like the story of the chemistry lecturer I recounted in the last chapter. Even the "fourth floor" part was the same.

Another student, one who had never been especially active, began in July to go on aimless walks by himself. His speech grew incoherent and his behavior unpredictable. One day he disappeared. People working on the freight rail line found him lying on the tracks, both legs severed at the thigh by a train that had recently passed. They rushed him to the hospital, but he had already lost too much blood and died within hours. By chance I was delivering another patient to the hospital that night, and I noticed some physics students standing guard at the morgue. They were on a twenty-four-hour watch. This was because wild dogs thrived in Anhui, and their sense of smell was sharp. Whenever a fresh corpse was brought into the morgue, they would gather in bunches in the bushes outside. When no one was looking, often in the middle of the night, they would use their heads to butt the door of the morgue open and go lick up the blood of the fresh corpse. The reason for the twenty-four-hour watch was to shoo away these dogs. The Chinese custom of "guarding the gates for the departed" had a new and literal meaning.

The departed spirit of this particular young man was in a lucky minority. The regime viewed suicide as a counterrevolutionary offense, and even after death a suicide victim could be targeted for denunciation—but he was not. In principle, the reach of the proletarian dictatorship had no limit. Counterrevolutionaries could be pursued even to heaven.

Heaven. Yes. The heavens remained. The final lesson in my course of reeducation at Bagong Mountain was in the value of studying the heavens. The human spirit, like the human body, seems to have an automatic tendency to seek balance. When falling to the left, a human body automatically leans to the right, and when falling right, it leans to the left. When immersed in darkness, a human mind automatically thinks of light. When surrounded by evil, it seeks harmony and beauty.

It was on that principle that my life at Bagong Mountain sparked in me a passion for astrophysics. What power, I asked myself, could rival the one that governs the heavenly bodies in their timeless movements and at the same time dispel the depression of a lonely physicist as he sits at the bottom of a mine waiting for quitting time? What could match the divine purity of a firmament packed densely and deeply with stars—and also wash away the stench of wild dogs haunting a morgue?

This was not the first time in my life that I had found the heavens attractive. The year I graduated from high school, when my youthful aspirations were at a peak, I had written down "astronomy" as one of my three preferences for a university major. Then at Zanhuang, in 1958, I learned to be a keen observer of the heavens, but less from passion than from necessity, because I was out on the roads a lot at night, where the constellations and the moon were the most reliable signposts. Later, at USTC, there was a time when I was in charge of the physics demonstration room. Keeping a 15-centimeter reflecting telescope in proper adjustment required that I spend many nights with it, focused on the skies. And finally, there was that alluring article I had seen in 1966 about cosmic microwave background radiation.

All of these were but glancing encounters, however. They did not penetrate into my inner self and grab hold. The heavens seemed beautiful to me, but they were, after all, very far away. Not until I reached the bottom of the mineshaft at Xiesan did I suddenly feel the urge to reach as far as I could in the opposite direction, far out of the squalor, in search of an uncontaminated sanctuary for my tormented spirit.

With the help of chance, and even as the mindless political denunciations continued, I was able to lay hands on a copy of *Classical Theory of Fields* by Lev Landau. It was a banned book, of course. Ironically, though, when the 516 struggles reached fever pitch and everyone was preoccupied with protecting their own persons, there was actually more space for reading. Because of the malaria problem, we all slept under mosquito nets, and once you dropped your net, you could read as you liked. And so it happened, during my months in southern Anhui, that Landau's book became my most beloved (and only) after-hours reading material. Each evening, as night arrived, my fatigued body retired under a net while my liberated spirit leaped toward the wide universe in pursuit of the beautiful and moving question of its ultimate origin.

Poincaré once wrote:

> The scientist does not study nature because it is useful; he studies it because he delights in it, and he delights in it because it is beautiful. If nature were not beautiful, it would not be worth knowing, and if nature were not worth knowing, life would not be worth living.

Yes, the universe was beautiful, and worth knowing, too. There was a reason for me to keep on living after all. I had found a new starting point. Bagong Mountain, with its 102-degree temperatures, its mosquitoes and malaria, its 516s and its suicides, its dead bodies and wild dogs—no matter how squalid, ugly, and tyrannical—could not touch the beauty that arose from my wonder and awe at the colossal thing called the universe. That beauty now owned me.

11. ARRIVAL IN HEFEI

In August 1970, when our terms at the Xiesan mine were up, all of us USTC lecturers in physics went to Hefei. So did USTC people from other departments when their sentences, in other places, were over. Our coming together marked the beginning of the Hefei chapter in the history of the university.

Hefei then was a small city, only about half a million, and by the standards of Beijing was only semi-developed. You could cover the entire commercial district on foot within an hour. The streets observed no distinction between slow and fast lanes—trucks, cars, bicycles, flatbed carts, horse and donkey carts, and pedestrians mingled as each saw fit. The city didn't have any famous historical sites. There was one park, called Ferry to Leisure—to which one trip was enough.

In history, Hefei and its environs had often been battlefields. Many strongmen had risen and fallen here, and the people by nature were a bit pugnacious. China's waging of wars over the preceding hundred years had depended heavily on armies from Anhui Province, and Hefei's heroes were mostly military heroes. Li Hongzhang, the founder of the Tianjin Military Academy in the late nineteenth century, and Duan Qirui, the famous Republican-era northern warlord, were both sons of Hefei.

USTC moved into the campus of Hefei Normal College, a school that had been disbanded during the Cultural Revolution and was not going to be restored. It had taught only the humanities—history, literature, music, art, and so on. Because it did no science, the campus had no laboratories or machine shops, and its supplies of electricity, water, and gas were not enough to support scientific research. Except for a few dormitories and classroom buildings, USTC would have to start from the ground up.

We battered scientists weren't afraid of starting from scratch so long as we felt we were really building something. From all our experience of being "sent down" and "reeducated" beginning in 1958, we had picked up abilities in quite a few lines of work. I daresay Chinese intellectuals of our generation, however they might compare with their colleagues around the world in their special fields, in terms of general worker skills would easily rank number one. All of us could present long lists of the kinds of manual labor we understood.

In this memoir I have already mentioned some of the items on my own list: farming (both the northern and southern varieties, which are different), well digging, pig raising, railroad construction, coal mining, and flatbed cart pulling. Here are some others that I haven't mentioned yet:

In the fall of 1965, I worked in the converter room at the Shijingshan Steel Mill in Beijing. My job—an obsolete task by now, because machines have replaced it—was to shovel raw material into the furnace. I have a small scar on my arm that is a souvenir of a tiny drop of molten steel that once came flying out.

In the winter of 1967, I worked in a vinylon factory at Niulanshan, in the eastern outskirts of Beijing. The entire plant was imported, and it was state-of-the-art, but my own work was routine and I didn't pick up any new technology there.

In 1969 Mao Zedong called for "digging deep tunnels" to prepare for nuclear war, and I joined several times in the digging. I can't promise that our tunnels did anything to protect against nuclear attack, though. We never had any experimental evidence.

When I got to Hefei in 1970, the list kept growing: brick making was next. During my first year in Hefei, physics was only my avocation; my main work was making bricks. USTC had its own brick factory, finished in March 1971. The chemistry building that stands on the campus today was built from bricks that we professors made there.

WORK HARD TO BUILD CHINA INTO
A STRONG MODERN SOCIALIST COUNTRY!
PUT BRICKS AND TILES TO WORK FOR
CHINA'S SOCIALIST CONSTRUCTION!

Slogans and banners such as these were everywhere in China in the 1970s. I feel a duty here to describe our brick factory, both its personnel and its process, in some detail, so that people in later times can get a feel for what "making bricks and tiles for socialism" was all about.

The factory had a staff of thirteen. One was an experienced brick maker and the others were "black element" academics drafted from a number of departments. I introduce them briefly below. The tags that follow their names were their titles as of 1971; when I say what they are doing "now" I mean 1990, as I write this.

- **Chen Xiru,** lecturer in mathematics. Chen was studying in Poland in 1956 when, because of rightist opinions he expressed there, he was sent home and became a "rightist who slipped through the net." Now he is a famous professor of mathematics, one of China's leading authorities on probability theory.
- **Qian Datong,** lecturer in mathematics. Qian had already published papers on statistics but, because of some wayward political speech, became an "active counterrevolutionary." He is now an associate professor at USTC.
- **Deng Weilian,** lecturer in mathematics. Deng had an illustrious background. There is a statue in Guangzhou in honor of his uncle Deng Zhongyuan, who, before he was assassinated in 1922, had been a military general and one of the earliest followers of Sun Yat-sen, the Nationalist revolutionary leader. Deng's father had been in charge of the Nationalists' government-owned airline and, in 1949, ordered that all airline staff fly from Hong Kong to the mainland, with their aircraft, and report to the Communists. This transfer of personnel and equipment became the kernel of the People's Republic's own airline. Deng Weilian himself went to study history at Yenching Uni-

versity in Beijing, and in 1950, with the outbreak of the war in Korea, he volunteered to go fight the Americans. After the war he came back to China and switched his field to mathematics. Then he said something that offended the authorities and became an "active counter-revolutionary." In the late 1970s he left China for Hong Kong. I have been told that after 1984, when the Sino-British Joint Declaration on Hong Kong laid out plans for the city's reversion to China, Deng moved again, this time to the Fiji Islands in the South Pacific.

- **Xu Jialuan,** associate professor of physics. Xu supported the Communists in the 1940s and in 1949 passed up a chance to go abroad in order to answer the Party's call to stay and build a new China. As I noted in chapter 9, though, he later mentioned his dream of studying in the United States, and that mistake brought him a label of "counterrevolutionary element." The authorities said he was planning treason. He was struggled and beaten. In 1981, while on a visit to America, he flew from there to Taiwan, where the Taiwan authorities welcomed him as a "righteous anticommunist." He is now a professor of physics at a university in Taipei.

- **Li Xianyu,** professor of mechanics. In the 1920s Li studied engineering in Shanghai, where he was a classmate of Lu Dingyi, who later, from 1954 to 1966, was chief of the Communist Party's Department of Propaganda. Li joined the Party back in those early days in Shanghai as well. Later, while a student in Japan, he resigned from the Party, and because of that act he received the label of "traitor" during the Cultural Revolution. He died in the early 1980s.

- **Huang Maoguang,** professor of mechanics. In the 1940s Huang went to Cornell University in the United States for a Ph.D., after which he returned to China and became famous in the field of thin plate mechanics. But he kept up correspondence with his American friends, and for this he received a "spy" label. After President Nixon visited China in 1972, some of Huang's acquaintances in the American scholarly community came visiting, too, and the authorities, embarrassed in front of foreigners, had to remove the "spy" hat. Huang is retired now and lives in Beijing.

- **Zhu Zhaoxiang,** professor of mechanics. Zhu at the time was one of

China's leading experts on the mechanics of explosions. He joined the Communist Party before 1949 while at Zhejiang University and did underground work against the Nationalist government, but in 1957 he was expelled from the Party for rightist opinions. His category in 1971 was "rightist who slipped through the net." He is now president of Ningbo University.

- **Lu Yang,** lecturer in chemistry. In the 1930s a group called the Federation for National Salvation called upon the Nationalists and Communists to resist Japan instead of fighting each other, and in 1936 seven of this group were arrested by the Nationalists. There was a great outcry on their behalf; even Albert Einstein sent a telegram of support. They came to be known as the Seven Stalwarts. The only female in the group, Shi Liang, was Lu Yang's aunt. The Communist Party was extremely enthusiastic about the Seven Stalwarts in 1936, but in 1957 Lu Yang's connection with Shi Liang did him no good at all. Indeed, two of the Seven Stalwarts were themselves labeled rightists. This is what people mean by the phrase "That was then and this is now." Lu Yang committed suicide in 1981.

- **Liu Lang,** a leading physician and president of USTC's medical school. Liu joined the Communist Party in his youth and worked in military medicine. Before working with the Communist armies, though, he had also worked in Nationalist organizations, and that was enough to get him the label "historical counterrevolutionary." In the 1980s he went back to Beijing, where he is now retired, and writing.

- **Guo Laofu.** In the 1940s, Guo went to study at a military medical school in Japan and later worked in the Japanese-occupied northeast of China. From there he joined the Communist Party of China and served in an army commanded by Lin Biao. He followed the army from the northeast all the way to Guangzhou in the south, but, because the circumstances of his original departure for Japan were "unclear," he, too, got a "historical counterrevolutionary" hat. Later he retired to Beijing and took up fishing.

- **Jin Yongtao,** technician in the physics department. Jin was the only one of the "black elements" who did not have a higher education. He got his rightist hat in 1957 when he was a technician in the Physics Research Institute of the Academy of Sciences. Now he is an engineer at the Beijing Science Technology Management College.

• Me.

So there it was: the average level of education and knowledge at this little brick factory could rival what might be found at any building materials plant anywhere in the modern world. Indeed, measured in terms of concentration, we might have ranked first. The difference between our pool of talent and others was that in our case the authorities wanted only our manual labor, not our knowledge. They were asking us to use a two-thousand-year-old method of firing bricks to fire up China's modernization.

"Qin bricks and Han tiles" is a cliché in Chinese. People use it to point to the early start that China got in technology. Chinese knew how to make bricks in the third century B.C., and a century later could do tiles. Technologically speaking, there's no real reason for me to expand on the USTC method of making bricks, because it's all laid out in a book by Song Yingxing called *Heavenly Creations*, published in 1637. Still, in order to clarify the ways in which traditional Chinese culture was put to use to build Communism as invented by Marx, I will have to recapitulate some of the processes that Song described more than three hundred years ago.

The first step in traditional brick making is to cast the raw bricks. This requires blending the clay and getting it into wood frame molds. The job takes two people. One grips the mold firmly on the floor while the other raises a ball of clay that weighs about fifteen pounds over his head, then thrusts the ball forcefully downward into the mold. The quality of the eventual brick depends upon the force of that thrust: the harder the thrust, the denser the clay and the better the brick. If the force is insufficient, the clay contains too many little bubbles, like a sponge, and the finished brick will not be able to bear weight, which means it has to be discarded. No person can throw down more than a hundred lumps of clay before feeling utterly exhausted. In our little work group, only the younger people—the lecturers—had the energy to throw clay. The professors and the associate professors held the wooden molds. Later we got a machine that made the raw bricks and we didn't need to throw clay anymore. That was a big advance, but there was only one machine for the whole brick factory.

Step two is to air-dry the raw bricks. A finished brick weighs about five and a half pounds, and in its wet, unfired form weighs more than double that. We carried the wet bricks, entirely by hand, to places that had a good flow of air—but it had to be in the shade—and set them down to dry. They had to be turned several times during the process so that the drying would be even.

Step three is to build a kiln, and this requires technical expertise. A kiln is a domed structure, about thirty feet across and twenty feet high, made of unfired bricks. It resembles a tent. The dome structure was a breakthrough in building mechanics that someone in ancient China invented. The 120-foot Zhaozhou Bridge in southern Hebei, built more than thirteen hundred years ago, uses the same principle of stone-on-stone arched construction. The senior brick maker who directed us in our kiln construction was passing along essentially the same know-how that had gone into building that bridge. He had no blueprints, took no measurements, and made no calculations. He did everything by eye. He glanced here, glanced there, telling us all what to do—and the result was a beautiful round dome, exquisite in design. The professors of mechanics were very impressed. The old worker may have spent five years of his youth mastering this technology, learning how to set each minor angle in order to get the beautiful arc just right. There was no way he could know, of course, that in a mechanics class at USTC a hundred students could come to understand in one hour a mathematical notation that rigorously expresses the curve of that same arc, and from that could deduce the optimal size for each minor angle.

The final step in brick making is to fire the bricks inside the kiln. This is essentially a technical task that requires little labor. All we had to do was add coal when the senior worker told us to—and then stop when he told us to, after eight or nine days. But right there were two great secrets of traditional brick making: when to add coal and when the bricks were ready to take out. The old worker didn't say what criteria he used to judge these questions. He preferred to keep personal vigil at the kiln day and night, allowing himself only a bit of sleep after each addition of coal. We twelve intellectuals divided into three groups to form round-the-clock shifts. The professors got the day shifts, so I was always on night shift.

It turned out, though, that the old brick maker was not a perfect keeper of secrets. Each time we added coal, we sat around the kiln afterward and listened to him talk about his techniques. He seemed to view us as disciples in his craft. We learned that the crucial skill was to judge temperatures inside the kiln. He referred to the "fire conditions," by which he meant the colors of both the flames and the bricks. Most people cannot discriminate color differences among flames of 1,100, 1,300, and 1,500 degrees, but experienced brick makers can. The more accurate their eye for these subtleties, the higher their rank in the trade.

Later I read in Sima Qian's *Records of the Grand Historian*, which was written about two thousand years ago, that astronomers in ancient times categorized stars by their colors: white, blue, yellow, red, and dark. People have expressed skepticism about that passage—the colors of a few planets might be discernible to the naked eye, but thousands of stars? Yet it is worth noting that modern astrophysics also classifies stars by color, and the colors correspond to different temperatures. Moreover, the color classifications of quite a few stars, as obtained by spectral measurement, match those listed in the *Records of the Grand Historian*. This finding, too, has drawn skepticism.

After my experience at the brick kiln, I came to believe there is a chance that the *Grand Historian*'s records might actually have some basis. Two thousand years ago China had brick-kiln artisans, it seems, who could discriminate extremely fine gradations in the color of fire; so might it not also be possible that astronomers of that era had trained their eyes to perceive extremely fine gradations of starlight?

But if Chinese astronomers ever did have this skill, it died out long ago. And it is not going to come back, because modern astronomers have no use for it. Spectroscopic analysis has exceeded, a thousand times over, what the best possible human eye could ever do. Today I feel a deep respect for that old kiln artisan who could see temperatures for himself, but I have no desire whatsoever to acquire his skill. A pyrometer could give me temperatures inside a kiln with much greater precision. During my work at the brick factory, I never went to the USTC physics lab to get a pyrometer, though. After all, we were being reformed. I just shoveled coal, as instructed.

In the dead of night, on my shift at the kiln, I stared into the fire and mused that human history itself might be something like a fire that constantly forges new things into being as it reduces old things to ashes. The extinction of traditional skills sometimes causes people who admire such skills to grieve, as if treasures have been lost forever, and as if today's world depends on whether they can be retrieved. I didn't think so, though. I felt, and still feel, that old skills do have archaeological value, but other than that, extinction is probably what ought to happen to them. The progress of humankind depends on retiring old technologies—and that means, in today's world, trading in eye skills for pyrometers. This is why I did not want to learn eye skills, even while admiring the man who had them. If my refusal to learn eye skills nudges humanity a tiny bit forward, so much the better, I thought. Is this "cultural revolution"? Yes, I mused—and that is what the term really ought to mean.

Oops! Time to add coal again.

There was not much politics in our work at the brick factory. In theory we were still targets of the dictatorship, undergoing "remolding." But other than assigning an old artisan to direct our labor, the authorities pretty much left us alone. They may have concluded by then that we were unreformable.

If so, they were largely right. Five years of Cultural Revolution had left me certain that there was no way at all I could accept the slightest remolding by the regime. This was as clear to me as the principle of not going back to eye skills once you have pyrometers. So farewell, political dreams of youth! I wrote in a letter to Li Shuxian: *In recent times we seem to be returning to those clear-headed days of the early 1950s. The innocence is gone, but that cool feeling of confident candor is similar.* Leaving the naïveté behind gave me a new sense of assurance.

With the illusions set aside, the mandatory pretense that one still believed them turned into farce. Every morning at the brick factory there was a five-minute exercise during which we were asked to "confess our crimes before Chairman Mao." The form of the exercise, as in some religions, was collective confession. The twelve of us who bore guilt stood in silence, heads bowed, before a portrait of Mao. In theory each of us was recounting our crimes in silence before the Great Leader. What was actually going on inside the minds of those professors and lecturers, though, was anyone's guess. There may have been no thoughts at all, but just an observation, perhaps, of a fly crawling across the sacred visage . . .

People like us were known to the authorities as "old oil oxen": "old" because we'd seen it all, so were not easily frightened; "oil" because using extreme tactics on us was about as effective as using a knife to cut oil; and "oxen" because trying to use ideological persuasion on us was like singing to a cow.

Right through the 1980s, when I exchanged letters with my friends from the brick factory days we addressed each other as "Dear O_3," which was our abbreviation for the English words "old, oil, ox." The incorrigibility of O_3 was, at bottom, the irreversibility of science. Science advances only on mechanics that are intrinsic to science; it does not—cannot—go into reverse because of any nonscientific force, however strong. The historian of science George Sarton has commented that of all the areas of human endeavor, science is the only one that always moves forward— even if, sometimes, the forward movement is slow. The brick factory was a crystallization of this principle: trying to use two-thousand-year-old technology to "remold" the precision of mathematical formulae simply does not work.

We objects of remolding did not mind moving backward in all sorts of ways as long as science remained pristine. On the outside, we looked every bit the part of criminals who were undergoing reform: ragged clothes, bodies covered in clay and coal bits, faces caked with ash and dust. Out on the streets, while hauling clay or coal, we usually wore those same dull expressions of indifference to dirt and exhaustion that people who have to haul for a living often wear. People who did not know us would never guess by looking at us that we were highfalutin professors. Unless, of course, they were suddenly to ask:

"Hey, you guys know about the Taylor expansion?"
"How about showing us a few Maxwell equations?"

I would have been ready. In my spare hours during those brick making days, I was deep into Maxwell's equations in curved space-time.

In August 1971, a severe heat wave put many departments into temporary shutdown. We labor convicts were not eligible for vacations, but because the master brick worker also thought the weather was too hot and wanted to take a few days off, the authorities had no choice but to declare a one-week "amnesty."

Great, I thought, *I'll go have a honeymoon!* By chance, Li Shuxian was able to put in for a vacation at the same time. We had been married for nearly ten years, but this was the first time we had had vacations that overlapped.

In those days our little family lived separately in three locations. Li Shuxian was in Jiangxi, I was in Anhui, and our two boys were in the care of my mother in Beijing. The chance for a vacation arrived so abruptly that it made it hard to arrange for the boys to come south to meet us. Moreover, they were young, and it was not clear that they would be able to keep the secret nature of our travel under their hats. So, all things considered, we just decided to take the "honeymoon" that we had missed the first time around.

Honeymoons are supposed to be both sweet and secret—and given our circumstances, both these elements were double in weight. It was still the high season of the Great Proletarian Cultural Revolution, and both of us were still targets of the dictatorship, so of course the trip had to be secret. But we weren't much afraid, either, because years of class struggle had already killed the zest for travel in the general populace. Never mind outcasts like us—even the politically acceptable population did not venture out much anymore, and the guardians of the dictatorship would never imagine that impurities like us would have either the interest or the nerve to go out sightseeing. We calculated that the tourist spots would be low-pressure zones for class struggle, and that turned out to be correct.

We chose as our destination the beautiful Huangshan mountain area. On August 12 we both set out, Li Shuxian from Nanchang and I from Hefei, headed for Shanghai, where we arrived the next morning. We met at the rail station, but did not behave as lovers normally do when they meet after a long separation. For one, time was short; we couldn't afford much of it for chat or shilly-shally. Moreover we had to be careful not to divulge our status. We gave each other smiles. I noticed that she had become as darkly tanned as I, and later learned that she had immediately noticed the same about me. Similar labor reform, similar sun exposure, similar tans. That was fine. Tans were good cover.

We stayed a night in Shanghai and then went to Hangzhou. The city was pleasant, as always, but it was not our destination so we did not stay long. On the morning of August 15 we took a long-distance bus from Hangzhou westward toward Huizhou. Outside the window the Fuchun River flowed gently and quietly through the hills. Its lines were delicate but sharp. Beneath the sun, glistening in its fluid brilliance, it resembled the patterns in Hangzhou's embroidered silk. It occurred to me that this route was probably the one my grandfather had traveled, but going in the opposite direction, when he ventured from Huizhou to Hangzhou at the end of the last century. As we proceeded farther west, into the mountains of western Zhejiang Province, the escarpment grew steeper.

Around noon the bus labored its way over the Yiling Pass and crossed the border into Anhui Province. The forests of southern Anhui were as luxuriant as ever, but there weren't as many rivers as in Zhejiang. A few little streams gushed through mountain crevices, but that was all. The roads were no longer paved; now they were brown dirt. The villages were simple, primitive, and isolated. At 1:00 p.m. the bus stopped briefly at a little town near Jixian—the birthplace of the great May Fourth intellectual Hu Shi—and the passengers got off to have lunch. Who would have guessed that modern China's strongest proponent of "thorough Westernization" would have been born in an isolated mountain village like this?

It was dusk when the bus arrived at Shexian and Yansi near the Huangshan Mountains. We felt lucky that there were very few tourists. In the whole of the Huangshan area, whose radius was about twenty miles, there seemed to be only about thirty of them. When we got to Shexian there were uncrowded shuttle buses ready to take us to the guesthouse at the foot of the mountains. When we got there, a slogan in giant characters—NEVER, EVER, FORGET THE CLASS STRUGGLE!—glared at us from the guesthouse wall, but the people at the reception desk did not look closely at our credentials and treated us the same as the revolutionary guests. The room rate was tiny: eighty cents per person per day. A meal cost fifteen cents.

The guesthouse, whose design mixed East and West, had a Chinese-style tile roof but a Western interior. It nestled well in its environment, resting in a tranquil nook inside a ravine, where you heard nothing but the music of a trickling brook that flowed past in front. After dinner we followed the brook downstream to a cavernous pool, where the sound of the water was louder. By then it was completely dark. The craggy rocks in the stream, the whitewater splashing against them, and White Dragon Bridge, vaguely visible in the distance, were all bathing in the gentle silver light of the moon. It was hard to see anything very clearly except the rocks at our feet and the stream water that flowed over them. The water was cool. The air was cool. The sticky heat of the day on the bus had melted away—no, more than that, the grime of two years of class struggle was also being washed away. We felt like lingering indefinitely at the cavern pool, letting the stream water wash our spirits clean, letting the gentle moonlight take charge . . .

But we couldn't. We had big plans for the next day.

On August 16 we were up and out at 6:30 a.m. After climbing for an hour, we reached Half-Mountain Temple. The trail grew much steeper after that, and the cliffs at the two sides were more imposing. We were getting into the heart of the mountains.

Huangshan rocks are a symphony of differences. Look this way and they are round, that way and they are angular. They appear huge in the distance, but small up close. Varying in length and in flatness, alternately soft or angry, they follow no rule. They seem almost alive, growing at will, free of bonds. It's a pity that so many rock formations at Huangshan have been given tacky, unimaginative names that liken them to human beings or to gods—"Boy Praying to Guanyin," "Prime Minister Watching Chess," and so on. Why do human beings have the peculiar need to anthropomorphize things that they find in nature? It is such a narrow view, so self-referential and silly. It is why Li Shuxian and I, at Half-Mountain Temple, did not wait to listen to the monks explain the name for every rock in sight. Instead we kept climbing. We thought the rocks themselves should keep their rights of self-expression and that the freedom to imagine should be left to individual hikers. Romantic footnotes should be left to pairs of lovers.

For the next two and a half hours we hiked up and down the two main peaks—Capital of Heaven Peak, which is about 5,740 feet high, and Lotus Blossom Peak, 6,167 feet at the top. Veterans of these climbs might reasonably suspect that I am in error here, because most hikers reserve one day for each of these peaks—or, at a minimum, half a day for each. The reason we could do both within half a day had much to do with the fit physical condition that our labor reform had put us in, but also something to do with our shortage of time. Our whole vacation had to be on fast-forward.

The weather was kind to us. Bright sun and gentle breezes made it possible for us to cover all the main sites at Huangshan within two days. Had it rained, we could not have gotten up Capital of Heaven, the peak with the steepest ascent. To reach the top you had to cross a long, rocky slope over which (in 1971, anyway) there were no steps to help you out. There were small indentations, enough to place your foot—or half of it—chiseled into the rock. In some places there were also hanging chains that you could grab onto as you went up or down. A place called "fish-back ridge," about three feet wide, featured drops into abysses on both sides. Once a year or so a careless climber lost his or her life there. We made it, though, and heaved a sigh at the top. (We visited Huangshan again in 1987 and rode to the top in a cable car. That meant we missed, of course, the beauty of the bare-handed climb.)

The peak at Capital of Heaven is the most beautiful in the Huangshan Mountains. The top is like a small island that juts out toward space, holding its own, bucking and tossing among the clouds that billow one moment and disperse the next as they blow by. The air is thin, the wind chilly; this is the frontier of the secular world, the edge where the cacophony of human loves and hates melts away. It reminded me of the "Paradiso" section of *The Divine Comedy*, where the highest level in Heaven is occupied not even by God but only by Dante, his lover Beatrice, and their limitless joy. Peering out and down as far as we could, we could still discern the rivers, streams, and land that lay below, lit by the bright sun and home to all of that noise that we had risen above. Chinese poets through the centuries have written many famous lines about mountain peaks of various sizes (including some, truth be told, that are not all that pretty), but for some reason there isn't any poem about Capital of Heaven. Perhaps the poets who ventured there were all shocked into mute stupor at sights that exceeded the bounds that the imagination could encompass.

At 1:00 p.m. we finished an ascent of the third main peak, called Brighttop, and then reached the Northsea Guesthouse, the highest guesthouse in the Huangshan range. We stayed overnight there.

We rose early the next morning to see the sunrise. I had seen so many sunrises at Lianggezhuang that this one did not do much for me. Then we headed down the mountain by a different route, arriving at the town of Dunxi, which is the commercial hub of Huizhou County and is divided down the middle by the Xin'an River. Dunxi was our home for the evening and night, but the 104-degree heat killed our interest in sightseeing and almost killed our ability to sleep. Early the next day we escaped northward by bus to Wuhu, Anhui's most bustling city, but I'm afraid that our deepest impression of Wuhu was a bowl of spoiled noodles that we bought. We continued on to Nanjing, but by the time we got there the only place to sleep was in the main hall of the rail station. No bed, no pillows, yet we slept soundly. Six days of travel had exhausted us.

On the morning of August 19 we reached Mingguang, also known as Jiashan, which is Li Shuxian's hometown and was the last stop on our honeymoon tour. Our final tourist visit was to the Tomb of Aunt Cao, which is just outside Mingguang. Aunt Cao was the younger sister of Zhu Yuanzhang, the founding emperor of the Ming Dynasty (1368–1644). As a major personage of the imperial clan she should, by rights, have had an extravagant burial. But she died too soon, before the dynasty was really up and running, and when there were more pressing priorities than burials. So her tomb is nothing special. There is no memorial arch and, in accordance with local tradition, no tombstone. To judge from the remnants that survive, the stone guardians and horses that had been sent to accompany her into the next world were not very big. The only really distinguishing feature of her tomb was the size of its lot, which was about ten times that of the adjacent tombs for commoners. Compared to the tombs of her descendants—the thirteen famous Ming Tombs near Beijing—this was frugal in the extreme.

This illustrates a general pattern with China's dynasties. The first generation is violent but frugal. Zhu Yuanzhang's own mausoleum in Nanjing is downright shabby compared to the opulent tombs of his successors. Succeeding generations keep the violence going, but turn profligate and corrupt. By the end of the dynasty they are violent, corrupt, muddle-headed, and incompetent. They fall, and then a new cycle begins: violence to corruption to mediocrity to annihilation, in a repeating pattern that has its internal logic.

I felt the Mao dynasty was observing the same trajectory. By the end of my belated honeymoon, my road ahead seemed clearer to me.

12. TURN TOWARD ASTROPHYSICS

MY WORK AT THE BRICK FACTORY CAME TO AN END LESS THAN A MONTH after I got back from Huangshan. The authorities reassigned me to the physics department. The decision arrived abruptly and for a reason I hardly expected. It was not that they suddenly concluded that I no longer needed reform, and it was not that the brick factory suddenly closed. It was that Lin Biao suddenly changed from Mao Zedong's "closest comrade in arms" to "traitor" and died.

In China's planned economy, everything was supposed to go according to a central plan. The reality for citizens, though, was very nearly the opposite. To plan one's life could be treacherous, because the core of the Party, while planning what would happen to everybody else, could not plan itself. Interminable struggles over the political "line" at the highest levels, and unpredictable risings and fallings of top leaders, happened quite outside any plan. The government regularly issued five-year plans for the economy, but never published a five-year plan for the intra-Party struggles over the political line, even though, for ordinary people, the consequences of the latter were far greater than those of the former. This proves that life in China's socialist system obeyed one of the fundamental tenets of Marxist "dialectics": it showed that A arises from a lack of A—a plan arises from the lack of a plan.

On September 13, 1971, Lin Biao met with his unplanned death according to plan. (Exactly what plan led to the death has been a topic for lively
debate among historians ever since.) After that, the Great Cultural Revolution entered its second half, which was a stage of decline. Slogans about
revolutionary struggle still rent the heavens, but to judge from the
exhausted look in Mao's eyes (apparent in photographs), the campaign was
on the wane. Soon the "Mao Zedong Thought Propaganda Teams," whose
job it had been to stir up class struggle, left the campuses, and after that
the "proletarian dictatorship brigades" (of which our brick factory group
was one) were disbanded as well.

A "new" revolution arrived, however. Its formal name was the Proletarian Education Revolution, and its slogan was "Return to class to make
revolution." My recall to the physics department happened under its aegis.

The new revolution turned out to be just another rubric for class
struggle, and I was once again sent to do factory work. But although the
reality was the same, the theory this time was different. Officially, the purpose was not to "reeducate" people or to "reform" them. It was to illustrate another of Marx's principles: that everything is created by labor.
Engels had said that all of the natural sciences arise from needs that
emerge in the course of productive labor. For science, one factory is more
important than twenty universities. Conversely, anything that is not necessary to the processes of productive labor is for that reason not science,
or at least not proletarian science. It followed that the first step in an education revolution in the natural sciences should be that scientists participate in productive labor.

Accordingly, a few of my fellow physicists and I were sent to a camera
factory in Beijing. The purpose was to get us to understand exactly what
kind of physics was needed by this factory whose importance exceeded
that of a university by twenty times.

The Marxist theory got at least one point right: the camera factory,
which produced Great Wall cameras, really did need some physics. It was
a new operation and the cameras were not very good. One of the many
problems had to do with the lens filter coatings. The factory had a special room where technicians applied a coating that was supposed to turn
the filter surfaces yellow; but they couldn't control the thickness of the

coating and the filters came out with hues of red, green, and other colors mixed in. So here indeed was a genuine need—control of coating thickness—that arose out of a production process.

It was a problem that modern physics could easily handle. The theory of optical thin film interference had been around for a hundred years or more, and I drew upon it to fashion a little device that we attached to the machinery. This kept the coatings even and the filters a uniform yellow. So my visit had not been entirely a waste. I had used the yellow filters of Great Wall cameras to prove that physics is in tune with Marxism: science indeed was "necessary to productive labor."

But the yellow filter incident was not the most important part of my stay in Beijing. The important milestone was a paper that I wrote on modern cosmology. It was the first such paper to be published in socialist China, and it turned out to show that physics and Marxism do not quite agree. It was also the beginning of new trouble for me.

Actually, cosmology has been a "pirate ship" for a long time. In 1989 a British cosmologist lamented that "cosmologists have an unhappy history of getting into trouble with the powers that be." He listed examples: Aristarchus, Copernicus, Bruno, Galileo, Sakharov, others. His theme was that authoritarian regimes have never gotten along with people whose profession it is to research the universe. Or to put it the other way: power elites who have disliked cosmologists have almost always been authoritarian.

My motive in choosing the field of cosmology was by no means to seek headaches for myself or to jump onto a "pirate ship" in order to irritate Communist authorities. It was (as I explained in chapter 10) my experience at the Xiesan mine, hauling malaria victims and seeing dead bodies, that caused me to look toward the heavens and to decide to head in that direction. Far from seeking political trouble, it was precisely an impulse to escape it, to soar toward the placid beyond, that ignited my interest. So when I moved from the brick factory to the physics department and began to have a bit of time for research, I set aside the solid state physics and laser physics that had occupied me in the past and turned to astrophysics.

It was not easy going. The university libraries had reopened, but their books and journals lagged well behind the times. They had almost nothing published after 1968, so it was impossible to know what colleagues

around the world had recently been doing. We did get a few little bro-
chures, and so could speculate, but that's all.

Another problem was that astrophysics, from its birth in the 1860s to
the present day, had never been needed in any process of productive labor.
No factory had ever used it to manufacture anything. So obviously it fell
outside what Engels had declared science to be, and there was no way it
was going to get any support from the Proletarian Education Revolution.
Professor Qian Linzhao advised me that it would be better if I continued
my work in either solid states or lasers, since those two fields were ones
the authorities still regarded as useful—whereas heaven only knew what
they would think of astrophysics. This caused me to hesitate for a time,
but then three things happened during the spring and summer of 1972 that
made me finally take the dive.

First, my assignment to the Great Wall camera factory gave me the
chance to go to research institutes and specialized science archives in
Beijing, where I could see professional literature that I couldn't get in
Hefei. Second, news that Joseph Weber had detected gravitational waves
coming from the center of the Milky Way generated great excitement
among physicists, and some of my former colleagues at the Physics Research
Institute of the Academy of Sciences had become inspired to test Weber's
theory by repeating his experiment. Most of them did not know gravitational theory very well, though, so they asked me to come give them a
systematic account of general relativity. I agreed, and that errand required
that I dig deeper into astrophysics. Third, *Acta Physica Sinica*, now simply called *Physics*, resumed publication. All of China's scientific journals
had completely closed in 1966, and *Physics*, resuming in the fall of 1972,
was the first to come back. So now we again had a place to publish.

When I got back from the camera factory I sat down to write my first
physics paper since the Cultural Revolution began. The piece was not
long, but its name was: "On a Cosmological Explanation for Matter and
Black Body Radiation Using Scalar-Tensor Theory." I wanted to squeeze
into the title the names of as many concepts in cosmology as I could—
"cosmological explanation," "black body radiation," and so on—so that
everyone would know this was a paper on modern cosmology. If I had used
a less explicit title, something like "A Rigorous Solution in Scalar-Tensor

Gravitational Theory," the story that unfolded next might have been different.

The article appeared quickly in *Physics*. Then, in the winter of 1972–73, I began hearing that the relevant authorities were incensed and were making inquiries. Someone was daring to talk about "cosmological explanations"? What temerity!

And sure enough, in the spring, a spate of articles in the Shanghai newspaper *Wenhuibao* and the journal *Dialectics of Nature* launched an all-out denunciation of the field of modern cosmology. One of the attacks, titled "Does the Universe Have an Explanation?" took straight aim at my article—even though my article had not contained even one political term, let alone any political content.

In case you, my reader, might be curious about exactly what words a proletarian dictatorship uses when it denounces a field of pure science, I record below some of what the attack said:

> Modern cosmology is "bourgeois cosmology." It is "counterfeit cosmology" and "shows only the degree of depravity that is reached when the natural sciences fall into the hands of the rotten and depraved bourgeois class."

> The model of an expanding universe "seeks to establish that the capitalist system not only cannot be overcome but will continue indefinitely to expand."

> The cosmos "has no mathematical or physical explanations, but it has a philosophical explanation"; "the proletariat has its own cosmic explanation"; "the proletariat will write its own new 'On the Revolutions of the Heavenly Bodies' and new 'Idea of a Universal History on a Cosmopolitical Plan.'"

("On the Revolutions of the Heavenly Bodies" is a work by Copernicus, and "The Idea of a Universal History on a Cosmopolitical Plan" is an essay by Immanuel Kant.)

In short, all of cosmology, from Copernicus on, was under attack. But invective of this kind was not an invention of China's Cultural Revolution;

it was a tradition in Communist ideology. Years before, on June 24, 1947, Andrei Zhdanov, the ideology commissar for the Soviet Communist Party at the time, made a major speech in which he announced an all-out war on "bourgeois science." He called on Communists, armed with Marxism, to "occupy" astronomy, physics, chemistry, biology, computational science, and other natural sciences. One by one, relativity theory, quantum theory, resonance theory, genetic theory, and others all came under fierce attack.

Cosmology took the hardest hit. In the Soviet Union it was completely eliminated; the very word "cosmology" was deleted from textbooks. The rationale was that because Marxism had already solved all problems concerning the cosmos, the entire field of modern cosmology was anti-Marxist. In the People's Republic of China, which was founded in 1949 with a "tilt toward the Soviet Union" while the Zhdanov campaign was at high tide, cosmology was doomed from the start. There were no cosmology textbooks, no papers on cosmology, and no mention of cosmology in any development plans for the sciences. It was as if the field did not exist. The 1973 denunciations of cosmology in *Wenhuibao* were, in short, orthodox Communism.

Wenhuibao had a unique position during the Cultural Revolution. Although not an organ of the Party center, it was under the direct control of Yao Wenyuan, the leading authority on Chinese Communist ideology at the time, so it carried special weight. The Cultural Revolution itself had been launched by a withering attack that *Wenhuibao* had published. The writer-historian named in that attack took the matter rather too hard and resorted to suicide.

Now *Wenhuibao* and *Dialectics of Nature* were turning their annihilation machinery against relativity theory, quantum theory, and cosmology. Everyone knew there were powerful political forces behind the move, and people waited to see what might happen. Would somebody take things too hard again? But alas, the murder effect did not travel well this time; the pressure was not enough to persuade even one person to give up on life. Maybe this was because astronomers, astrophysicists, and cosmologists, ever since Aristarchus of Samos (310–230 B.C.), have never been very big on suicide. Or maybe it was because seven years of Cultural Revolution had taught people that nothing is really that shocking anymore.

Still, the episode raises a question worth asking: Exactly why is it that the august ideology of Communism, while claiming to liberate the entirety of humanity, cannot swallow something like cosmology? In 1973, the number of people in all of China who understood relativistic cosmology could not have been more than a hundred. A paper in a physics journal could not possibly have had more than a hundred readers. So how could it threaten a proletarian dictatorship with a standing army of three million? How could the colossal Communist Party become as enraged as it was by a little paper on pure science? People in later times might look back and judge that the power holders of the day were daft. Something like Don Quixote?

Joking aside, insanity was a real problem during the Cultural Revolution. Quite a few people, wounded by events, were driven to madness. But the insanity of denouncing cosmology was not the result of any trauma; it grew out of Communist ideology.

Mao-era state socialism rested on a "Holy Trinity" of despotisms: in politics, a one-party dictatorship; in economics, a dictatorship of state planning; and in ideology, a dictatorship that resembled that of the medieval church in Europe. Each of the three powers needed the other two. Marxist texts had the status of sacred religious texts. No challenge, however slight, of whatever kind, from whatever person, could be tolerated. Zhdanov's point (in *Wenhuibao*, noted above) that we don't need modern cosmology because "the proletariat has its own cosmic explanation" was precisely that point—no challenges allowed.

Hoping to understand what could be meant by a "proletarian cosmic explanation," I did some research. What I found was that, although the Marxist classics use the terms "universe" and "cosmos" fairly often, there are only two sentences in them that could be said to offer an "explanation":

1. *Space in the universe is infinite.*
2. *Movement through space in the universe can go forward or backward, up or down, or left or right indefinitely; there are no end points.*

The two statements appear in two works by Engels: *Dialectics of Nature* and *Herr Eugen Dühring's Revolution in Science*. Neither of the propositions is accepted in the field of modern cosmology, because there is no evidence for either. But their presence in Engels means that a proletarian dictatorship must ban modern cosmology.

Actually, neither of the statements originated with Engels. They are only recapitulations of the most simple hypothesis in the cosmology of Newton's time—that the universe is an unlimited three-dimensional euclidean space. But these two propositions had the good luck of being understood by Engels, who copied them into his books. With that their value soared. They turned into the cream of the cream of human learning—a "proletarian cosmic explanation"! (One can only wonder what Newton would have thought.) In any case, Engels had driven a wedge between Newtonian cosmology and modern cosmology. They were now opponents: "bourgeois cosmology" and "proletarian cosmology."

There is an interesting precedent for this. The theory that the earth is at the center of the universe is not in the Bible and was not invented within the Christian church; it originated in a model of planetary movement that arose in ancient Greece. But when the medieval church adopted the concept, it got catapulted to the level of sacred, unchallengeable doctrine. That the earth was at the center was now the divine truth, and it was heresy to say that the sun is.

So the ideological dictatorships of modern socialism and the medieval church had several things in common. They both saw themselves as authorities on cosmology; both adopted an outmoded cosmology as their unchallengeable model; and both used the tools of tyranny to block scientific progress. This helped me to understand that the problem with Communist rule over science was not just those tools of tyranny themselves but an ideology that in its very nature is opposed to the conditions that science requires: free inquiry, a spirit of skepticism, and reliance on evidence.

A few years later, in 1981, I accepted an invitation to a conference on cosmology at the Vatican. The conferees were presented with the text of a speech by Pope John Paul II on the church's current position on the relation between science and religion. It said that "the cooperation between science and religion, so long as neither side undermines the autonomy of the other, is beneficial to both. This means that religion can ask for the freedom of faith, and science can insist on freedom of inquiry." But in 1990, as I write this, the dictatorial system in China still rejects in principle the notion that science can be free to operate independently of Communist faith.

Marxist writings often make the claim that Marxism expresses the essence of all previous learning and transcends all cultures. Because it stands as the most general of truths, any new creation or development in science or culture must accept its suzerainty. Earlier in my life I had blindly embraced this principle.

Once blind faith was gone, it became easy to see that this essence-of-the-essence doctrine was nothing but a garment in the wardrobe of the emperor's new clothes. Moreover, it has been one of the favorite garments of the great Communist teachers generation after generation. Only when they wear it can they criticize and guide all branches of learning without needing to understand them. Here are a few examples:

- Karl Marx's *Mathematical Manuscripts* has long been honored as a classic in Marxist natural science. During the Proletarian Education Revolution movement in China in the early 1970s, universities went so far as to adopt it as a mathematics textbook. In it, Marx uses dialectics to expound upon concepts in calculus, and specialists in Communist ideology have followed up with piles of articles on, for example, Marx's dialectical analysis of zero divided by zero. Unless one reads this literature conscientiously, one can get the impression that Marx actually does have a hold on some kind of esoteric argument. What a careful reading actually establishes is only this: that Marx completely failed to understand the limits theory that was already well established and available during his time.

- In 1908 Lenin wrote a propaganda pamphlet called "Materialism and Empirio-Criticism" in which he became very concerned with physics. He wrote with soaring passion about a "crisis in physics" and attacked a number of physicists, especially Ernst Mach and Jules Henri Poincaré. The overall message was that only Lenin can save physics. The claim of Mach and others that no absolute reference system exists was made, according to Lenin, only as a basis for asking their capitalist bosses for higher salaries. One might think that a personal attack of this sort would trigger a sharp response. But Mach replied only that "Mr. Lenin has yet to understand physics."

- In 1963 Mao Zedong decided to wear the "dominate physics" clothes as well. He had just invented the new slogan "Never, Ever, Forget the Class Struggle" when—perhaps inspired by Lenin's precedent—he was suddenly attracted to physics. He felt a need to instruct physicists in how to do particle research. He praised the Japanese physicist Sakata Shoichi, commenting that Sakata's research accorded with Marxist philosophy. Chinese Marxists swarmed to show how Sakata's results fit with Mao's philosophy as expressed in the essays "On Practice" and "On Contradiction" and in the Mao slogan "one divides into two." It's too bad for Sakata that he was Japanese; had he been Chinese, he could have soared to stratospheric heights. The actual impact of Mao's comment was not, alas, that all Chinese specialists in ideology should go in search of physicists in order to learn about Sakata's physics. It was the opposite: all Chinese physicists had to take initiatives to go absorb the guidance of Mao Zedong Thought.

It may be that this sort of hallucinatory megalomania in Communist culture had its origins in the all-embracing philosophical system devised by Hegel. In the years when I was trying to get into the Communist Party, I read some Hegel in order to better understand Marx. Most of Hegel's enormous system lies outside the scope of my special knowledge, and I have no opinion on those parts of it. But this much I can say for sure: every one of Hegel's theses on physics, without exception, is pure poppycock and utterly devoid of value for serious physicists. From his discussion of concepts in physics such as force and heat, it is plain that all he is doing is spreading a philosophical system that he regards as omnipotent over areas in which he has no understanding whatsoever.

Hegel's intellectual pushiness grew from needs that were intrinsic to his philosophy. In countries that practice proletarian dictatorship, however, the function of the megalomania in Marxism has been to exert ideological dictatorship over others.

In December 1974, I wrote to Li Shuxian that "we are governed today by muddleheadedness and ignorance . . . on this topic my thinking has now gone very, very far." It was around this time that the icon of Marxist ideology collapsed in my mind once and for all.

In 1973, the year in which the political attack on cosmology was launched, a few of my colleagues and I organized an informal group on astrophysics. At first there were only five of us, but we were the seed that eventually grew into USTC's Center for Astrophysics. None of us anticipated that such a thing would happen. In those days, when the Great Proletarian Cultural Revolution was waning but still dominant, the government had yet to resume support for academic research of any kind. Our little group lived only by interest and without any thought of where things might lead. We were lucky that the open-minded Liu Da had by then returned to be Party Secretary of USTC. Liu never disobeyed explicit orders from above but, down on the ground, was very good at "opening one eye and closing the other," as the Chinese saying has it. Our little group had his tacit approval.

The conditions for research were, of course, poor. We began with no budget, and our first grant, which came for ad hoc reasons, was only 200 yuan. But we didn't have many special activities and didn't need equipment, so budget was not a big concern. We had no office, so we held our seminars in a staff dormitory room that contained a ten-square-foot blackboard. It was hard to find professional reading material; astrophysics had not been in the original plans for USTC, so the library holdings in the field were paltry. Sometimes one of us traveled all the way to Beijing in search of what we needed. We were cut off from the international community of astrophysicists; there was no way we could send our papers for publication abroad, and it was extremely rare for any foreign colleagues to come our way.

Research activities begun in such conditions normally wither and die, but our little group thrived. Not only did no one quit, but a trickle of younger people kept arriving, wanting to join. Some of the "credit" for this continuing influx must go, ironically, to the political campaign against cosmology. That campaign lasted right to the end of the Cultural Revolution in 1976, and (although this was not its purpose) it provided a politically correct reason for Chinese astronomers to get back into action. After all, in a big campaign on the topic of astronomy, who should participate if not astronomers? Beginning in 1974 there were major annual conferences on astronomy. Denunciations of the wrong kind of astronomy topped the agendas, but in order to do that, someone had to read the texts of the papers that were going to be denounced. So real astronomy spread.

During the last three years of the Cultural Revolution, the power of the ideological dictatorship to intimidate people declined steadily. When it was launched in 1973, the attack on cosmology had considerable sting, but later it became more and more pro forma. Scholarly meetings on astronomy turned gradually into genuine conferences conducted under the banner of denunciation—and became opportunities for a bit of travel as well. This was how the field of astronomy got back on its feet in China. It grew from being attacked.

Universities and observatories around the country took turns hosting the conferences, and in 1976 it was our turn to hold one in Hefei. It was, as things turned out, the last to be held during the Cultural Revolution. Before it ended, though, the Cultural Revolution exerted once last kick. Repression intensified during its final year and grew especially strong after the "April Fifth" incident when protesters were forcibly evicted from Tiananmen Square by baton-wielding police. Well-positioned people began discreetly letting us know that the Hefei conference on astronomy would get very close attention from "the concerned parties"— meaning the government guardians of ideology—and that we should be careful. So we prepared meticulously and scoured our plans to remove every vulnerability we could imagine.

As a site for the meeting, we chose a building complex that had been constructed a few years earlier as a training base for officers of the Viet Cong. It was not open to the public. Its environs were pretty and it had good equipment, including a place to swim. Since it had been built for Communist revolutionaries, no one could accuse us of choosing a place with bourgeois comforts. The only drawback was that, since the Vietnamese don't mind heat, it had no air-conditioning.

The bigger worry was what to do for the customary conference excursion. We would obviously be denounced if we chose Huangshan. There was always Bagong Mountain, but who would want to go there? We finally settled on Huoshan County in the Dabie Mountains of western Anhui. This was known as "the county of the generals" because it was the native place of more Communist generals—several dozen of them—than anywhere else. It was also an early base of the Communist revolution. Neither of these points was the attraction for us, though; we were drawn by the rare natural beauty of the Plum Mountain Reservoir in that area.

All the preparations went forward as planned, and our meeting convened in July 1976. As expected, the "concerned parties" in both Beijing and Shanghai sent some neophytes in astronomy to attend. Some of the real astronomers nicknamed these interlopers "fishermen," because their purpose at the meeting was obviously to troll for politically incorrect speech. If you weren't careful you could be a "hooked fish."

The first fish to be hooked was Professor Dai Wensai of Nanjing University, who made the mistake of saying publicly that he thought there really had been a Big Bang. Since Professor Dai was a very senior figure in the field, the fishermen opted not to set their hooks right away, but to wait for others to nibble as well so that they could reel in a big haul. In that limbo, nothing happened as the conferees peacefully set off for Huoshan, spent two pleasant days at the Plum Mountain Reservoir, then returned to the Viet Cong training base. The fishing resumed, and everyone watched to see who might be hooked. The weather got hotter and hotter, the atmosphere in the un-air-conditioned conference tenser and tenser . . .

Then—oops, too bad!—right when tension was at its peak, the shocking news of the great Tangshan earthquake arrived. The conference ended, fish and fishermen dispersed as one, and that was that.

So our little research group on astrophysics muddled through, and eventually thrived, only by the grace of a counterproductive political campaign plus assists from a few weird, unpredictable events. In any case, beginning in 1974, our group produced more scholarly papers per person per year than any other part of USTC. The topics were cosmology, gravitational collapse, compact objects, and active celestial bodies, all of which fall into the general category of relativistic astrophysics. Soon thereafter the school authorities officially recognized an astrophysics research section in the Department of Physics, and from that time forward we were legitimate.

I find, looking back at what I have written in this chapter, that it contains rather too much stultifying detail about denunciations of cosmology. With this emphasis I might, without meaning to, actually be desecrating cosmology and astrophysics. The harebrained denunciations are, after all, only a minor sidelight in their history. One fact that I cannot change, though, is that those were indeed sorry times. It is the history itself, not my words about it, that does the desecrating. The fields, in their wisdom, just sparkle along as if nothing happened.

In fact I don't think cosmology and astrophysics will mind that I have written down this chapter in their history. Astronomy has never aimed at worldly fame or descended into hurly-burly over power. It doesn't need the sympathy that pity offers. Indeed, the flow of strength goes in the opposite direction. The more a human being opens to the universe and accepts cultivation from it, the more inspiration that person will receive and the more firm the person's confidence will be—especially that kind of confidence that cannot be had in other ways, the confidence of belief. Immanuel Kant chose these words for his tombstone:

> *Two things fill my mind with ever-increasing wonder and awe, the more often and the more intensely the reflection dwells on them: the starry heavens above me and the moral law within me.*

Indeed. The universe is quite as ideal, noble, and unbounded as this. When you stand face-to-face with the universe, in its ultimate depth and ultimate beauty, your spirit cannot but soar. As you grow clearer and clearer about how space and time are continually expanding, and how the universe is evolving:

What terror or timidity is not swept away by a current of joy?

What problem or puzzle does not melt in the beauty of wisdom?

What worry or anxiety does not dissolve in a celestial song?

13. MODERNIZATION AT THE
END OF THE 1970s

In July 1976, the great Tangshan earthquake killed about four hundred thousand people. It seemed, somehow, also the death knell of the Great Proletarian Cultural Revolution.

When USTC opened for classes in the fall of 1976, the Astrophysics Section of the Department of Physics received its first-ever budget allocation. We used it to buy a calculator. It wasn't much more powerful than the little pocket calculators that followed very soon thereafter, but in size and weight this one resembled an electric typewriter. The factory that made it did not do deliveries, so one afternoon a colleague and I set out by bicycle to go pick it up. The day was September 9. We were barely out of the university gates when we—and all the rest of the city— were overwhelmed by mourning music. It blared from every public loudspeaker, large and small, in unprecedented volume. In that era, the volume of funerary music was strictly calibrated to the political status of the deceased, so for us the inference was obvious: Mao was dead.

We picked up the bulky machine, loaded it onto a bicycle, and headed back to campus. The mourning music boomed unabated. I found it strange, though, that nothing else seemed different. The little flatbed carts streamed through the streets just as before; no cars honked horns in sympathy with the mourning (as they often did on other occasions); pedestri-

ans walked past giant banners that read LONG LIVE CHAIRMAN MAO! as if
no banner were there. This is how the passing of this man from the era
before calculators—no, let's be clear, this *emperor*—was observed by his
subjects.

A month later Mao's wife, Jiang Qing, and her political allies known
as the "Gang of Four" were arrested. With no ceremony beyond that, the
curtain fell on ten years of the Great Proletarian Cultural Revolution and
the stage was set for China to attempt modernization again.

The end of the Cultural Revolution brought an effusion of levity all
across society. News of the collapse of the Gang of Four sparked a spontaneous celebration at Beijing's Tiananmen Square. Cymbals clanged,
drums banged, and people's spirits soared. The clouds of so many years
of "denunciations" were floating away. What joy!

It was easy to reach a new consensus that China should pursue modernization. Everybody wanted the country to move beyond Mao Zedong's
approach of fight-heaven fight-earth fight-humanity. When it came to questions of what modernization was, though—how to pursue it and where
best to start—there was not a lot of consensus. Everyone had his or her
own notions. Estimates differed, too, on the questions of exactly what China's current position was and what the prospects were. Most people were
cautiously optimistic. But the ones who had been most badly battered in
the Mao-era campaigns remained skeptical and fearful. They just waited,
watched, and kept their mouths shut.

Some people who had relatives overseas, or in Hong Kong or Macao,
rushed to emigrate as quickly as they could. The government was now
permitting emigration, but approvals were not easy to come by. My old
friend Deng Weilian from brick factory days and my colleague A, whom
I had known for twenty years, were both indefatigable in their determination to get out to Hong Kong. Both had cheerfully left Hong Kong in
1949 to be part of the new China. Now, the two major episodes of elation
in their personal histories formed a stark contrast: in 1949 they were elated
to go in, and in 1977 they were elated to get out.

Deng Weilian came to see me before he left and we talked about how
things looked for China. He was pessimistic. He said the reason he wanted
out was that China's future looked bleak, and the reason for his gloom was

that Deng Xiaoping had returned to power. This was not how most people (including me) saw things. The common view was that because Deng had been purged by Mao and had felt the brunt of the proletarian dictatorship personally, he would be different from Mao.

But Deng Weilian said that we were all hoodwinked, and he had an extraordinary analysis to support his view. Drawing a parallel to a famous military trick in the ancient novel *Romance of the Three Kingdoms*, he reasoned this way: Mao had not really persecuted Deng; Mao and Deng had conspired to present the appearance of persecution, the purpose of which was to deceive the Chinese people into welcoming Deng on precisely the assumption many of us were now making—that Deng, detesting Mao, would be different; the hidden goal was to continue the Mao dynasty; in essential matters there was no difference between Mao and Deng; Mao's official "successor," the mediocre Hua Guofeng, was but a stalking horse. Weilian buttressed his interpretation with the observation that every other time Mao had carried out the purge of a rival, he had not rested until the rival was dead. Never before had there been a case like Deng Xiaoping's— you get purged and you still get to play bridge. After listening to Weilian's analysis I remained unpersuaded. I had to admire the rigor of his logic, though.

The people most eager to leave were those who had ties outside China. The ones who were born and grew up in China—like me—found leaving harder to think about. Our default position was to stay put and hope things would improve. The end of the Mao dynasty might be a turning point.

My own first response to the new modernization ethos was to throw myself into teaching and research in physics. However the cards play out, I told myself, physics is essential to modernization. Before 1977, I published an average of four papers per year. After 1977, it was eight. Astrophysics was consuming my life.

In October 1976, our astronomy research group went to visit the Xinglong Observation Station located one hundred miles northeast of Beijing in the Xinglong Mountains. During the Qing period the area had been a hunting reservation for the aristocracy, and even now almost no one lived there. Pollution from electric light was near zero and atmospheric conditions were good, so it was an ideal place for "optical observation," as we astronomers call it. The station's equipment, though, left much to be desired. The main pieces were a 60/90-centimeter Schmidt telescope and a 60-centimeter reflecting telescope. In 1958 construction had begun on a telescope with a two-meter diameter, but the later tides of "revolution" doomed that project.

Chinese astronomy has a few thousand years of history. Because ancient kings and emperors claimed that their authority came from heaven, astronomy from the very beginning was a government-sponsored branch of learning. It is interesting, though, that the most eminent premodern Chinese astronomer, Guo Shoujing (1231–1316), did not emerge in one of the great Chinese dynasties—the Tang, the Song, or the Ming—but during the Yuan, when China had been invaded by Mongols and its own civilization was at low ebb. I find this interesting because it shows that the fortunes of Chinese astronomy did not parallel the rising and falling of the rest of Chinese civilization. Astronomy may have been the first science in the world to transcend nationality and make progress across cultures.

The Beijing Observatory, which was built in 1279 by order of Yuan founder Kublai Khan, was the capital observatory of what was then the largest empire in the world. It was also, for its time, the world's most modern observatory, and Guo Shoujing was its first director.

Time does not stand still, however, and seven hundred years later, the Beijing Observatory telescopes were nowhere near the best in the world. At the Xinglong observation site we could do only the most ordinary observations. We were lucky, though, to observe the BX Andromedae, an eclipsing binary star, at the time of its minimal brightness. Based on that observation, I was able to infer that the rotation period of this binary is gradually increasing, and I wrote a paper about it called "The Period Increase of BX Andromedae." This is the only paper I have ever written based on data from my own observation.

When we got back from Xinglong, some of my friends in space physics invited me to join in a two-month observation of whistlers. This was not astrophysics, but it is a very interesting phenomenon. Whistlers are electromagnetic waves of audible frequency that are generated by thunder in the southern hemisphere and then, following the earth's magnetic field at high altitude, arrive in the northern hemisphere. Southern hemisphere thunder, by the time it reaches the northern hemisphere, becomes a wonderful whistling sound. When you hear a volley of whistles at a listening station, you know that somewhere in the southern hemisphere, at that very moment, thunder is rolling. The length and pitch of the whistle can tell you about the magnetic field configuration high above the earth.

The whistler observation point that I visited was in a geomagnetic station in a northwestern suburb of Beijing. Interest in geomagnetism, like astronomy, has ancient roots in China. The legendary Yellow Emperor is said to have led his fighters in 2690 B.C. through a thick fog that had been breathed out by Chi You, the mythical beast who commanded the barbarian enemy, by riding in "south-pointing chariots" that apparently used geomagnetism to tell direction—and could do so even through a fog. Those were the most advanced war chariots of the time, and they assured total victory for the Yellow Emperor. But the descendants of the Yellow Emperor did not, alas, follow up with military applications of this breakthrough. The "south-pointing needle" (a compass) became, instead, a tool in the geomancy called *fengshui* and was used primarily in the layout of gravesites. Chinese coffins, almost without exception, were laid out with the head to the north and the feet to the south, like little magnetic needles lying in line with the earth's magnetic field. Physical magnetism had merged with moral magnetism; the earth's magnetic field became a blanket of loving care.

Our objective in studying whistlers was closer to the Yellow Emperor's. We speculated that when man-made objects like satellites or intercontinental ballistic missiles penetrate the earth's magnetic field at high altitude, they might leave behind ripples that could show up in whistler patterns. If we could analyze those ripples, we might be able to detect satellites and missiles and trace their courses. And if that worked, the breakthrough would obviously have great military value—just as the Yellow Emperor's "south-pointing chariots" had. But it didn't work.

These two excursions into observation—one of the heavens and one of the earth—were but eddies next to the mainstream of my interests, however. My main interest was deeper in space, mainly in quasars. In November 1977, Professor Dai Wensai invited me to Nanjing University to lecture on general relativity. Professor Dai attended all of my lectures, and so did other luminaries in the astronomy field at Nanjing's Purple Mountain Observatory, such as Professor Gong Shumo, so I took my responsibility very seriously. By that time, the political fishermen were gone. Modern cosmology, rising under the mantle of "modernization," had moved from underground into the open for the first time in socialist China.

How a society understands the cosmos is one way to measure how advanced it is. There are many unanswered questions in cosmology, but the forefront of the field, at any given time, does stand as the most advanced understanding we human beings have of the universe we live in. Because cosmology was repressed for so long in socialist China, Chinese people have not been able to keep up with advances. Grade schools and high schools, and even universities, for decades got no further in reporting the matter than Immanuel Kant and Pierre-Simon Laplace—only because that is exactly as far as Engels got. As of the late 1970s, after the severe erosion of Chinese education during the Cultural Revolution, many teachers and students in physics departments in China knew nothing at all about Big Bang cosmology. Popular understanding of the universe fell even to the level of *fengshui*, which taught that "the sky is round and the earth is square." People had no idea what kind of universe they were living in. This is why some of my colleagues and I decided to write some books for the popular reader in China.

Thoughts about the shape of the world were, in fact, what brought Chinese people their earliest glimmerings that modernization is something that they might need. In the late sixteenth century, when the Italian Jesuit Matteo Ricci came to China to do missionary work, the Bible that he brought with him didn't arouse much interest among the Chinese, but the world map that he presented to the Ming emperor—the "Comprehensive Map of the Geography of All Countries"—caused quite a commotion. Until then, the maps of the Ming showed the world as flat, with China in the middle. There were some labels for barbarian tribes and alien regions around the edges, but no place was nearly the size of China. No words indicating Atlantic Ocean or North and South America were even on the map.

Ricci's map was shocking in China not only because China was not in the center (Ricci said the world didn't even have a center) but because the celestial empire was only a small piece of the whole. The world had other parts, and they were huge! A small group of Chinese intellectuals resolved right then to pursue this new learning, and their efforts, as I see it, were the first sprouts of Chinese modernization.

In May 1987, during a visit to Rome, I went to the Vatican Library to take a look at that "Comprehensive Map of the Geography of All Countries." (What they had on display was a replica, of course.) The map is very rudimentary. A lot of the distances are way out of proportion. Australia barely shows. Still, in its day it had been far enough ahead of Ming maps to make Chinese people want to go and hide. I felt a sudden respect for those late-Ming intellectuals who reacted not in petulant rage but by reaching out to embrace new learning. China's first book on astronomical telescopes, *On Telescopy*, was published in their day, only fifteen years after Galileo built the world's first example of the device. You can see how quickly they were willing to learn.

If we draw a parallel between mapping the world and mapping the universe, cosmology in China in the late 1970s was not even up to the level of Ricci's rudimentary map. Ricci's understanding of the world was far, far ahead of Kant's and Laplace's understanding of the universe. Now consider this: Kant and Laplace weren't even Chinese, so why were Chinese people feeling ashamed to admit that the Kant-Laplace map of the universe was out of date? But they did feel that shame. Truth can be stranger than fiction.

In July 1977, Beijing hosted the first conference on natural dialectics to be held after the Cultural Revolution. University teachers of courses on Marxism and related topics came from all around the country to attend these annual events. The title of the conference that year, "Dialectics of Nature," was the same as it had been in the immediately preceding years when the "great denunciations" were in high gear. But the content of the conference this time was very different. What the organizers were trying to do now resembled Matteo Ricci presenting his map: they wanted to introduce the teachers of Marxism to what had actually been going on in various fields of learning during the years when China was bottled up. The conference was held at the Party School in Beijing, which was, by odd coincidence, on the very site where Matteo Ricci was buried after he died in Beijing.

The organizers asked me to be the main speaker for the field of modern cosmology. More than a thousand people filled the auditorium of the Party School to hear me. This was the first time I had ever needed to explain cosmology to people who lacked basic knowledge of physics, so I put a lot of care into planning the lecture. But I was still afraid that people would not have patience to keep listening, especially because the weather was hot. After an hour and a half of lecturing, there was a fifteen-minute break.

The break made it clear that people had not been bored. The official who was chairing the session passed me a big handful of notes that audience members had sent up to the dais. "Never mind these," he said softly as he handed them to me. "Just keep going; say what needs to be said." I unfolded the notes and took a look. They said things like:

> *May I ask the speaker if his intention is to deny Engels?*
>
> *Do you or don't you believe in Marx's theory of an unlimited universe? Please answer!*
>
> *Mr. Chairman, why do you invite speakers full of counter-revolutionary ideas like this? I hope the organizers will reconsider.*

I was elated. Here was pay dirt! Modern cosmology was striking a blow at the hard core of contemporary ignorance. So when the fifteen minutes were up, I did as the chair suggested and just kept going. I had not originally planned to say much about the tiresome topic of ideology; time was limited, and there were several facets of the cosmology field that still needed explanation. But because of this new inspiration from the audience, I saved a few minutes to address ideology explicitly, and I raised the volume of my voice a bit to do it.

"Engels's concept of the universe, in my view, is out of date."

This was the first time I had challenged classical Marxism in public. When the lecture was over, an excited crowd besieged me for quite some time. My challenge had struck a chord.

I gave similar lectures in other places—Shanghai, Hangzhou, Chong-qing, Nanning, Guiyang, Kunming, Anqing, Urumqi, and elsewhere—and got virtually the same responses: the same indignant notes and the same after-lecture crowds. I noticed that, as a rule, the more backward the place, the stronger the opposition. In 1984, at Nanchong Normal College in Sichuan, a student in the physics department stood up after listening for a few minutes and announced, placidly confident in his cor-rectness, "This stuff is all counterrevolutionary."

It made me sigh. This was the fruit of thirty years of socialist educa-tion? What can one say? Perhaps only that the sealing off of China under the Mao dynasty was little different from its sealing off for two centuries under the Ming. In one case the blind faith had been that "we are the great heavenly dynasty of the Ming" and in the other it had been that "we are the great center of world revolution." Indeed, the Mao dynasty was the more benighted of the two; the Ming had that little group of open-minded intellectuals on its historical record, the Mao not even that. Prolonged cul-tural starvation had desiccated people's minds so severely that they were simply incapable of absorbing new things. Hallucinatory megalomania had inserted an impervious membrane between people and things that arrived from the outside; the society could feed only on its own offal, recycling it internally.

I concluded that the main problem facing modernization in the late 1970s was not that people were ignorant but that they did not even know that they were ignorant. Without public acknowledgment that Marxism was out of date, to imagine the modernization of science in China was folly.

I reflected that my fate in this society had little to do with the logic of surface appearances. In 1958, when I was in Zanhuang laboring hard and studying Marx in order to reform myself, my political status plummeted. I was expelled from the Party and became a pariah. Two decades later, as I went around the country lecturing on the theme that Marxism is out of date, my status actually got better and better and I was invited back into the Party. This showed that "belief in Marxism," as the authorities under-stood it, was nothing but a pretty banner. You could parade it to the left, then parade it to the right—all on whim. I had been slow to grasp this fact.

In 1977 the parade was heading to the right. Word was spreading that

Party Central was preparing to exonerate victims of the various political campaigns of the Mao era. My political trajectory continued upward, in tandem with the increase in the rumors. It was as if I had "bounced" off the bottom. In March 1978, I was invited to attend a huge National Science Convention in Beijing. This was the sign that my pariah status had been lifted and I was once again a member of "the people"—meaning politically acceptable people. The convention was held in the Great Hall of the People, into which only "people" were ever invited. That great structure, facing Tiananmen with its Greek columns, had been built in 1959, the year after I was expelled from the Party, and it had taken nearly twenty years for me to enter it for the first time. It really was true, as some said, that there were essentially two castes in China, the people and the non-people.

In the spring of 1978, the authorities organized a big campaign to push the idea that "practice is the criterion for determining truth." There were big meetings, little meetings, newspaper and magazine articles, and more. It was quite a scene. They invited me to join and I agreed. For a physicist, this modest sentence was like confirming that, yes, ABC is ABC. The true significance of the authorities' invitation to me was not that my expertise could confirm their idea. That much was obvious. The significance lay in the political facts: that I had been invited at all, that I could have a platform from which to speak, that my words could be printed in the newspaper, and that my name could appear in number 5 size print. Each of these was a mark of rising political status. By the summer, my bounce from the bottom went high enough that my name could appear in number 3 size print (a size used in small headlines)—but this was permitted only in provincial newspapers, not central ones.

The university promotion system, which had been sidelined for two decades, was restored in 1978. In September I was promoted to full professor. The promotions were based on evaluations by colleagues, but the authorities wanted it clear that the policy change was their doing. Deng Xiaoping said several times in those days that "I want to be the Minister of Logistics for the intellectuals."

In the fall of 1978, Hu Yaobang (whose death would spark the Tiananmen protests a decade later) took over the Organization Department at

Party Central and began the process of formally exonerating 1957 "rightist elements." He oversaw the drafting of Central Document No. 55 of 1978, which provided that Communist Party members who had been stripped of membership because of "rightist speech" should have it restored. The guidelines included me. The contents of Document No. 55 leaked in advance and spread widely among intellectuals. But as I saw it coming, it presented a dilemma. My Party status would likely be restored, but I had given up, long ago, on the idea that the Communist Party of China represented the progressive forces in society. I now saw it as a symbol of backwardness. My faith in Marxism was gone as well. So should I accept an automatic restoration of Party status or not?

In early October I went to Guilin, the small city in southwest China famed for "the loveliest landscapes under heaven," to attend a conference on "The History of Microphysical Thought." Most of the papers were on philosophy of physics, an area in which I was not especially interested, but I went anyway, in part because the organizer, my old friend Hou Depeng, urged that this was a good chance to come see the famous scenery. Guilin was not at its best during my visit, though. Its stunning beauty depends on the graceful Li River that snakes through its mountains, but the river during our visit was almost dry, and the barren riverbed robbed the mountains of their charm. We could still visit the famed Dissolving Cavern and Reed-flute Crag, but these held no attraction for me. My time at the Xiesan mine had given me more than I needed of tunneling into caves. No hole, on either flat land or a mountainside, appealed to me in the least; it only brought back bad memories. I left the conference before it ended.

During the three days I was there, the hottest topic of conversation—hotter than any of the conference papers—was Document 55. There were quite a few rightists and "rightists who slipped through the net" at the conference. Everyone was exchanging stories and speculating on what Document 55 might do. The three rightists at the meeting whom I knew best were Hou Depeng, Xu Liangying, and Fan Dainian. They, like me, had joined the Communist movement early, and I wondered whether they felt the same dilemma I did.

Hou Depeng was labeled a rightist while working at the Central Propaganda Department in 1957 and was then "sent down" to work in Guangxi. His experience during the Cultural Revolution paralleled mine. In 1970, political fighting in Guangxi had reached such a pitch that bodies of people beaten to death were simply tossed into the river. Even live people were sometimes tossed in, tied in gunny sacks. More than a thousand corpses floated downstream all the way to Hong Kong. When British authorities in Hong Kong complained to Beijing about this, Beijing ordered officials in Guangxi to pull corpses out of the river. Hou was a member of the brigade assigned to that work. After the Cultural Revolution, he taught quantum mechanics at Guangxi University. Now, he said, he was ready to accept reentry into the Party with no conditions, if that was what Document 55 was going to offer him.

Xu Liangying, in the 1940s, had been a teaching assistant in physics at Zhejiang University, where he headed the Communist Party's underground campus organization and organized several student movements. After 1949 he did research at the Institute of Philosophy of the Academy of Sciences. He was fired from that job in 1957 because of his rightist "hat" and returned to Zhejiang, where—like me, briefly—he became a farmer. But while working the soil he also collected and translated everything that he could find by Albert Einstein—papers, lectures, letters, records of conversations—and in the end had amassed 410 items that, in translation, totaled 1.3 million Chinese characters. Between 1974 and 1979 he published the collection, in three volumes, as *The Works of Albert Einstein*. It was the world's tenth collection of Einstein's work.

I met Xu in 1974, when he came to ask my help in translating an astronomical term that appeared in an Einstein text. After that we became good friends. In 1978 he was reassigned to his post at the Academy of Sciences, where he planned and organized the Academy's new Institute for the History of Natural Sciences. Although he had begun as a very orthodox Marxist, from the time I knew Xu he was always a fiercer critic of the Communist Party than I was. His stance toward Document 55 was that he would accept restoration of Party membership, but "My purpose in going back to the Party will be to change the Party."

Fan Dainian had been a colleague of Xu Liangying at the Institute of Philosophy and had been declared a rightist at the same time as Xu. Fan, too, was sent next to farming. After that he worked briefly in the library at USTC, then went back to the Academy of Sciences, where, in 1978, he helped to organize the Institute of Management Sciences. He, too, was ready to reenter the Party with Document 55. His reasoning was that if you want to get anything done these days, you have to begin inside the Party.

After I left Guilin I pretty much decided to join these friends in accepting reentry into the Party in order to work inside it to change it. Four months later I received the formal document that restored my membership. Here is the full text:

Decision on the Correction of the Expulsion from the Party of Comrade Fang Lizhi

Fang Lizhi, male, 42 years of age. Original family status: staff. Personal status: student.

Entered the Party in June 1956 while studying at Peking University, in 1956 came to our institute to work, served as a research intern, was a member of the branch committee inside the Party, on 18 October 1958 because of Rightist speech during the times of rectification and opposing the Right was designated by the Party committee of the Academy of Sciences organization for expulsion from the Party, now teaches at the University of Science and Technology of China.

In accordance with the spirit of the central dissemination of Document 55 (1978) of Party Central, the question of Comrade Fang Lizhi's expulsion from the Party for Rightist speech has been reviewed. During the rectification of 1957, Comrade Fang Lizhi was able to participate in the movement actively, and in an outline for "A Letter to Party Central" offered his own opinions on the direction and policies of the Party and the government and related questions; this accords with the organizational principles of provisions of the Party Charter. Most of the opinions in the outline are correct, even though some of the opinions, classifiable as cognitive problems, not Rightist speech, are inappropriate in places. Therefore his expulsion from the Party was not right, and it is

decided to do a correction, to rescind the original punishment, to restore his political reputation, and to restore his
Party status.

> Provisional Party Committee of the Communist Party
> of China for the Institute of High-Energy Physics of the
> Chinese Academy of Sciences
> *23 February 1979*

Just like that, I was a Communist Party member again, and moreover a senior member with twenty-four years of membership credit. It didn't count that I had been outside the Party for twenty-one of those twenty-four years, and it didn't matter that not a trace was left of the Communist idealism that had originally brought me into the Party. It had taken the Party twenty-one years, the time of nearly one human generation, to reach the conclusion that "offering one's own opinions on the direction and policies of the Party and the government" is permissible. How arduous were China's steps toward modernization going to be?

In the summer of 1978, I was invited to attend the Ninth Texas Symposium on Relativistic Astrophysics, which was to be held in Munich, West Germany. This was my first invitation abroad. Chinese regulations, which had been in place for thirty years, were that any Chinese citizen traveling abroad for a work-related purpose, no matter how important or trivial, could not depart without approval from the country's premier. So my invitation to Bonn needed review and a decision at the highest level. In November, the good news arrived. Premier Hua Guofeng had approved. How many of my colleagues in astrophysics around the world enjoy the benefit of such high-level solicitude?

By chance, China's own First Conference on Relativistic Astrophysics was taking place in Guangzhou on the eve of my departure for Bonn. I went to Guangzhou and gave a presentation on the cosmology of the early universe. On November 23, the day of the midconference break, a group of us boarded a minelayer of the Chinese navy's Southern Fleet and toured the Pearl River Delta. The area has no scenery to speak of, but plenty of history. It was where, in 1839, the Opium War broke out. British gunboats defeated Qing soldiers and the dynasty was forced to sue for peace, surrendering sovereignty and accepting disgrace. From then on people throughout the country (not just a few intellectuals, as in the late Ming Dynasty) began to see China's backwardness, to let go of the myth that they were inhabitants of an unmatched celestial empire, and to accept that modernization was needed. The Pearl River Delta can be seen as the site from which modern China originated.

We went to Huangpu harbor to board the naval vessel. The small ship's first stop was Tiger Gate Fortress, which guards the Pearl River inlet and is where the British military knocked China's door open. The second stop was Taiping township, where Lin Zexu, a Qing high commissioner, destroyed British opium in an attempt to end its sale and spread. The lime pit that he used for this purpose was still on display. After lunch we went to the Shajiao Fortress, where we saw a huge, mind-boggling Chinese cannon. Its shaft had an external diameter of about 2.3 feet and it was about sixteen feet long. The guides said that this great gun, after arriving in place and shooting one cannonball, went "blind," as they put it. Its bore somehow got clogged and now it was used only for display.

The Opium War caused some Chinese to conclude, *If we can just chase the British and the other foreigners out of China, we can revert to being the great celestial empire that we once were.* In essence, this is the pattern the Chinese Communists observed. True, they held Marx, Engels, Lenin, and Stalin—foreigners all—in the highest regard; from the point of view of Chinese nativists like the Boxers, they "ate Western food." But when they took power in 1949, they were extremely thorough about chasing out foreigners and cutting off normal ties between foreigners and Chinese.

Here is a very small example of how effective that cutoff was: In 1977, even with the Cultural Revolution over, postal workers in the largest post office in downtown Hefei didn't know how to send a letter outside the country. People who asked about doing such a thing were met with stares of startled disbelief. It was as if the post office were using maps from the Great Ming. Foreign countries? What?

By the time we took our delta tour, the original mission of that great but ill-fated cannon had long been accomplished. The ship we had boarded was a Chinese military vessel; Chinese were in charge at the mouth of the

Pearl River; British warships had long ago retreated to Hong Kong. But while that useless cannon rested on its haunches, the modernization that was supposed to flow in automatically if only we could chase out the foreigners—didn't happen. This truth seemed now to be dawning on certain people. Having sealed China off, they now favored "opening." Good. Meanwhile, though, we had paid the price of a near thirty-year delay.

In October 1977, the American Astronomical Society sent ten astronomers to China. This was the society's first official visit ever. Soon, more and more Western astronomers were coming, and the applications of Chinese scientists to go abroad were also more easily approved. The long-standing barriers were gradually falling. I found it interesting that when Chinese and Western colleagues met, it didn't seem to matter that they had been separated for so long, did not know each other personally, and had been through some very different life experiences. They just dived straight into professional talk. There were sometimes a few language difficulties, but no other barriers. Except as locators for items in the heavens, words like "Eastern" and "Western" were useless. This was further evidence that astronomy transcends cultures. Its vision is universal.

How could it be, I thought, that modernization is not also universal? The keys to modernization are neither Chinese nor foreign, neither Eastern nor Western. They are the ability to absorb advances—advances called science and democracy—that are available to anyone, anywhere. That, in a nutshell, is it.

Otherwise, a useless cannon will forever be a useless cannon.

I returned to Beijing on November 27 for a few busy days and a hurried visit with my family, then headed for Bonn.

14. STEPPING OUT OF CHINA

ON DECEMBER 6, 1978, AT AGE FORTY-TWO, I STEPPED OUTSIDE CHINA for the first time. I was accompanied by two colleagues from the Beijing Observatory on a flight to West Germany, and we arrived in Bonn the next day.* December 7 was, by chance, the twentieth anniversary of the founding of the Institute of Astronomy at the University of Bonn, and our hosts were in high spirits. After an evening reception, they took us to see a special little library that contained some original works by Johannes Kepler.

I was aware that Kepler had drawn on concepts of musical harmony to explain patterns of planetary motion, but I had never seen any of his original manuscripts. I was surprised to learn that some of them were actually written on musical scores—and moreover without words, only in musical notation. Kepler saw the solar system as a system in "harmony" and used intervals and rhythms to describe the speeds and reversal of directions of planetary movement, rather as one might describe a movement in music. In his own words:

---

*Translator's note: Li Shuxian did not accompany Fang on this trip because she could not get a work release from her teaching at Peking University. The authorities would not allow two spouses to leave the country at the same time for fear that they would not return.

The heavenly bodies are nothing but a continuous song for sev-
eral voices, perceptible to the intellect, not the ear; a figured
music that seems to use cadences and a fixed, predesigned six-
part chord to set landmarks in the immeasurable flow of time.

One thing Kepler's musical scores helped me to understand was that in order to perceive the earth's orbit clearly, one's perspective had to be from outside the solar system.

When I got back to Zum Treppehen, the hotel where we were staying, Kepler's solar system music was still ringing in my ears. But now it had a new variation: in order to perceive China clearly, one needed a perspective from outside China.

After that trip to Germany, I made several more short-term visits to institutes of physics or astrophysics in other countries. By the summer of 1980, I had been, in this order, to West Germany, Italy, France, Romania, Switzerland, England, Ireland, the United States, and Pakistan. China was just opening up after being cut off for four decades, and Chinese people were largely unfamiliar with the rest of the world. The rest of the world was, if anything, even less familiar with Chinese people. I got used to being the first person from China anyone had seen in forty years: *An authentic Chinese, and he's a physicist!*

In the spring of 1979, I visited Palermo, the capital of Sicily. On the night I arrived, the local radio station broadcast that "today the first professor from China has arrived in Sicily." It did not try to say "counting from when?" though. It was certainly true that there hadn't been many Chinese people in Sicily for quite some time. I couldn't argue with that. Perhaps we can say this: I was likely the first Chinese physicist to visit Sicily since the time of Carthage.

It was the same in other Italian cities. Every time I arrived at a new place, a clutch of reporters was waiting for me and I had to take questions. The questions were almost always on the same topics: Marco Polo and spaghetti. It was as if no Chinese had been to Italy since Marco Polo returned in 1295. It also seemed that other than to address the question of which came first, Chinese noodles or Italian spaghetti, there was no particular reason why Italians should think about China.

Around Easter of that year, I went to Monaco. I wanted to see what Monte Carlo looked like. I don't mean the gambling—I didn't have any money for that in any case. I was just curious, I guess—maybe because the computational algorithms known as the "Monte Carlo methods" were becoming more and more important for physics in those days. Anyway, when I crossed the border, the immigration officer picked up my passport and peered at it first this way, then that, as if loath to lay it down, rather like a philatelist enthralled by a rare stamp. He said it was the first time he had seen a passport from the People's Republic of China and he wasn't sure where he was supposed to apply his stamp. In the end he decided not to stamp the thing anywhere and just let me in. I had the impression that a Chinese citizen was a rarer sight than a Chinese panda.

Oddity though I was, I never felt isolated, because my hosts were always physicists or astrophysicists. Physics is the same everywhere, and this makes it easy for physicists to get onto the same wavelength. For example, I was not personally acquainted with Professor Remo Ruffini of the University of Rome before he invited me to visit him. Then we discovered that, without the other knowing it, we had published papers on a similar topic—in fact had done this three times! Our conclusions were similar, too. Physics has had its own community ever since Galileo and Newton founded the field. Some people have even called it a kind of worldwide "religion," with Einstein as pope.

March 14, 1979, was the hundredth anniversary of Einstein's birth. For more than a year before and after that date, there were a variety of events honoring the memory of this great man. When I got to Rome, just before the anniversary, Einstein shows were on television every day. I stayed at the Lincean Academy, one of the centers of the commemorative events, and reporters from Italian National Television Station Two came there to interview me.

"What's the relation between Einstein and China?"

China again. And it was a challenging question. Einstein actually had very little direct contact with China. He spent only two days of his life there, in 1921, when a ship that he was taking from Japan to Germany

docked for two days in Shanghai. There was no way his China experience could yield the big scoop these reporters were digging for.

I could, of course, have said, "Einstein was denounced during the
Cultural Revolution." That would, in its own way, have been a scoop.
But wouldn't it be just too embarrassing for China, with its worldwide
reputation for honoring teachers and following the Way, to reveal that a
supremely respected scientist had been denounced? I could have taken
another tack and said, "I have a good friend who compiled three big
volumes of *The Collected Works of Einstein* while farming." But I was
afraid that that would cause the Italians to wonder if I knew the first thing
about relativity theory. Their next question might well be, "And the use
of relativity theory in farming is . . . ?"

I was lucky to have been studying superdense stars at that time. This
allowed me to risk the following answer: "Twentieth-century Einstein has
a connection with eleventh-century China." I said this because one of the
important pieces of corroboration for the prediction of the existence of
superdense stars—neutron stars—in Einstein's relativity theory has been
the observation by Song Dynasty court astronomers in 1054 of a supernova explosion. But even as I gave my answer, I feared privately that it
might seem a bit far-fetched to the TV journalists. I hardly imagined
that it would be a big hit with them—but they were delighted! This might
have been because my answer spanned ancient and modern as well as
East and West. And it might have appealed particularly to Italians, because
of their love of antiquity.

That special regard for antiquity struck me in another experience. On
a trip to Venice in 1983, I noticed an exhibition entitled "Seven Thousand
Years of Chinese Civilization." In elementary school in China, we had
been taught that China is a "five-thousand-year-old ancient land." So how
did that get bumped up to seven thousand in Italy? I guess the organizers
of the exhibit needed to attract visitors, so they tacked on another two
thousand. If my comment about Einstein and the eleventh century was
far-fetched, this was worse.

Far-fetched associations happen a lot when great people are being com-
memorated, because most people like to highlight their own slice of life

and display their own special regard for the great person, perhaps as a way to share a bit in the glory. Science itself, though, is built on an opposite principle. It is a global project that has no national or geographic borders. Instead of spotlighting localities, it brings people from different cultures and places together, making ties across cultures not far-fetched at all but very real. Einstein in particular pursued projects globally, made discoveries that were universal, and called himself a "citizen of the world." So when I mentioned Song Dynasty observations as contributions to the discovery of neutron stars in order to show how a field inaugurated by Einstein was global, I was not really out of bounds.

Later I was inspired to compile a list of the major events that went into the discovery of neutron stars so that I could use it whenever I needed to show that science is global. Here it is:

- *The general relativity of Albert Einstein is established (1915)*
- *The statistics of Enrico Fermi and Paul Dirac are established (1927)*
- *James Chadwick discovers neutrons (1933)*
- *Lev Landau predicts the possibility of neutron stars (1933)*
- *Walter Baade and Fritz Zwicky conjecture that neutron stars result from the explosion of supernovae (1934)*
- *Robert Oppenheimer theorizes that neutron stars are formed from gravitational collapse of larger stars (1939)*
- *Antony Hewish and Jocelyn Bell discover radio pulsars (1967)*
- *Historical records from 1054 to 1056 in China, Japan, and Korea support the hypothesis that pulsars are neutron stars*

Plainly, our understanding of neutron stars has international origins.

In April 1979, Italian National Television Station Two asked me to go before the cameras again. They were doing a series to probe more deeply into Einstein's work and were including a section on the origins of his concept of relativity. It is widely accepted that the following passage from Galileo has had crucial importance in the development of relativity theory:

> *Shut yourself up with some friend in the main cabin below decks*
> *on some large ship, and have with you there some flies, butter-*

*flies, and other small flying insects. Have a large bowl of water
with some fish in it; hang up a bottle that empties drop by drop
into a wide vessel beneath it.*

*With the ship standing still, observe carefully how the insects
fly with equal speed to all sides of the cabin. The fish swim indif-
ferently in all directions; the drops fall into the vessel beneath;
and, in throwing something to your friend, you need throw it
no more strongly in one direction than another, the distances
being equal; jumping with your feet together, you pass equal
spaces in every direction.*

*When you have observed all these things carefully, have the
ship proceed at any speed you like, so long as the speed is constant. You will discover not the least change in all the effects
named, nor could you tell from any of them whether the ship
was moving or standing still. In jumping, you will move across
the floor the same distances as before, and you will not make
larger jumps toward the stern than toward the prow even if the
ship is moving very rapidly.**

The Station Two people had arranged for someone to read this famous
passage in the city of Pisa, where the Arno River flows into the sea. They
chose the site because Galileo lived many years in Pisa, and he was imprisoned there as well. It is quite possible that the discovery quoted above
was made on the Arno River.

The program director had heard me say, in a talk at the Lincean Academy, that Galileo's discovery about relativity may not have been the first
of its kind. A passage in *The Book of Documents: Kaolingyao section* from
the Han period in China (206 B.C.–A.D. 220) says:

*The earth moves at constant speed but people are unaware. It
is as if people are in a ship with the windows closed; the ship
moves and people do not notice.*

---

*Translator's note: This translation has been adapted from *Dialogue Concerning the Two Chief World
Systems*, translated by Stillman Drake (Berkeley: University of California Press, 1953), pp. 186–87.

The insight is quite the same as Galileo's, but it came more than a thousand years earlier. The Italian TV director, showing not the slightest bias, changed his script right after he heard my talk and included that line from *The Book of Documents*. Moreover, he asked me to be a temporary actor—to go to Pisa, stand in front of the Tower of Pisa, and pronounce the line *zhou xing er ren bu jue ye*—"the ship moves and people do not notice."

It was an invitation I found hard to refuse, so one day in early April I went to Pisa with him and his crew to record those words on tape. It made for an incongruous scene. I would forgive Italian television viewers, for whom the Leaning Tower is a national treasure, if they found something a bit absurd about a Chinese guy standing in front of their tower pronouncing strange sounds about the movement of boats. It may have been the very bizarreness that left deep impressions on people. Later, when I visited the International Centre for Theoretical Physics in Trieste, some of the secretaries recognized me right away. "Here comes the TV-star professor," they said.

My few seconds of electronic stardom showed Italian viewers that sprouts of thinking that resemble relativity theory had appeared in China even earlier than in Italy, but I never felt any nationalistic pride about that fact. Galileo's thinking, as a whole, was the true progenitor of modern physics; it unleashed an unstoppable scientific tide. That early burst of brilliance in China was like a meteor: one flash and it was gone.

Why did modern science not emerge in Chinese civilization? Historians have offered various answers to this question, but for me, as a physicist, it does not seem very hard to understand. There is no way that isolated, authoritarian societies can advance very far in science. Science needs free exchange. Einstein said that "everything that is really great and inspiring is created by the individual who can labor in freedom."

The International Centre for Theoretical Physics (ICTP) at Trieste illustrates this point. It began as a United Nations project, and its founding director, Professor Abdus Salam, told me that his main reason for starting it was to help physicists from Third World countries move out of their isolation and into an environment of free research. The People's Republic of China had been a member of the United Nations since 1972, but its government had not allowed Chinese physicists to work at the ICTP, or even to visit it. In 1979, things loosened. I was the first Chinese physicist to visit the ICTP, and I was able to help more to come by serving on the ICTP's International Scholarship Committee. I did what I could to get as many Chinese physicists as possible to the ICTP, to enjoy the right to "work in freedom." It was just what they needed. In the years before the Tiananmen events of 1989, the number of Chinese who went to the Center reached as high as two hundred per year, and many of them did so on my personal recommendation. I feel far, far prouder of this accomplishment than of my television appearance on behalf of *The Book of Documents*.

I spent a somewhat longer time in England—fully a half year, from October 1979 to April 1980, except for a visit to Ireland for Christmas. Most of my time was spent at Cambridge, where I was a visiting senior researcher at the Institute of Astronomy. Professor Martin Rees was director. My life in Cambridge was far more quiet, routine, and unvarying than it had been in Italy. Every morning about nine o'clock I rode my bicycle to the Institute of Astronomy and worked till noon, when I ate lunch at the dining hall of the Cavendish Laboratory. Then I went back to work, later took afternoon tea, then resumed work again until about seven, when I went back to my apartment. I lived on Cranmer Road, in a quiet, elegant area not far from the famous strip of green called The Backs on the west side of the River Cam. Since King's College was my official host, I sometimes went to dinner at the dining hall there, but other times I just went back to my apartment and made noodles. If nightly noodles was monotonous—*well, all right*, I thought. Monotony seemed normal in England.

There was social life, but not much. At King's College the social life was in the dining room, but the formal dinners were too solemn—especially for the members, like me, who sat at "high table" wearing gowns. People who sat there had to observe decorum, and that meant keeping chatter and laughter within bounds.

There was a small community of Chinese at Cambridge who had been there for many years, but most of them were from Hong Kong or Singapore, and I didn't have much contact with them at first. In February, four months into my stay, their "Chinese Society" invited me to give a talk on

astronomy in ancient China, and after that I got to know them a bit bet-
ter. Only a few mainland Chinese were in Cambridge at the time; the one
I knew best was Zhu Cisheng, from the astronomy department at Nanjing
University, and I occasionally went to his place to chat.

I did not go to church on Sundays. I did go once, at the beginning of
Advent, to join in the singing of hymns at the King's College chapel, and
I attended an Easter service at St. Matthew's Church. I was struck on these
occasions by the similarity in form to some of the inner-Party activities of
the Communist Party of China.

My daily life was nothing special. Outside my windows I saw what one
often sees in England: lawns, groves of trees, meadows, horses, cows,
squirrels. So I have no amusing anecdotes to pass along; everything just
unfolded on track. But this only proves the wisdom of the saying "No news
is good news," because those six months at Cambridge were extremely
productive in my research. My conclusion was that the placidity and regularity of Cambridge life are forces that both oblige and induce a scholar
to make progress.

At one point a student of mine, Wu Zhongchao, arrived to do a degree in
theoretical physics and applied mathematics. He used to come looking for
me on Sundays, and we went for strolls. We would walk northward along
the river until it was almost dark, then turn back. I occasionally went bike-
hiking with friends as well, either to a botanical garden near to the Mullard
Observatory (the place where pulsars were discovered) or to a cemetery for
American soldiers who were killed in action during World War II. The latter had been a U.S. Air Force base during the war, and now it had a wonderful lawn. The roads around Cambridge were (just as Professor Qian
Linzhao had told us in 1969) indeed hilly, and one had to be careful. I was
reminded of the professor's unfinished story about the runaway bicycle.

Cambridge has a long-standing reputation in the Chinese academic
world. The Chinese poet Xu Zhimo wrote a famous essay about it in the
1920s, and Chinese scholars had been visiting the campus even before that.
One of my teachers had been here—and indeed, one of *his* teachers had
been. It seemed that each time China opened its doors, another new group
of scholars headed to Cambridge, retracing steps that their predecessors
had trod. Would the next generation have to do it once again? Just

before I left Cambridge I wrote an essay, which was published in May 1980 in the Hong Kong *Dagongbao*, expressing the hope that the next generation would be spared that fate.

Some of my experiences left me less than optimistic, though. On December 14, 1979, for example, the Italian Cultural Institute in London, still commemorating Einstein, held a public symposium on relativistic astrophysics. Martin Rees chaired, and Remo Ruffini and I were speakers. The goal was to introduce this difficult but exciting new field to the general public. I arrived at the meeting hall early, having traveled from Cambridge, and found more than a hundred people already there. The organizers had sent invitations to the Chinese and Italian ambassadors in London, and the Italian ambassador, Roberto Ducci, was there. But there was no sign of anyone from the Chinese embassy. Then, just before the event began, the Chinese ambassador, Ke Hua, made his appearance. He greeted the event's organizers, shook hands with the Italian ambassador, and then rushed off, explaining, "I'm sorry, I don't understand the subject, so I'm not going to stay to listen." Two Chinese diplomats—science and technology attachés—did stay.

After the seminar there was a brief reception at which a group of elderly British ladies surrounded me and peppered me with questions about this or that point in the presentations. They had found some parts puzzling, which is understandable. The jargon alone—black holes, accretion, time freeze—might be enough to spin one's head. For these ladies, "not completely understanding" was the reason for coming up afterward to learn more. To them, a new frontier was exciting. For our Chinese ambassador, though, the reasoning had gone in the other direction: "not completely understanding" was the reason for *not* listening.

My stay at Cambridge ended on April 19, 1980. I went to London and the next day boarded an airliner that flew over Greenland and Canada and arrived at San Francisco at 3:00 p.m. My schedule in the United States was tight from the moment I arrived. I had originally hoped that it would be relaxed, because there were many places, from the West Coast to the East, that I had wanted to enjoy. But the Chinese Academy of Sciences notified me, rather abruptly, that I was to be in Pakistan by mid-June for the International Nathia Gali Summer College, where lectures by me had already been scheduled. This turned my U.S. stay into a fifty-day barn-storm. My itinerary was San Francisco, Los Angeles, Austin, Houston, Boston, Washington, Charlottesville, Chicago, New York. There was very little leisure. I did a lecture every five days, on average, and that doesn't count the seminars and colloquia, or the travel time, so hardly any time was left for sightseeing. Still, I took every chance I could to glimpse this expansive New World. Between Los Angeles and Austin, I should, prop-erly speaking, have stopped at the Kitt Peak National Observatory near Tucson, Arizona. But the temptation of the Grand Canyon was too great, so I settled on the following whirlwind tour:

April 25: at night, boarded a long-distance Greyhound bus in Los Angeles.

April 26: arrived in Phoenix, Arizona, at 5:00 a.m., Flagstaff at 9:00 a.m., and the Grand Canyon at 11:00 a.m.; looked around, but had no time to descend into the canyon; at 5:00 p.m. reboarded Grey-hound for Flagstaff, arriving at 7:00 p.m.; left Flagstaff at 10:30 p.m.

April 27: arrived at Albuquerque, the largest city in New Mexico, at 5:00 a.m.; after breakfast and a three-hour tour of the cityscape, boarded another Greyhound at 11:30 a.m. and arrived at 7:45 p.m. in Lubbock, Texas; stopped for a hour and half and then reboarded Greyhound.

April 28: arrived at Dallas at 4:50 a.m.; after breakfast and another quick tour, got back on the bus and arrived at Austin at 12:50 p.m.

April 29: gave a lecture at the University of Texas on "Phase Transi-tion in the Early Universe."

It was one of the most densely packed four-day periods of my life.

May 24, 1980, is a day I must call "wasted" from one point of view, inter-esting from another. A friend in New York, whom I will call T, took me to Long Island. We went first to Old Westbury Gardens, a park of landscapes in the European style. Then we went to Old Bethpage Village, a full-scale restoration of life and buildings—tavern, inn, craft shops, and others—from mid-nineteenth-century America. Artisans dressed in the garb of earlier times demonstrated blacksmithing, boot making, broom making, dyeing, and other skills. The tourists were fascinated. A bootmaking demonstration drew a crowd of people who craned their necks to see how the shoe was fitted onto the last, how the leather was cut, and how it was then nailed to the sole. They were enthralled to see these ancient (for America) skills.

As I watched, an irrepressible resentment of T invaded my mind. Why had he brought me to see *this*? T was Chinese, but, separated from China for too long, was apparently unaware that these very methods of shoe-making were still in use on the streets of Beijing. Why would I need to fly thousands of miles over the Pacific Ocean to view demonstrations like this? If the tavern at Old Bethpage is a valuable antique, then those shops all across Zanhuang County that hang out their "tavern" signs ought also to be protected as national treasures. In any case I was amused, at least, to note how the value of a thing could vary so much with its context.

I then reflected that the same is true of words. Words could have different, even opposite, meanings in different ideological contexts. For example, during my travels in the United States, from West Coast to East, I was always meeting American intellectuals who couldn't understand why Chinese intellectuals deplored the Cultural Revolution. These Americans were not Maoists, or even believers in Communism, but they felt that Cultural Revolution slogans like "Intellectuals Should Serve the Working People" expressed high human ideals. Dubious of what I was telling them, they kept asking me, "What *was* the Cultural Revolution, after all?" and "What were you doing at the time?" I felt that there was no alternative but to go to the root of the matter and try to explain how the same words could have very different meanings. This might be the only way these curious Americans could see what those slogans, built of words, actually meant in China. It was a considerable challenge, though, because the distortions were so many and so systematic. I started here:

> *The People's Government = authoritarian rule*
> *liberated people = debased subjects*
> *Cultural Revolution = destruction of culture*
> *scientific worldview = dictatorship over science*
> *intellectuals serving the working people = distribution of labor*
>   *assignments to intellectuals*

These truisms were things that good-hearted, naive Americans like those tourists at Old Bethpage Village found inordinately hard to understand. It occurred to me that the only way to get them really to understand would be to go to Long Island and build an Old Bethpage Village of the Cultural Revolution that featured living reenactments of typical scenes (short of the suicide scenes, of course) and let them crane their necks for a while.

Before I had seen nearly enough of America, I had to rush to Pakistan, the next stop on my journey. I arrived in Rawalpindi on June 14 and headed immediately to Nathia Gali, a cool, elegant summer resort in the northwestern part of the country. The summer program on physics began on June 15. I was not late, and I gave my lectures as scheduled.

On June 22, during the first weekend break, I went with two colleagues, one Italian and one American, to look for the ruins of a Buddhist temple that lay between the towns of Butkara and Malam Jabba, not too far away. It was said that the Chinese pilgrim Xuanzang, who traveled to India in the seventh century A.D. in search of the true Buddhist scriptures, had once been in charge of this temple. The trip required us to descend from the cool hills, and the weather was torrid that day. Even before noon the temperature reached 113 degrees Fahrenheit. At one point we had to walk, under a fireball of a sun, and without umbrellas, along a dirt road lined by very few trees. There was no breeze, and the heat was so intense that it was almost hard to breathe.

The area was the Indus River Valley, where the mighty mountains of the Karakoram range rise to the west and the Hindu Kush stands to the east. On his way to India, Xuanzang had crossed the Karakoram and followed the Indus down to the Indian subcontinent. On his way back to China, he stopped temporarily at this local temple to wait for summer to arrive, because only then could the snowy ridges of the Karakoram be challenged. By that time the name Xuanzang was so famous that the local monks decided to honor him with the status of temporary temple chief.

Let me explain what helped me to press on, despite the heat, in search of those ruins. I imagined that the place might be the country of so-and-so as described in *Journey to the West*, the charming Ming novel about Xuanzang's journeys; an image floated before my mind of the four intrepid pilgrims in the novel, the monk and his three assistants, Sun Wukong, Zhu Bajie, and Sha Wujing, traipsing through 113-degree heat, and I felt that our little troupe of twentieth-century physicists were somehow their confreres in torture.

The image that floated to the mind of my Italian friend was quite different. In the day when all roads led to Rome, this same area was where the Roman empire abutted the Chinese empire of Han. If that were not enough attraction, the Oxus valley, slightly to the north, was where Marco Polo had crossed the Pamir plateau on his way to China in the thirteenth century.

Our American friend was probably the one who suffered the most that day. He, too, had to take the 113-degree heat, but he could not enjoy the compensation of these rich historical associations. For him, the seventh century probably seemed somewhere back there not far from the Big Bang.

We found the ruins about 11:30 a.m. The temple structure was entirely gone. All we could see were the foundation and a few stone carvings. This was in a Muslim area, but the people guarded this Buddhist site with the strictest of care and had nothing but praise for Xuanzang. My Italian friend noticed that the broken stone carvings had an unmistakable Greek flavor. In particular there were carvings of the body of Buddha that bore a striking resemblance to ancient Greek and Roman statues of the naked human body. Sculpture of this kind apparently did not come back to China with Xuanzang—or, if it did, it must not have been accepted in Chinese society. But historians have confirmed that China did accept many other things that Xuanzang brought back.

For example, the temple ruins were surrounded by rice paddy, and I noticed some Pakistani farmers heaping rice stalks into piles. From my farming days in China I knew this activity well, and I noticed that the forks the farmers were using were exactly the same three-pronged kind that Chinese farmers use—and that they apparently were prototypes of the nine-toothed rake that Zhu Bajie used as a weapon in *Journey to the West*. The way the farmers piled the stalks was also exactly the same. I couldn't help wondering whether Xuanzang's transmission of culture included some agriculture.

When our visit was over we took a car northward along the valley of the Swat River and, as dusk fell, reached the foothills of the glorious snowy peaks of the Kalam range, where we spent the night. We got up early the next morning to hike. By the time we reached a point about three hundred feet below the snow line, I felt utterly exhausted. I lay on my back, gazed at the sky, and fell into a reverie. The vault of heaven was tranquil; wisps of white cloud floated silently by; the towering peaks of the Hindu Kush, capped with snow, rose against the deep azure sky.

My thoughts returned to Xuanzang and his three disciples. Unfortunately the novel *Journey to the West* doesn't tell us what happened after he had gathered his sacred texts. How did he manage to lug hundreds of them over those snowcapped mountains and get them back to China? Anyway, when he did get back, he refused the high posts that the emperor of the Tang Dynasty offered to him and devoted himself instead to translating his precious trove. This was the right decision. What China needed was not tribute offerings of rare Sanskrit texts to its emperor. What China needed was a way, as the Buddhists say, for all sentient beings to transcend to a spiritual plane.

Humanity has always sought to transcend. Right now China was facing another such effort, calling it "reform."

15. IN THE TIDES OF REFORM

AT THE BEGINNING OF THE 1980S, *REFORM* WAS THE MOST FASHION-able word in China. The first thing I did after I got back from Pakistan in July 1980 was to attend a conference on how USTC was going to do reform. But even though everybody was talking about reform, and even though it seemed to touch everywhere, no one could say exactly what it meant. Deng Xiaoping himself, the "initiator" of reform, could speak only of "crossing the river by feeling the stones." Crossing what river? To reach where? He didn't say.

For me, a major concern was to get rid of the "forbidden zones" of the Mao era, and in the early days of reform a lot of progress was being made on that score. In August 1980, for example, cosmology suddenly was no longer a forbidden zone: there was to be a First National Conference on Cosmology. Our research group at USTC was assigned to run the conference, and it was radically different from the one we had run just four years earlier. We didn't have to hold it at a training base for the Viet Cong. We held it in the Lu Mountains in Jiangxi, a place famed for its beauty. A great banner draped in the lobby of the elegant Lulin Hotel read CONFERENCE ON COSMOLOGY.

When school opened in September, USTC instituted a system of elections for positions at the lowest levels of authority. It was largely a symbolic move, but still it was progress. I was elected to head the university's Interdepartmental Program in Physics. The program was responsible for all physics courses—in general physics, theoretical physics, and physics laboratory—for all majors on campus. More than a hundred staff were involved.

USTC began sending a large number of physics students overseas. Professor Tsung-Dao Lee of Columbia University had set up something called the China-U.S. Physics Examination and Application (CUSPEA), which was a program that let Chinese undergraduates apply for Ph.D. programs in physics at American and Canadian universities by taking an examination in China. I was on the CUSPEA selection committee, and in October we held a meeting at which we chose 102 students from across China for the first group.

In November I went to Beijing and spoke at a conference on the philosophy of science. I criticized Lenin again, for his abuse of Ernst Mach and others, and this time there were no ripples. No one handed in notes saying "Stop the counterrevolutionary talk!"

Everything went smoothly until December, when I ran afoul of a "forbidden zone" that was still in place. A national conference called "Study of Science, Study of Human Talent, and Study of the Future" (abbreviated "The Three Studies") was scheduled for Hefei. About four hundred people had registered, but I had not. I was teaching electromagnetism six hours a week and didn't have much time for outside activities. The chair of the conference came to me, though, entreating me to give a talk in the section of the conference called "Study of the Future." "It's all right if you haven't actually studied the future," he said. "Everybody is at least entitled to a view of the future." He had a point, I had to admit.

So on the morning of December 7, 1980, I went to the Three Studies conference to give a talk. I offered a view as plain as day. I said science had progressed into an era that was radically different from what had gone before; China's future could not possibly stay cooped up in the Marxist era. I ended with this:

The three fundamental elements in Marxism—philosophy, political economy, and scientific socialism—are all out of date.

Humankind has passed through a number of stages of civiliza-
tion, and Marxism can be viewed as one of them. The passing
of an historical stage may not be a bad thing, because human-
ity passes into a new future only by shedding old ways of
thinking.

In the midst of reform, I thought, who would still believe that nineteenth-century Marxism was the cutting edge? Today's world was living proof that some of the theses in Marxism were simply wrong.

I did not anticipate that my little talk would stimulate something of a replay of what happened in 1955 at the Youth League Conference at Peking University. But it did. I again threw a conference into buzzing confusion. Some people were in favor and some were opposed, but almost no one lacked a vigorous opinion and there was no way the program could proceed as scheduled. By the time the Communist Party Secretary for Anhui, Zhang Jinfu, gave a speech in the afternoon, things had settled down a bit. Zhang did not criticize what I said directly, but commented only that the conference should set aside questions of whether any things are "out of date." So my ship had run aground again, even if the reef this time was soft.

Then there was a second soft collision. Early in 1981, some students in the USTC mathematics department formed an organization that they called Student Voices. They had no political agenda, at least not at first. They invited me to give a talk and I agreed. But then, after the posters went up, the Party Secretary at USTC paid me a special visit. He urged me not to go. He couldn't come up with any good reasons, though, so I went.

At the talk I presented a principle that I knew students of mathematics in particular would appreciate. To say that reform can proceed only within fixed bounds amounts to saying that reform cannot take place. This is because there is a theorem in mathematics that says that when the boundary conditions of a domain are specified, solutions within the domain exist and are unique. Not long thereafter, as if to confirm the theorem of unique solutions within bounded domains, Student Voices was forced to close—not because of my talk, as it turned out, but because the central authorities had sent a strongly worded internal memorandum to universities nationwide instructing that they find ways to shut down all autonomous student organizations. In December 1979, Deng Xiaoping had ordered the closing of Beijing's "Democracy Wall," where essays and poems calling for freedom and human rights had been appearing since the fall of 1978. After Deng's order, no independent student groups of any kind were tolerated.

Right from the beginning of reform, a fissure had separated science students from the regime. The students were expecting that there be no limits on scientific inquiry, while the regime was prepared to allow "reform" only inside a birdcage. In the heady initial days of reform, everybody was too excited to notice the fissure. But as it widened, one couldn't miss it.

In March 1981, I was elected as an academician in the Chinese Academy of Sciences. There were about four hundred academicians; it was the highest honor a scientist in China could receive. The selection process, when it began in 1956, was modeled on the way other countries choose their honorees. It was supposed to be free from politics, and the scientists had certainly seen it that way. But elections to the academy were halted in 1957 by the politics of the Anti-Rightist Movement, and then, as the status of intellectuals fell, some members who had already been elected were expelled. During the Cultural Revolution the entire institution was suspended. It was revived in 1980, but it was still not independent of politics. The president of the academy was a Party official, not a scholar.

So, although I had received the votes to be a member, the authorities could still block me on political grounds, and some of my friends were worried that this would happen. The authorities had not been pleased with my talks at the Three Studies conference and at Student Voices.

The worries did not pan out, but that was not because the authorities had forgotten about my two talks. On April 29, the Communist Party Second Secretary for Anhui Province, Gu Zhuoxin, invited me for a "chat." The president of the Party School of Anhui Province was there, too. Their topic was the Three Studies conference. I was ready for them to criticize my "anti-Marxist" speech, but after they invited me to recapitulate my views, and after I did so, I sat waiting for them to hold forth and they hardly said anything. The meeting just ended. The point of the session was to show the regime's "concern" for me.

A second expression of concern came on May 12 at a meeting of academicians in Beijing. Fang Yi, a member of the Communist Party Politburo, a vice premier of the State Council, and the highest government official in charge of science, wanted to talk with me. Our exchange lasted more than an hour, and at no point did Fang Yi say that any of my views were incorrect. He said only that "some things, although not wrong, must not be said too casually." Then, just as abruptly as the last "chat," this one ended.

It was pretty clear that the regime's objective was to mollify and co-opt me. These high officials, while cautioning me to watch my words in public, were at the same time conceding in private that my views were not wrong. When they advised me to "be careful how you put things, rightness or wrongness aside," the message was that if I mastered this skill of how to put things, I could have a future in the system. Success as an official in China requires one to make words "fit"—whether or not they make sense.

The problem was that I had no desire to be an official. I had already said as much in a letter I wrote to Li Shuxian from Cambridge in March 1980:

> My hope from here on out is not to be an official but to work
> to strengthen science in China. In the system that we have, an
> official, even a science official, has to ride in the flow of some
> very foul water, and has to sacrifice one's independence. If I
> stand outside, on the other hand, I can be useful as a gadfly.
> One reason I've been able to do some good in recent years,
> and have gained the support of others, is that I have dared to
> let loose with my criticisms. If Chinese society is going to move
> ahead, somebody has to do this. And I personally feel much
> more free in this role.

It was true. Somebody did have to do it. Neither science nor China could progress without independent voices. I wanted to explore this freedom more.

Much of my energy in those days—outside of normal teaching and research—was spent in strengthening the ways in which my colleagues and

I stayed in touch with people in our fields around the world. This activity was essential to "reform," in my view, and is reflected in my travel log:

> **June 12** to **July 3, 1981,** to Islamabad.
> **September 23** to **October 7, 1981,** to Trieste.
> **November 3, 1981,** to Japan for half a year.

The visit to Islamabad was to attend a "Third World Symposium on Physics," to which the Chinese Academy of Sciences sent a ten-person delegation that included me. The trip to Trieste was to plan for the Third Marcel Grossmann Meeting, which was to be held in China the following year. (Grossmann was a pioneer in relativity theory and a onetime tutor to Einstein.) The meeting in China in 1982 was to be my responsibility.

My stay in Japan was as a visiting professor at the Research Institute for Fundamental Physics at Kyoto University. This institute had been founded by Yukawa Hideki, the first Japanese physicist to win a Nobel Prize. Yukawa loved classical Chinese literature. His calligraphy graced the walls of the institute's seminar room, and one of the pieces was the famous dialogue in Zhuangzi about the happiness of fish.* My host, Professor Sato Fumitaka, told me that this was one of Yukawa's favorite pieces of Chinese philosophy.

During my stay at Kyoto I lived in the university's guesthouse called Kitashirakawa, which was close to campus and very convenient. I didn't know Japanese, but Chinese characters were everywhere. I felt I could guess about 50 or 60 percent of what was meant, so I didn't have that completely alien feeling that I had in Europe.

In Japan I had another feeling that I never had in Europe. Everywhere in Japan I saw things that seemed like recapitulations of Chinese culture, and this made me feel, as a Chinese, rather like a cultural or spiri-

---

*Translator's note: Fang is referring to the story in which Zhuangzi and Huizi, his friend and rival, are on a bridge and see a fish swimming in the water below.

Zhuangzi: "See how the minnow swims around as it pleases, so at ease? It is happy."
Huizi: "You're not a fish; how do you know the fish is happy?"
Zhuangzi: "You're not me; how do you know that I do not know?"

tual ancestor. The city of Kyoto was modeled on China's ancient capital of Chang'an during the eighth century A.D., and its layout today still bears a strong resemblance to that of Xi'an, as Chang'an is now called. The names of some of the city gates in modern Kyoto are the same as those of ancient Chang'an. When Japanese friends took me to visit their shrines, our roles were sometimes reversed, with me doing the explaining to them, because the auspicious phrases were in classical Chinese. When we went to watch classical Japanese drama together, my Japanese friends had to rely on Japanese subtitles whereas I could read directly from the original Chinese phrases that were projected. These were usually poems in the traditional pattern of five syllables per line—not very well done, actually, but they did rhyme. One read:

> I grab the tail of a green snake
> A few inches below its big blue head.
> There must be something weird in me;
> Stiff things I love, supple things I dread.

In a letter to a friend five days after I arrived in Japan, I wrote that "back when the Japanese were importing all kinds of things from China, they must have assumed that 'anything originating from the Great Tang must be good.'" Even today, for example, Japanese shops have Chinese names like "Great Immortal," "Kingly General," and "Pleasures of the Mystical Way." These names are auspicious. But others are not. I also saw "Mountain Thieves," "Southern Barbarians," and even "Dwarf Pirates." The latter was especially odd, because in recent times Chinese have used it to denigrate Japanese. To see shop names like these written seriously, in neat characters and hung at roadsides, made me unsure whether to laugh or cry—or perhaps to feel guilty that Japanese people might have held the Great Tang in such high regard that they copied literally everything they could from it, including verbal abuse of themselves.

That spirit of copying might seem laughable, but it probably deserves some respect. The Chinese, in borrowing from the West, have favored the motto "Capture the cream and toss out the dregs," and compared to that, the Japanese might seem insufficiently discriminating. But the Chinese approach, I'm afraid, has gone too far the other way. We have been excessively choosy.

The longer I stayed in Japan the more I became aware of the civilization's ability to borrow. My boyhood experiences during wartime had left me with a deep wariness about Japan. Although I treated my individual Japanese friends exactly as I did other friends, when I thought of Japan as a whole, a vague grudge was still lodged in my mind. Now I felt a need to try to complicate that impression in certain ways. Japan's prosperity was no accident; it was a major success of the Japanese people. Their ability to absorb foreign culture was far better than China's. If "reform" was going to succeed in China, there would need to be a similar spirit of "opening all doors."

On December 26, 1981, I sailed to Okinawa for a vacation. I rode a 7,500-ton steamship that left from Osaka. It was the holiday season, and the only tickets available were for space in a large open cabin for fifty people. The cabin floor was covered in Japanese tatami and was very clean, but the crowding was severe. Some people even slept in the corridors. It reminded me of year-end crowds in China, but not as noisy.

We sailed forty-one hours past Cape Toi and Cape Sata on Kyushu Island, then went past Yaku Island, Amami Island, and some others, with the Pacific Ocean to the east and the East China Sea to the west. This was not far from the route that the Chinese Buddhist monk Jianzhen took when he crossed to Japan during the eighth century. China has no popular novel like *Journey to the West* to tell about Jianzhen's travels, so he is not as well known as Xuanzang, but I did notice this comparison: in the Japanese city of Nara, the Tōshōdai-ji temple, where Jianzhen explained Buddhist texts, is very well preserved and very famous; by contrast, the Xingjiaosi Temple in Xi'an, where Xuanzang translated Buddhist texts, is dilapidated beyond recognition. Very few people in China even know that this famous temple still exists.

Our ship docked at Naha, Okinawa, early in the morning of December 28. The next day I took a tour that covered the whole island. When we got on the bus, our tour guide, speaking English, asked each of us to say what country we were from. When it came to me I said, "China."

"Yes, Taiwan," she said, in a friendly effort to show that she knew what I meant by "China."

"No, Beijing," I said.

She looked startled. As in Sicily, I must have been the first specimen of my kind to arrive in quite some time. On one point, though, Okinawa was very different from Sicily: many ancestors of the Ryukyu islanders, including Okinawans, had come from China. Our tour guide pointed to a number of ways in which Chinese culture had affected Ryukyu civilization, and said that the early Japanese pirates in the area had actually regarded the Chinese as their overlords. We visited Shuri, the capital of the Ryukyu Kingdom from the fifteenth to the nineteenth centuries, and saw the Chinese-style arch at the city gate. Its inscription—THE GATE OF OBSERVING ETIQUETTE—was written in the style of the famous Tang calligrapher Yan Zhenqing (A.D. 709–785). Another example was that in Japan, roof tiles are flat, but in Okinawa they had interlocking notches like the ones used in China. On our tour, we visited a pineapple farm and its attached sugar factory, where the hosts explained to us that their methods of producing sugar from pineapple originated with thirty-six families of early Chinese immigrants. When the owner of the hotel where I stayed learned that I was from China he became extremely friendly; he said his own ancestors had come from the Chinese mainland—but he couldn't say exactly how many generations ago that was. He and his family said they liked the sound of my spoken Chinese, even though they couldn't understand it. They seemed to like it only because it was the language of their forebears.

Chinese people like to call themselves other people's ancestors. As soon as children learn to write, they like to scribble on walls that "so-and-so is my grandson"—as if being a grandfather were somehow a great thing. Now, on the Ryukyus, when I found myself everybody's "ancestor," it suddenly was plain to me that being an ancestor was nothing to be especially proud of. It is true, of course, that ancestors lead the way chronologically; but in almost all other ways, it is usually descendants who are more advanced. Okinawa was a barren island in the days of the ancestors—but now the descendants had prospered and were much further along. Chinese also believe that the achievements of descendants show how wonderful the ancestors were. But that can't be, either. To say that every good thing today is the result of merit in earlier times is to over-look that the entire universe rose from nothing to be something. The innovations of humankind, generation by generation, seem to follow the same principle—each generation creates something that did not exist before.

On the last day of 1981, I flew from Okinawa to Nagasaki, where I spent New Year's Eve. In the days when ocean travel was done in sailing ships, the Chinese merchants who traveled back and forth between China and Nagasaki, the Japanese port closest to China, were obliged by the wind patterns to spend the turn of the year there. They crossed to Japan dur-ing the six months when the winds blew eastward and returned during the six months when the winds blew the other way. Several Chinese native-place guild halls still stood in Nagasaki. The Worship Blessings Temple was the hall for Fuzhou people, and the Rising Blessings Temple was for people from the Yangzi delta. Sage Blessings Temple, Flowers and Moon, and Roofs for Tang People were other places where Chinese had gathered. I could picture the bustle of those bygone days. But now the buildings stood deserted. No one honored their past and few tourists noticed. They were ghosts of forgotten times.

I stayed in Japan until April, then passed through Taiwan and Hong Kong on my way home. I spent three weeks at the University of Hong Kong. After that I threw myself full time into preparations for the Third Marcel Grossmann Meeting.

The Grossmann Meetings, which are devoted to topics in general rel-ativity and relativistic astrophysics, occur every three years. By inter-national standards their size is nothing special. About three hundred people attend, which makes them about midsize. But this was the first time an international meeting on physics of anywhere near that size was going to take place in China.

Shanghai had been designated to be the site. Forty years earlier, Shang-hai was the largest city in East Asia, grander than Nagasaki or even Tokyo. But now, after forty years of separation from the world, we couldn't find a hotel anywhere in Shanghai that had any experience with international academic conferences. We finally settled on the Jinjiang Hotel. It was Shanghai's best—the place where foreign leaders stayed. But the Jinjiang people were clueless about the needs of an academic conference. There was, for example, no overhead projector anywhere in the hotel.

The meeting was scheduled for the end of August, and I began to work full time on it in mid-June. Officially I was only the "academic" organizer, but in fact I had to handle meals, lodging, and much else. China was still locked into a central planning system. The authorities stipulated that hosts of all foreign visitors—be they heads of state or scientists—must, for each visitor, submit a detailed itinerary including where every meal was to be taken and even how much food would be needed. The plans were then printed as "red-letterhead documents" (i.e., official documents with government seals affixed) and sent to all relevant departments. This meant that we, the organizers, had to estimate exactly where—and how much—two hundred or more visiting scientists would eat during the week of their stay. You can imagine the complexity. Professor Sato Fumitaka at Kyoto University had experience in China and knew how to be helpful. He wrote to me explaining that his wife and daughter would accompany him to Shanghai but noted specifically that "you may schedule the three of us for two portions of food—that will be enough."

The most serious crisis was over the Israeli participants. The policy of the Chinese government at the time was to refuse visas to all Israelis. We wrote well in advance to the Foreign Ministry recommending that, in accordance with accepted practice for international scientific conferences, visas for the Israeli participants be allowed. By June the authorities had not yet replied. Some American physicists, who had been chafing over the matter, announced that they would skip the conference if the issue of the Israeli visas was not resolved. The chair of the international organizing committee for the conference became agitated at this point and made a special trip to Beijing to make it clear that he would consider moving the entire meeting to another country if the problem persisted. We Chinese hosts went to the Foreign Ministry to restate our own appeal. We finally reached a compromise that allowed two Israeli scientists, Tsvi Piran and Gerald Tauber, to enter China. Just to be sure that nothing went wrong,

I went to meet them personally at the Shanghai airport. It was the first time an Israeli had entered China since 1949.

It seemed that every little detail of the conference had to be fought as a "reform battle." In the end, though, it all worked out and the meeting went smoothly. "Smoothly" does not mean easily. It means a myriad of irksome snags were overcome, one by one, with labor.

Broadly speaking, China's reforms at the time faced two kinds of obstacles. There were the outmoded regulations and bad habits left over from the Mao era, and these were gradually being overcome. But there were also the new obstacles and pressures, and these cast a worrisome cloud over the prospects for reform.

In each year after reform began in 1978, strident new noises that were very much at odds with reform issued from the government. In 1979, the noise was Deng Xiaoping's announcement of the "Four Basic Principles"— demands that everyone "persist with" four things: "the socialist system, the dictatorship of the proletariat, the leadership of the Communist Party, and Marxism-Leninism-Mao-Zedong-Thought." These principles flatly contradicted the slogan "Practice is the sole criterion for testing truth" that Deng had recently invented and had been spreading everywhere. What's worse, they were no different in their essential meaning from the "class struggle" principles of the Mao era, and they were put immediately to use in suppressing Wei Jingsheng and others at Democracy Wall. In 1980 the new noise was the order to suppress organizations and elections among university students. In 1981 the noise was the denunciation of the film *Unrequited Love*, which had dared to suggest the question "You love the government, but does the government love you?"

Still, and despite the continuing background static, reform moved forward. It was being pushed by the populace below much more than being led by the Communist Party from above. In several places farmers had taken the lead to make changes in their villages before Communist officials caught up and declared the changes to be official. You might say that a popular gale for reform was muffling the government's discordant noises. People hoped the authorities would just be less noisy, go with the flow, and hand out more ex post facto approvals.

What happened, though, was that quite a few powerful people inside the Party decided to talk about "reform" on the one hand while manipulating state-owned resources to build their private wealth on the other. As this pattern became more obvious, respect for the Party steadily declined. University students, especially the ones with good grades, became less and less interested in joining the Party. It no longer seemed a "glorious path." Near the end of 1982, the Party Secretary of the Department of Applied Chemistry at USTC asked me to speak to his students on "Why Join the Communist Party?" This topic was a first for me. But I accepted, and I did encourage students to join. My pitch was this: Precisely because the prestige of the Party has been falling, the only effective way to change it is to get more educated people inside. If all the talented people refuse to join, then we'll be led by a Communist Party that not only lacks popular respect but is bereft of modern knowledge as well—and how will the society get anywhere if that happens?

I made this argument often. I told people that to get anything done in China—even a harmless thing like a scholarly conference—every single detail has to go through the Communist Party. You can't avoid this fact even if you want to. So rather than scheming about how to get around it, it's better to join the Party and change it from within. Everyone in my astrophysics research group joined the Party around that time.

In the fall of 1983, I went to Europe again, and this time Li Shuxian could come with me. We arrived in Rome on September 8 and worked in the physics department at the University of Rome for three months. We lived in Castel Gandolfo, an ancient, elegant town that rests in hills just to the south of Rome and is the site of the pope's summer palace. The Vatican Observatory and a huge flower garden are there as well. Pope John Paul II, avoiding the final days of the summer heat in the city, was in residence when we arrived. He returned to St. Peter's Basilica on September 18.

The hills of the town descend to an oval volcanic lake called Lake Albano, which is expansive, deep, calm, and rimmed by thick forest. Olympic crew races once were held there. It takes about four hours to walk around the lake, and people who live in Rome flock to it on weekends to enjoy the outdoors.

The trip to or from Rome takes about forty minutes by rail, and Li Shuxian and I made the trip daily. The train station at Castel Gandolfo is at the base of the hills, next to the lake. To get there we took a shortcut down a long set of stone steps that descended through a thicket of greenery. In the early mornings, the steps were usually deserted as we made our way down—except for a few stray dogs. Pretty soon the dogs became our friends. As soon as we appeared at the steps they would dart and prance to meet us and escort us all the way to the station. This was entirely voluntary on their part.

For a time our Castel Gandolfo residence, which was spacious, served as an activities center and sort of boardinghouse for Chinese students and scholars who were visiting Italy. There were quite a few by then—in Sicily, Sardinia, and elsewhere—including about ten who had been my friends or students back in China. At one point an official delegation led by the president of the Science Association of Xinjiang stayed with us. This was all very different from the way things had been just four years earlier on my first trip to Italy.

Whenever Chinese outside China got together, the favorite topics of conversation were reform in China, the future of China, and comparisons between China and foreign countries. On one occasion, I remember, our topic was Italian sloth. We were reviewing a variety of examples of the phenomenon and noting how it contrasted with Chinese diligence. We were describing it almost as a difference between heaven and earth. A few Italians were listening in, and they didn't seem to mind our criticisms. They laughed at the funny examples as hard as we did, as if they felt comfortable with their worldwide reputation for indolence. Then one of them offered, in turn, a criticism of China that I will never forget: "Chinese people are very diligent at keeping China undeveloped." The words stung. But when I reflected on it for a moment, I had to admit he had a point. Even the "lazy" Italians had achieved a developed society, so whatever force was holding China back must indeed be the result of very hard work by somebody.

In October, we got word from China that another of those movements by "people who are very diligent at keeping China undeveloped" was at hand. It was the Anti-Spiritual-Pollution Campaign, whose goal was to purge China of all polluting influences from the capitalist world. The campaign did not reach as far as Castel Gandolfo, of course, but "spiritual pollution" was a favorite topic at mealtimes nonetheless. One of our Chinese houseguests came up with a trenchant opinion. He said the biggest piece of pollution that the capitalist world ever sent to China was Marxism. The capitalist world produced Marxism but declined to take it for itself. Instead it shipped it off to Russia and China, where its pollution has caused backwardness ever since.

In November 1983, we went to Germany. First we visited Munich, where we were hosted by Professor Gerhard Börner at the Max Planck Institute for Astrophysics. I gave a seminar on the morning of November 15 on "Dark Matter," which was one of the topics I had been working on. In the afternoon, the German president, Karl Carstens, made a sudden appearance at the institute. He was walking the length of Germany north to south on what he called a "long march," and by coincidence he arrived at the Planck Institute the same day as my talk. He delivered an informal speech, to a gathering of about twenty people, in the foyer of the main building. Apparently aware that some Chinese were in the group, he asked if Chinese leaders were still on a long march.

That evening we flew from Munich to West Berlin. It was late by the time we reached the downtown area. The Kurfürstendamm, which normally bustled, was already deserted, and most of the hotels had no vacancy. We wandered around for a while before we found a small hotel that could take us in.

About ten o'clock the next morning, we passed through the Berlin Wall at the Invalids' Cemetery and entered socialist East Germany. We went with a tourist group, but personally I had no interest in the tourist sites. I wanted to see what Marxism looked like in the home country of Marx. Much as I expected, East Germany resembled China—both in what it had and what it lacked.

As soon as we crossed the border, some of the guides began peddling East German postage stamps to us, and even though our passports clearly showed that we were from a fraternal socialist country, they hoped we would pay in hard Western currency, not East German marks. Next we visited a monument to the Soviet army, which struck me as oddly familiar. China had been a victor in World War II, and Germany was among the vanquished; but their war monuments were almost the same.

When our bus crossed from West Berlin to East Berlin, no one checked anything; when we crossed back to West Berlin, though, the East German border guards spent fully five minutes searching the vehicle inside and out for illicit human cargo. On the west side of the wall a few wreaths had been hung; they were for innocent people who had been shot to death while trying to scale the wall.

That was enough for me. The police and the wreaths said it all. We flew back to Munich at 5:30 that evening. Our trip had taken twenty-four hours and had cost us one thousand marks. I felt I had never spent money better, though, because I had been shown an irrefutable conclusion: the socialism invented by Marx, Lenin, Stalin, and Mao Zedong was a failure. It could not save China. Forget it.

16. VICE PRESIDENT OF THE UNIVERSITY OF SCIENCE AND TECHNOLOGY OF CHINA

IN THE EARLY 1980S A RUMOR AROSE THAT I WOULD BE NAMED A VICE president of USTC. While I was still away in Kyoto, in 1981, a USTC colleague wrote to me with the "secret" news that the university's Party Committee had sent to Party Central a list of recommended appointments and that my name was there as vice president.

In 1982, Hu Yaobang was promoted to be General Secretary of the Communist Party, and one of his priorities was that leadership groups become younger, better educated, and more professional than before. Institutions across the country started looking hard for people who met these criteria, and this helps to explain why USTC intensified its focus on me. I was one of the youngest full professors in the country as well as one of the youngest members of the Academy of Sciences. Added to that was that my seniority in the Party—twenty-six years, from 1955 to 1981— was at the high end for people of my age. (Having been expelled for twenty-one of the twenty-six years did not, at this point, count.)

I frankly felt ambivalent about the prospect. Part of my hesitation was purely selfish: I liked to work on science that interested me and preferred such work to putting in hours for the common good. My friends were not of much help with the problem, because they fell into two camps. One group thought I could create a better campus environment for everyone and that this would be a better overall contribution to USTC than my own work. The other group said my brain was suited for physics and using it on administration was a waste. A colleague in the latter group got so worried that he wrote an article titled "Fang Lizhi Is Unsuited to Be a Vice President" and published it in the magazine *Study of Science.*

That friend might have worried less if he had known that Party Central had its own doubts about me. USTC's nomination of me in 1981 remained stuck at the top for three years, until the summer of 1984, before anything happened with it. The authorities never explained what their misgivings were, but these are not hard to guess. My unorthodox public talks in 1980 had not sat well.

When the appointment finally did come, it arrived abruptly, with no sign of either what had delayed it or what, now, had precipitated it. In the Chinese Communist system, hirings and firings are among the most guarded of secrets, and it is often very difficult to fathom what is going on. Certain background facts, though, must have been relevant. These, for example: that students at Nanjing University had recently taken to the streets to demand that the president and the Party secretary on their campus be replaced, because, the students said, they were incompetent both as administrators and as scholars; and, at USTC, some students were already planning events to demand that Fang Lizhi be appointed vice president. They said they, too, were ready to take to the streets if this did not happen.

The authorities moved quickly to appoint Qu Qinyue, a genuine scholar and not a Party member, to be the new president of Nanjing University. Qu had once been a colleague of mine; we had coauthored a paper on abnormal neutron stars. By chance, he, Li Shuxian, and I were all in the same location when he learned of his appointment. We were lecturing at Nanchong Normal College, a campus not far from Deng Xiaoping's hometown in Sichuan. When the lecturing was over we took a three-day boat trip down the Yangzi River from Chongqing through the famous Three Gorges to Wuhan. Our second-class cabins were next to each other, and Qu shared with me the obvious observation that the authorities had selected him in hopes that he could settle down the Nanjing University students. Then, as soon as we got off the boat, I got word of my own little glorious assignment to the imperial ranks.

In the early 1950s, Chinese university presidents, especially those at the elite "key" universities, had high social status. Their standing in the bureaucracy was on a par with ministers in the central government. But after the attack on intellectuals in the Anti-Rightist Movement, that standing fell sharply. In 1984 the president of a key university corresponded to a bureau chief in the central government. Deng Xiaoping said repeatedly that intellectuals should be "emphasized," but in fact the highest salaries for professors under Deng were 20 percent lower than they had been in the early Mao years, and university presidents never recovered to the minister level, either.

What did get restored to the minister level was the *process* for appointing university presidents. Universities were possible sources of trouble, so the General Secretary of the Communist Party of China had to approve all hirings and firings of their leaders. That did not mean, though, that university presidents had actual power on their campuses. The practice was that minor decisions were made by campus Party committees and major decisions by the State Education Commission in Beijing. University presidents were "responsible" for campuses over which they had no real authority.

An anecdote can show what I mean. When I visited Jiaotong University in Shanghai, campus administrators told me about a project whose budget, as determined by a formula that the State Education Commission had approved, included the number 44.4 percent. This was a problem. Should they round the number down to 44 percent or up to 45 percent? In the end they had to ask for guidance on the question from the State Education Commission itself. The power of a university president was insufficient to decide even a matter of four thousandths.

By these standards, I enjoyed unusually good conditions during my tenure as vice president of USTC between September 1984 and January 1987. USTC had no Party secretary during those years and did not even have much of a functioning Party committee. Perhaps the General Secretary in Beijing was just too busy to get around to such a small task. USTC was one of the ten "key universities" in China, but it was in Hefei, a small city that was off the beaten track, so perhaps it is not strange that we were overlooked for a while.

USTC got a new president at the same time it got me as vice president. He was Guan Weiyan, another physicist—a specialist in low-temperature physics—who had been a student of the Soviet physicist Pyotr Kapitsa. I had known Guan from the early 1960s when I was at the Academy of Sciences working on solid state physics. Our common background made it very easy for us to cooperate. Guan served simultaneously as deputy Party secretary, but we always talked to each other the way physicists talk.

The happy coincidence meant that, for two years, two physicists who were president and vice president of USTC saw eye-to-eye, had no Party committee looking over our shoulders, and had some freedom to make innovations on campus. Later in our tenure, after USTC students orga-nized protest demonstrations—and students on other campuses (156 altogether) followed their lead—Party Central finally got around to the matter of naming a Party secretary at USTC. A bit late?

On the other hand, it was probably not a question of lateness. With or without a Party secretary, frictions on the campus were growing. Quite a few professors, including me, had already stated publicly that we disagreed with the State Education Commission on a key question: Had Chinese education in the seventeen years before the Cultural Revolution—from 1949 to 1966—been on the right track? The State Education Commission said yes; many professors said no. In our view, the destruction of Chinese education was one of the disasters on Mao Zedong's historical record. Not only had ten years of Cultural Revolution caused an entire generation to miss one or another part of its schooling; in important ways, even the 1949–66 years had been aimed at keeping people ignorant. The evidence for this, in our view, was clear. Illiteracy in the 1980s was still around 30 percent. More important, young people who did know how to read had been trained in a slave mentality that was very much the opposite of mod-ern education. Chinese universities in the early 1960s openly called for molding students into "docile tools of the Party." One model for emu-lation was the soldier Lei Feng, whose goal, in his own words, was to "become a stainless-steel screw for the Party."

Now, in the 1980s, the State Education Commission wanted to resume the policy of training docile tools. It had no intention of restoring genuine education. For university students, it even offered a new, freshly minted model for how to be a tool. He was Qu Xiao, a 1957 rightist who went to jail for twenty years, during which time his wife and children left him. For that part of his life, he certainly deserves sympathy. But in 1985 he began going around to universities giving lectures in which he said that the Communist Party's punishment of him was "like a mother spanking her son." It is a mistake, he said, to assign blame in such matters; spanking is a form of love, meant for a child's good. He urged that others view the matter as he did; we all should be willing to be the continually spanked children of the Party.

Are university students children of Communist parties? To people who live in modern societies, the question might seem bizarre. But in Chinese universities in the mid-1980s, it was not only a real question but an active one that was argued on both sides. One of the things I worked hardest on as a university vice president was to try to establish that university students are not children of the government.

I spoke to students about it many times. I used a standard template for my speeches, and I copy it below as a memento of the era:

> You are constantly told to study hard in college—the Party has given you this wonderful opportunity, so how can you not study hard?
>
> As citizens, of course, you would be right to work hard in school. But to say that the Party gave you the opportunity, or that the country gave it to you, or that you are "children" of the Party or government, is entirely incorrect. First ask these questions: Where did the Party come from? And in what sense does it "give" you something? We were all born with the rights to think and to be educated. We are the owners of that right; it is not something the Party gives us. To say the Party bestows these things is a reflection of a feudal mind-set.
>
> Let's look at the economics of it: Workers in China are paid less than the value that they produce. The difference, in fact if not in name, is a tax, and that tax more than covers the costs

of our educations. The Party does not donate our educations. It is more accurate to say that the government is obligated to give us what we have paid for. All of you here are students, I know, so you have not yet personally paid much in these de facto taxes; but your parents have paid plenty.

This can be calculated, and we can take USTC as an example. The ratio of teaching staff to students at USTC is about 1:2, and it takes an average of five years for a USTC student to graduate. This means that, on average, one teacher produces two students every five years. Now let's ask: What is the average lifetime economic value to the state of the education of one student? The state denies that there is a labor market, but that does not mean that this value cannot be calculated, and I have done so, and we can put it conservatively at 20,000 yuan. That means that one USTC teacher produces, on average, 40,000 yuan of wealth for the state every five years. In return, the state pays a teacher on average one hundred yuan per month—or, in a five-year period, 6,000 yuan. So where do the other 34,000 yuan go? Some, of course, is needed for capital expenditure, equipment, maintenance, and the like. Those costs, too, can be calculated, and they amount, on average, to somewhere between 15,000 and 20,000 of those 34,000 yuan. But this means, still, that each year the state takes from each USTC teacher, on average, about 3,000 yuan in a de facto tax. That is a tax rate of about 70 percent.

So you can see that your education is not something that the Communist Party bestows from above, but rather a process by which money flows upward from us toward the Party. At the time of the revolution, we Communists always liked to ask the question, speaking of the old regime, "Who is feeding whom?" Today we have to be very clear on that same question, and we must change the way we conceive things.

I also kept telling students that the role of universities is not to train loyal children but to produce independent adults.

In October 1984, at the occasion of my first speech as vice president of USTC after Guan and I were installed, a student asked me what kind of university I wanted to see USTC become. I answered that "a university should become a thinking center." What I meant was that China needed creativity more than it needed anything else. My answer was the beginning of a protracted confrontation with the State Education Commission.

Later, when Guan and I were fired—"removed" in his case, a more severe "revoked" in mine—the authorities charged us with pursuit of a "bourgeois line" in education that was leading USTC toward "liberalization." To me, by that time, the word *liberalization* sounded more like high praise than malfeasance. And in fact the charge was true: both of us had consciously tried to bring a freer atmosphere to USTC. Our only regret was that we hadn't had enough time to get very far. We could get done only some of what we wanted, and when we stepped down USTC was still far short of what our goals for it had been.

Those first steps that we did take included:

- Communist Party administration and academic administration were kept separate. Party committees at all levels had to stay out of professional decisions about teaching and research.
- Budget allocations, teaching assignments, and promotions were decided by committees of professors only.
- Representatives of teachers and students had the right to evaluate and to monitor university administration and to voice their criticisms at the department and university levels and beyond that at the levels of Party and nation.
- The system of "political advisers" for students was abolished.
- Political censorship of academic conferences was abolished.

USTC was not very big. It had fewer than four thousand undergraduates and just over one thousand graduate students. Teachers and researchers totaled fourteen hundred and support staff was fifteen hundred. The campus covered thirteen acres and its buildings comprised a bit more than two million square feet of space. It had more than thirty research units and these turned out about eight hundred articles or other research products per year.

The quality of the students was very high. Average scores for USTC students in national examinations of various kinds consistently put the school among the top three in the country. USTC physics students showed well in the nationwide competition for the one hundred spots offered every year, beginning in 1980, in Professor Tsung-Dao Lee's CUSPEA program to pursue doctoral studies in the United States. One year, thirty-six of the one hundred were from USTC.

I learned that being a university vice president is easier than being a physics professor. This was perhaps especially so in a country that uses central planning, in which the government in the national capital specifies all the crucial numbers concerning personnel, pay scales, standards for admission, building plans, and the like. The university president is spared the burden of having to decide such things.

My initial charge as vice president was oversight of expenses for scientific research. A bit later I was named first vice president, and that brought more duties. When Guan Weiyan was off campus, I needed to stand in for him.

The first thing I learned was that many things didn't need any management. The university was full of educated people, and results were much better if you let people decide things for themselves than if you ran around trying to micromanage. Of course this meant that you couldn't flaunt your know-it-all "leader" image. But if you were okay with that, it also meant that your workload fell by about 40 percent.

The next thing I learned was that most of an administrator's workday is taken by saying yes or no to all kinds of applications. It reminded me of the true-or-false questions on physics tests. I found that 80 percent of the questions were ones I could decide in less than a minute; 15 percent of the decisions needed ten minutes; and only 5 percent raised issues that needed more time than that. I had never been able to go that fast on physics tests.

Allocating funds was less easy. The school's budget at the time was about twenty million yuan, which, on a per capita basis, was one of the highest in the country. But it still was not enough to cover ever-expanding needs. This meant that every year at budget time there were a few days that had to be spent entirely on calculating, arguing, persuading, and negotiating. It was tough going. But we always did get through, because everyone knew that in the end compromise was inevitable.

Another very time-consuming activity was eating. China has a custom—it's hard to call it a bad habit—that says that any time a guest appears, a host offers a meal. For a university vice president, the problem was that university procedures required one to host—or at least to attend—too many such meals. Guests were arriving at USTC in ever-greater numbers in those days. There were nearly a hundred per year from foreign countries and even more from inside China. Eating and drinking was becoming a burden. I had to comfort myself with the thought that eating was still easier than teaching. Even the most elementary classes were harder than eating.

This is part of why I say being an official was not very hard. Communist functionaries sometimes appear, on the surface, to be extremely busy: attending meetings, giving speeches, issuing directives, and continually appearing in all kinds of places, large and small. We scientists, though, can observe one empirical regularity: they usually put on weight. Moreover, there is a positive correlation between the height of the official position and the weight added to the body.

Right from the start I had a sense that I would not be an official for very long, so I adhered to two principles: one, every meal that was not an official banquet I ate in the student dining hall; two, I always taught beginning physics, four hours per week. I also kept up with my astrophysics research—I could not do without that. I produced about ten articles per year while serving as vice president. In 1985 I coauthored a paper with Professor Sato Fumitaka of Kyoto University titled "Is the Periodic Distribution of Quasar Redshifts Evidence of a Multiply Connected Universe?" that won first prize in a competition sponsored by the International Society on General Relativity and Gravitation.

On average, I spent about four hours per day working in the vice president's office on administration. It was pretty clear that if I had just remained a functionary—a screw in the machine—I could have expected routine promotions every few years. The normal career path for Communist officials is "up only." So long as you manage to do literally nothing, you can expect to float a level higher in rank every few years. I learned this principle for bureaucratic success from a Uighur official, and the story is worth telling.

In the fall of 1983, the president of the Science Association of the Xinjiang Uighur Autonomous Region, whom I will call Ah-X-X, visited the International Centre for Theoretical Physics in Trieste. Abdus Salam, the ICTP's director, was Muslim, as was his Uighur guest, and this led Salam to want to do something special for the Uighurs. He proposed that every year two physicists from Xinjiang visit his center—all expenses paid. He asked nothing in return. Ah-X-X, though, repeatedly declined to put his name to any formal agreement. A colleague of mine from Xinjiang was puzzled and asked him what was wrong. Ah-X-X then revealed the secret of his success: "Never, ever, do anything. Even more important—never take an initiative." Soon after that Ah-X-X got another routine promotion.

The underlying reason why things did not work out for Guan Weiyan and me at USTC was that we violated Ah-X-X's principle, and in a big way. We took initiatives. I devote the rest of this chapter to an extended example.

In 1983, on a visit to the Vatican Observatory, I learned that many of its telescopes had been sidelined because the night skies of Rome were too bright with man-made light for the telescopes to be effective. One of these was a one-meter Schmidt telescope of very high quality; in a suitably dark location, this instrument could be extremely useful to researchers. I suggested that the observatory might donate that telescope to China. China had a number of observation sites at latitudes very close to Rome's, and it would not be hard to find a good spot for it. Professor George Coyne, the director of the Vatican Observatory, happily agreed.

It was to be a purely scientific gift, nothing more. But since it involved China and the Vatican, we approached the matter very cautiously. We thought it better that the telescope be donated from the Vatican to some kind of international organization, which in turn could donate it to China.

A full year of talking back and forth ensued, and in the end the authorities at the Chinese Academy of Sciences agreed to a plan. They determined a specific physical site at an observation station in Urumqi, Xinjiang, where the telescope could be mounted. Then, in the spring of

1985, they dispatched a delegation of five (not including me) to the Vatican to discuss the particulars of dismantling, packing, and shipping the telescope. The science attaché at the Chinese embassy in Rome joined the group, and the two sides signed a memorandum of understanding. So far, so good.

The next logical step was to identify an international organization to be the intermediary. It would need to be a group that worked with both China and the Vatican. That summer, I traveled to Rome for the Fourth Marcel Grossmann Meeting. This happened to be right when the University of Rome was setting up an International Center for Relativistic Astrophysics (ICRA) that was going to include the Vatican Observatory, the physics department at Stanford University, the U.S. Space Telescope Science Institute, and many other groups. It would be hard to imagine a better conduit for the telescope transfer. I took the initiative to list USTC's Center for Astrophysics as a supporter of ICRA.

I thought this was the least a university vice president could do—it would not only help with the telescope transfer but would also enhance a funding opportunity for USTC. Just the year before, the Italian government had established a fund for projects in developing countries, and it seemed to me that ICRA membership for USTC could only help in applying for them. I was, after all, USTC's "financial vice president."

I will set down the rest of the story in log form:

June 17: ICRA is formally founded. The chairman of the University of Rome's Department of Science and Engineering, Antonio Ruberti; Vatican Observatory Director George Coyne; and USTC Vice President Fang Lizhi, each representing his own institution, sign their names to a draft of the bylaws of the new center.

June 18: Discussions are held on ICRA's composition and research plans.

June 19: The Italian newspaper *Il Messaggero* reports on the founding of ICRA, referring to the founding roles of the University of Rome, the University of Science and Technology of China, and the Vatican Observatory. *Voice of America* also does a short report.

For the journalists, the "news value" was that people from China and the Vatican were doing something together. None of them viewed my role in signing USTC into the ICRA as having anything to do with the political relationship between Beijing and the Vatican, though. ICRA was seen as a purely academic activity. It was, moreover, not the first time China and the Vatican had officially been in the same organization—both were members of the International Astronomical Union, for example. So USTC's support of the ICRA was not actually much of a precedent, and press interest didn't last long.

June 20: No more media reports. No comment or analysis, either.

June 21: Pope John Paul II holds an audience for scholars attending the Grossmann Meeting. All of us, including me, shake hands with the pope and are photographed as we do so. The international media make nothing of this.

June 22 and 23: The Chinese newspaper *Major Reference News* [a classified publication, accessible only to high officials, that contains news stories reprinted from the international press] runs stories about ICRA on consecutive days, putting both in the "politics" column. The fact of repetition shows that somebody high up is getting very nervous about ICRA.

June 24: The Ministry of Foreign Affairs in China sends to the Chinese Academy of Sciences a formal inquiry about ICRA and the Vatican Observatory's telescope. The implication is that these matters have to do with Chinese foreign policy toward the Vatican.

As I noted above, authorities at the Academy of Sciences had been intimately involved in the plans for the telescope from the start. If they, at this point, had simply shared their records with the Foreign Ministry, it would have been obvious that only academic exchange was involved, and the matter might have ended there. But in Chinese Communist bureaucratic culture, whenever the question "Whose fault was it?" conceivably arises, the first response is always to deflect the question elsewhere. Accordingly, the Academy of Sciences "referred" the question without comment to USTC. In Hefei—luckily for me—many of my colleagues had been highly appreciative of my efforts to find funding for USTC in Italy. So

USTC simply set the inquiry aside and meanwhile informed me about what was going on. USTC had been planning to select me as "model Communist" of the year, and it went ahead with that plan.

June 27: The Chinese Ministry of Foreign Affairs sends an inquiry about the telescope to its embassy in Rome. The embassy's science attaché (as noted above) had approved the memo of understanding when it was written. He well knew that the whole project was only about academic exchange, not foreign policy. But the embassy's reflexive reaction, just like that at the Academy of Sciences, was to deflect responsibility. So they referred the matter to me, and I had to sit down and write down every detail of the whole story to show that nothing had violated any principle in Beijing's relations with the Vatican.

If I committed any indiscretion, it was only that I did not tell the Chinese embassy in advance that I was going to sign on behalf of USTC in the launch of ICRA. But I am willing to take that rap, because that indiscretion was partly intentional. I knew at the time that to ask permission in advance would cost half a year of waiting for all the buck-passing to take place. The matter was both simple and reasonable, and my view was that it was better to present it as a fait accompli than as a request.

In any case, the embassy accepted my detailed report, and that should have ended things. Everything was now in black-and-white. No hijacking of diplomacy had occurred, and the fears of certain people in Beijing were but chimerical self-delusion. I left Rome and headed back to the International Centre for Theoretical Physics in Trieste. I was looking forward to the elegant atmosphere of the Adriatic coast and to finishing a preface that I had begun for a little booklet called *The Creation of the Universe* that Li Shuxian and I had written. But—and it's hard to say why—the self-stimulated agitation in Beijing persisted.

June 29: Beijing again interrogates the Chinese embassy in Rome. This time the inquiry apparently comes from a place higher than the Foreign Ministry. The Vatican telescope apparently has been discussed at the Central Committee of the Communist Party.

July 1: Today is the sixty-fourth anniversary of the founding of the Communist Party of China. In Hefei, at a celebration of that milestone, it is announced that Fang Lizhi has won an award as "outstanding Communist of the year." I am swimming in the Adriatic when the announcement is made and know nothing about it. As soon as I get back to my room at the Galileo Building, though, and before I even have time to wash the saltwater from my body, I hear that the Chinese embassy is urgently looking for me and demanding that I report to the embassy on the morning of July 3 no matter what. I wonder what the emergency can be. An order is an order, though.

July 2: I board an overnight train for the four-hundred-mile trip to Rome.

July 3: I go to the Chinese embassy in the morning, and it turns out that the urgent matter is only that Professor Lu Jiaxi, the president of the Chinese Academy of Sciences, is arriving in Rome that day from Beijing. I am to meet him at the airport.

As a member of the Academy of Sciences, I might have wanted to do this anyway, if I had been nearby; but to ask me to make a special trip all the way from Trieste seemed a bit much. Later I learned that the decision that I must meet Lu Jiaxi had been made in Beijing. The Foreign Ministry had envisioned that he would be engulfed at the airport by journalists demanding to know more about the Vatican telescope. It was important that I be there to help handle the crowd.

At 2:00 p.m. a few embassy officials and I left for Rome's Leonardo da Vinci airport to meet the president. The flight was late, and by 6:00 p.m. he still had not arrived. I kept looking around the terminal for journalists lying in ambush, but didn't see any. The atmosphere at the airport was, to be sure, tense—policemen were patrolling with dogs. But this had nothing to do with Lu Jiaxi; the day before, July 2, Palestinian guerrillas had set off a bomb at the airport.

Lu did eventually arrive, but no journalist, either then or at any other time during his stay in Italy, showed any interest in asking him about ICRA. The Foreign Ministry had prepped him on answers to every question they could imagine—and the efforts went to waste.

July 10: I take a side trip to Venice with Lu. The gentle breezes wafting across Saint Mark's Square finally help him to conclude that he is in no danger from aggressive journalists. He is almost as relaxed as the pigeons that strut on the pavement all around us. He opens up and tells me how, on July 3, the day he left for Rome, the Ministry of Foreign Affairs had held one of its regular biweekly news conferences. The government spokesperson had carefully rehearsed what to say when foreign reporters asked about ICRA. But there, as in Rome, none of the reporters asked the question. Lu even wondered whether they had forgotten what the letters ICRA stood for.

From all of this evidence it was clear that both the understanding and predictions of the Beijing authorities had been utterly wrong. A great kerfuffle over nothing. Yet a problem remained for them, because to admit a gaffe like that would be a serious loss of face. What to do? They canceled the telescope project. But they could find nothing wrong with the ICRA agreement, or with the door that it opened for USTC to apply for funds from the Italian government, so they let that part go—in form, at least. In actuality, the way they put the project through the political wringer injured it internally, and even though I did my best for two more years to save it, in the end it failed.

Its "internal injury" was that it always carried the heavy stigma of having sprung from an unauthorized initiative. As Ah-X-X well knew, the authorities are averse to initiatives from others. Any independent proposal that runs counter to their wishes they of course oppose. But the deeper problem is that they oppose even initiatives that *do* accord with their wishes, because these are examples of someone "usurping authority"—which, to a power-jealous superior, is the most taboo of errors an underling can commit. A Chinese proverb has it that "a great sage resembles a simpleton." One facet of its meaning, I think, is that a wise man pretends stupidity in order to keep the emperor unaware that he, the wise man, can guess what is in the emperor's mind before the emperor has said it.

Early July: The Chinese government releases a Vatican-appointed Chinese bishop after more than thirty years of incarceration.

July 21: In his regular Sunday address at Saint Peter's Square, the pope offers a special salute to China.

July 31: In another of the Chinese Foreign Ministry's regular Wednesday biweekly news conferences, a spokesman says, "China has taken note of the pope's salute to China."

Some of my younger colleagues in astrophysics became very happy when they saw these last three news items. Maybe the telescope could be saved after all, they thought. Wouldn't the project fit perfectly with the regime's new rapprochement with the pope? But my older colleagues, who were more experienced in how things work, said no—precisely because the telescope project accidentally matched the regime's posture, there was absolutely no hope of saving it, they said.

Both the telescope project and our ICRA membership perished because they ran afoul of the great taboo against taking initiatives. We failed not because we were smart enough to guess that the authorities were on the verge of "noticing the pope." No, we failed because we were stupid enough to forget the imperative to pretend stupidity. So we deserved it.

My friend who wrote the article had it right all along: Fang Lizhi indeed was unsuited to be a vice president.

17. BOURGEOIS LIBERALISM

COLLEGE STUDENTS PROTEST. ANYONE WHO HAS HELPED TO RUN A university campus knows that there is no way to stop student protests entirely. Still, one of the standard instructions that the government in China gives to university presidents is that they must be vigilant about preventing protests. At USTC Guan Weiyan and I periodically received lists of Chinese campuses on which student demonstrations had "broken out." The tone of these circulars was that little disasters had occurred—something like fires—and that the causes of the disasters were failures of duty by university officials. When university presidents greeted each other at meetings, they often opened conversations by asking, "Anything happened at your place?" An answer of "nope, nothing" might be followed by a knowing smile. Everyone knew what the word *anything* meant: it meant student uprisings.

In my view, what student movements do for a society is akin to what sneezes do for a person with a cold. They perform a useful function. A more apt analogy might be to typhoons, which can be very destructive in the areas where they occur but at the same time are essential to the maintenance of balance in global temperatures. Student movements can be seen as society's temperature regulators. If you solve the problem that is causing them, they will settle down on their own. In cases where there really is no underlying problem, you're in even better shape: you just wait for the movement to run its course and peter out naturally. As long as nobody gets hurt and no property is damaged, student movements are benign.

Guan Weiyan saw things pretty much as I did. During the first year of our tenure at USTC, 1984–85, demonstrations took place at several dozen institutions of higher learning in China. The average was about one per week. Even though Guan and I had a "hands off" policy toward demonstrations, USTC had a perfect record that year—zero incidents.

When school opened in September 1985, students at Peking University were starting to fidget. Wall posters reading REMEMBER SEPTEMBER 18 went up. September 18 was the day in 1931 when Japanese troops invaded China's northeast provinces. The Communist Party, not in power in 1931, back then had said "Never forget!" and had called for resisting Japan. But now, in 1985, the same Communist Party was stoutly opposed to remembering September 18. Now it wanted to do business with Japan, and this student initiative might ruin things. Both the students and the authorities understood, too, that the real issue behind the student protest was not the memory of the 1931 invasion; it was that high officials in China were taking big bribes in business with Japan in 1985.

September 18 came and went, and the authorities were successful in bottling the students up. The students, unwilling to accept defeat, then announced a plan for nationwide protests on December 9, the anniversary of the day in 1935 when the Communist Party organized a nationwide student movement against Japan. The date was a red-letter day of glory on the Chinese Communist calendar, but the authorities began two months in advance to deter students from marking the anniversary.

On October 21, the Communist Party Committee of Anhui Province sent orders to Guan Weiyan and me about preventing student demonstrations. We were instructed to go mix with the students and talk with them. We were to express our concern and soften their impulse to demonstrate. For me, the mixing part was easy, because I ate in the student dining hall every day anyway. I did not have to deal with the problem (that I had encountered at Cambridge University in England) of faculty eating at a "high table" and students at low tables. The student dining hall at USTC had no tables of any kind. They had been destroyed in the Cultural Revolution. Everybody ate standing up.

Second, the document instructed us to show movies and to arrange other recreation for the students as the December 9 anniversary approached. The purpose was to dissipate their interest in demonstrating. We were further instructed to home in on the students who were most likely to be active and to invite them to buffets on the evenings of December 7 or 8. (There was no mention of where the dining tables would come from.) The students, comparing notes across campuses, discovered a principle: The more nervous Party Central was about a campus, the more elaborate its meal preparations were. They boiled this down to "The tenser they get, the fatter we get." Even though USTC was not at the top of Party Central's nervous list, we administrators were asked to invite more than a hundred students to buffets. At Peking University, Party Central sent in a whole work team to take charge of demonstration deterrence. Still the campus was tense.

In the end, December 9 passed without event. By that time, though, I had been caught in an imbroglio of another kind. It began in early November when I went to Beijing for a symposium of the Chinese Physical Society to mark the hundredth anniversary of the birth of Niels Bohr. The meetings were held in the main auditorium at Peking University. My own lecture, on November 2, was on semiclassical methods in Bohr's quantum theory and quantum cosmology. The professional physicists came, but so did many students. The room filled to standing room only. My lectures on physics often drew a great many students, and, partly for that reason, they also drew the attention of the "concerned parties." They would dispatch people to listen and "take notes on trends." I had a friend who worked in Party affairs who knew a lot about these things. He would come up to me after my lectures and say, "You-know-who were here again today; I'm not sure they understood much, but they were here."

After my lecture on Bohr, students surrounded me, asking questions. One of them—the chair of the student association in the Department of Radio Science—asked if I would give another talk, and I said okay. We agreed on a lecture title of "The Social Responsibility of the Intellectual" and fixed the time for the evening of November 4. The "concerned parties" picked up on this tidbit of information very quickly.

I was not surprised to learn that people from the work team on demonstration deterrence would be coming to my lecture to monitor and record it. How should I respond? My experience in such situations was that provocative language is seldom necessary; gentle irony and humor are usually quite enough to get one's points across. Nothing brings a clumsy and overbearing ideology to its knees more deftly than the glee of an audience laugh. Moreover, the concerned parties—normally a dull-witted bunch—almost never understand why students are laughing.

That night, though, my satire did get perceived, and the authorities were furious. The work team sent a recording of my lecture straight to Party Central. The staff of Hu Qiaomu, the Party's top-level guardian of ideology, combed it for political error. I had chosen my words carefully, however, and the theoreticians had trouble pinning down exactly where my arguments had gone wrong. What most irritated them, in the end, was my reference to a scandal about a deputy mayor of Beijing who had pretended to be a physicist in order to go have a good time at a conference on synchrotron radiation that was held on Long Island, New York. I named the man—Zhang Baifa—and in that detail, in the authorities' view, had gone too far.

I went back to Hefei the next day, and as soon as I got there Guan Weiyan told me that my speech in Beijing had caused dissatisfaction at the highest levels. Party Central had called to demand that USTC apologize to the Beijing Party Committee for my criticism of Zhang Baifa. Guan had refused to apologize. As it happened, he was one of the physicists who had been denied a place on the trip to Long Island in order to make room for Zhang and other non-physicists; moreover, he himself had been the first to expose the Zhang scandal at a meeting of the Chinese Physical Society. He replied to Beijing that the evidence was conclusive and there was no reason to apologize.

Guan's answer further infuriated Hu Qiaomu, who sat down to draft a proposal: Fang Lizhi should resign from the Communist Party. He circulated his draft among other top leaders, many of whom affixed their little circles at the bottom. (Such circles, in Communist Party culture, indicate concurrence.) The situation was grim.

During the week of December 6 to 13, the provincial Party leadership in Anhui Province summoned me three times for "chats." Anhui had a population of forty million people and a geographic spread comparable to England's. That its highest-ranking officials could devote three days in a week to a single speech by one physicist is one indication of how much time China's authorities spend working conscientiously for China's development.

My talks with provincial leaders were only the overture to a symphony whose theme was "Advise Fang to resign." On December 16, I received a notice from the provincial authorities that Wang Heshou, the deputy director of the Central Commission for Discipline Inspection, would receive me that same day. This commission was in charge of "rectifying" Party members, so I was expecting more advice to resign. But when the appointed hour arrived, the meeting was abruptly canceled—with no reason given.

I went to Beijing the next day, by prior arrangement. As soon as I arrived I was called to an audience with Professor Yan Jici, the man who in 1965 had helped to save me from exile to Liaoning Province. Yan was now eighty-six years old. He lit into me for my "untimely" speech to the students. I had been scolded by elderly people before and had learned that the best strategy is to offer no defense but just to wait until they get tired and stop. What surprised me in this case was that after a tirade that lasted forty-seven minutes, Yan stopped suddenly. His attitude changed immediately. He reverted to the way he had always treated me before. He cheerfully pulled me away for a couple of drinks and acted as if the harangue of a few moments earlier had never occurred. I don't drink, but on this occasion I did my best to keep the old man happy.

The next day, December 18, I was summoned for yet another exhortation. This one came from Academy of Sciences president Lu Jiaxi, the same man I had accompanied in Italy the previous summer. Lu made his face as stiff as possible for his oral performance, and I had to purse my lips hard to keep from smirking during this most austere of ceremonies. Near the end, Lu pronounced that my punishment would be indefinite postponement of my proposed trip to the United States. (I had been planning a visit to the Institute for Advanced Study at Princeton for half a year beginning January 2, 1986.) So there it was: my criticism of an illegitimate trip abroad had finally resulted in the loss of my right to take a legitimate trip abroad. I guess I had it coming.

Okay, I thought—I don't go to the United States. Anyway, that should bring the exhortations to an end. I slept well that night. The next morning, seeking a break from the ordeal, Li Shuxian and I went to a friend's home to relax. When we returned to Peking University at noon, we saw notes—posted in several conspicuous places—saying, "Li Shuxian, tell Fang Lizhi as soon as possible that Party Central is looking for him." It turned out that the office of the Central Committee of the Communist Party of China, beginning early that morning, had been sending a stream of messages to both the Academy of Sciences and to Peking University, searching for Fang Lizhi.

The person in Party Central who wanted to see me was Hu Qili, whom I had met in my college days when I did my ad-lib speech at the Youth League congress in 1955. Now Hu had risen to be—at least in theory— number five in the Party. I didn't know what to expect from him. Another exhortation? A scolding? I arrived at Zhongnanhai, the cloistered compound that holds the offices of the highest Party and government leaders, at 3:00 p.m. on December 19. The guards outside were expecting me and immediately let me in.

Hu greeted me with a beaming face, the exact opposite of the face the president of the Academy of Sciences had worn the day before. This was my sign that Hu was going to play the role of "good cop." The alternation of good and bad cop—in Chinese, called "white face" and "red face," in a metaphor that derives from opera roles—is a standard control technique. A white-face treatment often follows a red-face treatment. Hu's talk to me was entirely explanatory in nature. He made no criticism of what I had said in my speech to the students. He kept repeating that "Party Central has noticed [the same corruption problems that you have noticed], but such problems are not easy to solve, so don't worry, just be patient." His attitude, I have to say, was commendable. I later learned that it had originated with instructions from Hu Yaobang, the General Secretary of the Party. I also came to understand what had happened on December 16 when the Discipline Inspection Commission had wanted to see me and then abruptly canceled: Hu Yaobang had issued a directive saying that three times is enough to press a person to do something, and he did not agree that there should be any further efforts to urge Fang Lizhi to resign from the Party.

At the end of my meeting with Hu Qili, he made a special point of saying, "We in Party Central trust you, and you are free to go on visits abroad. My direct telephone line is 397007. Call me personally if you have any problem." So just like that, the light was again green to go to Princeton. The Academy of Sciences reversed course and approved the visit for March. The "indefinite postponement" announced to me in person by the Academy president had lasted indefinitely for twenty-four hours. The reason for the about-face in policy was nothing more than a clog in the information flow between Party Central and the Academy of Sciences. The Academy received an order that "Fang should resign from the Party" and began to act on it without knowing that another order—"Don't pressure Fang to resign from the Party"—was in the pipeline. The clog in the message tube had made a 180-degree reversal inevitable. I had to feel for our Academy president. Nearly ninety years old, he still had to be so nimble afoot. It must have been exhausting.

That is how my near-miss with political trouble ended in 1985, but there was more to come in 1986. During my meeting with Hu Qili, he asked if I would write an open letter to students that he would recommend to the *People's Daily* for publication on New Year's Day. I understood, of course, that he wanted me to counsel students to stay calm during the year. I wrote a piece called "How to Be Responsible When Sensing a Crisis" and sent it to Hu a week later, but it never appeared in *People's Daily*. My views apparently were still unwelcome at the top. Here is part of what I wrote:

> *Someone predicted to me, partly in jest, that "you astronomers" are in for more crises in the new year, because Halley's Comet is making a return visit in 1986. Astronomers do not believe in astrology. And yet there have been, in fact, some historical coincidences between the return of Halley's Comet and noteworthy shifts in human societies . . . Might it be that the return of the*

comet this year will coincide with a turning point in the march
toward prosperity that China's reform is bringing?

I did not imagine that I would personally play a role in causing my "astro-logical prediction" to come true.

March in Princeton was still very cold. Li Shuxian and I set up a tempo-rary household at 23 Hardin Road at the Institute for Advanced Study. We kept it simple, because we were not planning to stay long.

Pretty soon, though, friends began advising us to figure out how to remain in the United States, and there were some fairly easy ways we could have done this. More and more Chinese scientists, especially younger ones, were making this choice. Some in our own generation, including people at the Institute for Advanced Study, were doing so as well.

I am not, in principle, opposed to emigration. It is a normal phenom-enon, and every person should have the right to choose where he or she wants to live. It had already occurred to me, moreover—more than once—that living in a developed society would offer advantages in my research as well as in daily life for my family. Whenever I ran into political troubles, I sensed how liberating it would be to live in a place where academic free-dom and freedom of speech were assured. By 1986 I had traveled outside China more than ten times, and each time could have stayed outside if I had chosen. But I always opted to go back.

The reason I always went back was not that I am in love with Chinese soil. Words like "Great earth, my mother!" are the playthings of poets, in my view. For me it was just that life feels very different inside China and outside. Inside, all kinds of trouble and interference are constantly caus-ing worry and disgust; but outside, although life is steadier and more peaceful, it somehow is less engaging. I found that political trouble could be oddly addictive. A person who grows up with it, when suddenly released from it, can feel somewhat at sea. It can even seem that it would be better to be back in trouble-land earning the sense of achievement that comes from doing battle with obstacles. At the end of 1985, when I was still smart-ing from recent political exhortations, I was very much in escape mode. But after a while in Princeton, my "addiction to trouble" slowly grew back.

Princeton was enjoyable, of course. It had no "red" or "white" opera faces, no exhortations, no post-exhortation banquets, no Zhongnanhai and no sly smiles inside Zhongnanhai. It had only the free-roaming spirit of Einstein. Not far from where we lived in Princeton there were some woods, and it seemed, somehow, that free souls were roaming around in there as well. At dusk there were deer—does and their fawns, usually— that ventured out to graze around; they behaved as if they, too, were aware that this was the home turf of a great spirit who enjoyed free wandering.

Still, I did not want to stay here long. Li Shuxian and I decided to go back to China in July as scheduled. One factor that drew me homeward— perhaps in satisfaction of my "addiction to trouble"—was the challenge of organizing the 124th symposium of the International Astronomical Union (IAU). In a developed country, a meeting like this would be a rou- tine matter, but not in China. No IAU symposium had ever been held in China before, and the topic this time was "Observational Cosmology." Only a dozen years earlier, modern cosmology had been a forbidden zone in China, so the very meeting itself was important. It was a statement that cosmology had officially arrived in China.

As of 1985 it was still not entirely safe to write about cosmology. In May of that year, I published an article in the Chinese journal *Science* in which I introduced quantum cosmology and referred in passing to the view that "the universe arose from nothing." In November, when Hu Qiaomu cir- culated his proposal that I be removed from the Party, he simultaneously wrote a letter to the editors of *Science* stating that Fang Lizhi's ideas on quantum cosmology were non-Marxist "subjective idealism" and advis- ing that the editors publish an article "that took a different view from Fang Lizhi's." (In such contexts, "take a different view from" is a synonym for "denounce.") Science of course thrives on criticism and denials—but it does not welcome political interference. I was a deputy editor of *Science*, and my fellow editors resisted Hu's interference. What the incident did show, however, was that even as late as 1985, top ideologues in China felt entitled to rule with authority in the field of cosmology.

When I shared this story with some colleagues at Princeton, one of them, the possessor of a sly wit, suggested that this great teacher of ideology be invited to the 124th IAU symposium to speak on the topic "Cosmology Today." It was a joke, of course. The great teacher fell well short of the minimum standard for symposium participation. The ABCs of the field were over his head.

Cosmology as a field was hardly alone in this predicament. The problem illustrated a much broader paradox that was hampering China. Almost everyone was strongly in favor of "modernization," seeing it as a goal that the country had been pursuing for more than a century. But at the same time, a modernization phobia was loose in the land, especially in ruling circles. Any noun that followed the word "modern" was automatically suspect: modern cosmology was "objective idealism"; modern physics (quantum mechanics) was "subjective idealism"; modern art was emptiness and decadence; modern music was profligacy and spiritual pollution; modern Western countries were founts of bourgeois iniquity. Modern technology wasn't so bad, and moreover, much of it had been invented in China long ago. The upshot of this line of thinking was that if you wanted modernization, Chinese tradition was the place to look for it.

So, as I saw things from Princeton, the project of getting modern science and civilization accepted in China still seemed urgent. I felt fortunate to have played a role in getting cosmology accepted. I reflected on the fact that three centuries earlier, five of my predecessors at the Beijing Observatory had been executed for attempting to use modern methods of astronomy to figure out calendars. Those pioneers had paid with their lives, and today we were luckier. Still, it was our job to keep diehards like Hu Qiaomu from messing up an IAU symposium.

The IAU meetings in Beijing went smoothly. The forms and procedures of these symposia are always the same, so I needn't review them here. The high point in our case was a banquet, done to the standards of a state dinner, that was held on the evening of August 29 in the State Dinner Room of the Great Hall of the People, next to Tiananmen Square. The Chinese proverb "Money can make ghosts turn millstones" in recent times had acquired a new version: "Money can make the Communist Party turn millstones." This was why we scientists, even though we didn't have any state-level guests, could get state-banquet treatment. We had the money to buy it.

At the end of the banquet the astronomers—sated, slightly inebriated, and heady with the sense of being national-level guests—virtually floated out of the Great Hall and into Tiananmen Square. The gentle winds of the autumn evening may have magnified the inebriation, because Allan Sandage, a forty-year veteran in the field of cosmology, was led to make the immoderate pronouncement that "this meeting marks the true beginning of observational cosmology." The next day Malcolm Longair, the distinguished British physicist, invoked Sandage's words to open his summary remarks on the meetings, and the line later appeared prominently in the published symposium summary. It had become famous. It seemed to add a new item of glory to Tiananmen's storied history: the great square was now the official birthplace of observational cosmology.

In retrospect, Sandage's colorful remark seems to me not only the climax of that IAU symposium but also coincident with an apex for China in the 1980s. From that point on, the society slipped toward crisis.

The storm clouds gathered quietly, and hardly anyone noticed them at first. I for one had no sense at all in the summer of 1986 that any blow-up was imminent. On my way back from America I had chosen to take a little detour to visit the Arctic Circle. I went to Stockholm for the Eleventh Conference of the International Society on General Relativity and Gravitation, and when the meeting was over I went up to a little town in northern Sweden called Kiruna to see what the "midnight sun" was like. Like most people living on most parts of the earth, I was accustomed to the alternations by which it is always either day or night, and either a warm season or a cool one, so my first impression of the Arctic was that everything had gone haywire. A day did not divide into light and dark hours, and all four seasons were present at once: the flowers of spring, the long days of summer, the layered clouds of autumn, and the cold of winter all shared a stage. The normal borderlines had been erased.

Kiruna's indeterminacies led me to recall a letter that a friend in Beijing had sent to me, shortly before then, about the "culture fever" that had arisen in China. People were debating whether China's reforms should be based in Chinese culture or be an explicit step into Western culture. The premise of the debate seemed to me the same as the day-or-night pattern that most people live within. It had to be either light outside or dark outside, one or the other. The friend who had sent me the letter about culture fever wanted me to express an opinion about it, but I had never replied. I hesitated in part because culture is not my special field and I felt less than fully qualified—but also, in part, because I am always confused by the imprecise definitions in such discussions. What should we say about the "socialism" that China had been practicing for thirty-seven years, for example? Was that "Chinese culture" or "Western culture"? For a scientist trained to work with definitions and evidence, debates on culture could be hard to follow. We scientists, moreover, like to focus on questions of truth versus error, or more advanced versus less advanced understanding; we very seldom raise questions of East versus West. At the earth's poles, in fact, the very concepts of north, south, east, and west are useless. So why do we have to worry so much about Easternness?

As I watched the ever-circling sun in the sky over Kiruna, it suddenly dawned on me how I could reply to my friend: what China needs is precisely to get away from confining questions like "East versus West." Our reform should "open up in all directions." We should welcome anything that is good, not asking whether it is "East" or "West." This was the origin of what the authorities later called my "bourgeois liberal thinking"— which, in their view, did so much to disturb the peace in China.

A few days before the IAU symposium in August, a group of young scholars had pulled me away to a one-day conference in Qingdao on "Chinese versus Western culture." That was where I first spoke publicly about the idea that had occurred to me in Kiruna. Later, at the IAU meetings, journalists of many kinds wanted interviews, and they kept asking what I thought about reform. Sticking with my principle of "opening in all directions," I said China should begin with academic freedom, freedom of speech, and freedom of the press.

The "errors" in my speech and behavior at the end of 1985 must have been still fresh in the minds of the authorities, because they were very quick to pick up on my new advocacy of these freedoms. The ideas were not my invention, of course; they were already inscribed as rights in China's constitution and could hardly be viewed as illegal. My innovation was only to say that on-paper rights should be actual rights. Later, when students realized that the constitution could be invoked in this way, they began to refer to their "right to demonstrate" and their "right to assemble" in places like Tiananmen Square. Those claims in turn led Deng Xiaoping later to charge, in fury, that "people are taking advantage of our constitution!" Here Deng established in a single blow that one characteristic of "Chinese democracy" is that citizens lack the right to take their constitution literally.

The idea of "opening in all directions" began to spread, and when it did, it collided repeatedly with Deng's "Four Insistences" (on Marxism, the socialist system, the leadership of the Communist Party, and the people's democratic dictatorship). On those four points, anyway, opening up was forbidden. By unfortunate coincidence the *People's Daily*, around that time, published an article on four principles we had been promoting at USTC: science, democracy, creativity, and independence. This made it seem (although we had not conceived them as such) that our four principles were being offered as alternatives to Deng's four.

Not wanting to go near that explosive problem, I headed back to USTC to begin teaching in the fall term. I began a course on atomic physics that met four hours per week. That left me little time for travel, so I turned down a good number of speaking invitations. I did make an exception, though, to go for two days to Zongyang in southern Anhui to attend a memorial for Fang Yizhi, a scholar whose book *A Physics Primer*, published in the seventeenth century, was the first in China ever to use the word "physics" in its title. His surname was the same as mine, and Yizhi was almost like Lizhi, so I really had to go. The event was unrelated to politics, and September and October went by smoothly for me.

In the larger society, though, unrest was growing. The reforms were stagnating, graft and other corruption were spreading, and a deep dissatisfaction was building up, especially among students. In November these things caught up with me. I traveled again to Rome, for a conference on Halley's Comet as observed from space, and on my way back I stopped for a few days in Shanghai and Ningbo. Li Shuxian and I wanted to visit Shanghai Jiaotong University, where I had been an adjunct professor since 1984, and Ningbo University, where the president was an old colleague from USTC.

As soon as I arrived in Shanghai I got a message that originated inside the Shanghai Department of Propaganda: I should cut back on what I say in public. I don't know whether the message was an attempt by the authorities to deter me or a tip from a friendly insider who knew that the authorities would be scrutinizing me. The bottom line, in any case, was the same. My arrival was not welcome in the eyes of the Shanghai authorities.

That did not bother me much. By then I was accustomed to government monitoring, and the students who had invited me to speak were clear-eyed about what they were doing. In those days the students seemed to have a principle that the less the authorities welcomed somebody, the warmer their own welcome would be. The result, in this instance, was that instead of cutting back on my words, I ended up speaking more than had originally been planned. At Jiaotong University I gave a seminar for colleagues on "Particle Astrophysics" and then gave a talk to graduate students entitled "Intellectuals Have Both Duties and Strengths." From the questions the students asked during Q&A it was obvious that they were intensely dissatisfied with the way things were going in China:

"What do you think of the fact that the Party worms its way into every possible cranny?"

"What percentage of Chinese officials would you say are corrupt?"

"Are the Four Insistences blocking China's progress?"

Things got even tenser at a subsequent lecture at Tongji University on November 18. My topic was "Democracy, Reform, and Modernization," and thousands of students showed up. They even held up a banner that read THE REPUBLIC NEEDS YOU, FANG LIZHI! They were itching for action, and I was lucky they didn't carry that banner out into the streets. But now I had been drawn in. I was at the center of another storm and there was no way out.

This time the highest officer in charge of monitoring me was Wan Li, First Vice Premier of the State Council. When I arrived in Shanghai, Wan Li arrived in Shanghai. Four days later I went to Ningbo, and Wan Li flew to Ningbo. He was collecting recordings of my lectures as he went. At Ningbo, though, the university people, from the physics department right up to the president, were my friends, and when Wan asked for tapes of my lectures, everyone politely declined. They pretended they didn't have any. Wan responded by saying that, all right, then I won't leave Ningbo. My official aircraft will stay on the ground until the university gives me recordings of Fang Lizhi's speeches. In a bind, the university did hand over a partial set of tapes.

I arrived back in Hefei on November 22. Wan Li followed a week later and announced that a roundtable on higher education would take place on November 30 at the Hall of Rice Fragrance—the grandest conference site in all of Anhui. The conference began that day about 9:00 a.m., with about a hundred people in attendance. In addition to Wan Li and his entourage, all of the highest officials in Anhui were there, as were the Party secretaries and presidents of all the Anhui universities. Some professors came, too. Television reporters and other journalists were at the ready, set to record the august pronouncements of the First Vice Premier.

Wan Li opened with some formalities but then moved quickly to the cold remark that "Someone has been saying that the State Education Commission should simply allocate funds to campuses and then leave them alone." Hah! Those words of "someone" were exactly what I had said just a few days earlier in Shanghai. Wan Li had come with an agenda—it turned out that the whole reason for this big meeting was to criticize Fang Lizhi. Fortunately, my lifetime of experience with criticism allowed me to remain calm. I sat there thinking "Bring it on!," opting to say nothing.

But that wouldn't do. About two hours into the meeting, Wan Li referred to me by name and invited me to come sit next to him to offer a response. The television crews, seeming eager for a dramatic clash, homed in on the two of us as I took a seat to Wan's right. I noticed he had a little notebook in his hand. It turned out to be a record of things I had said in my speeches in Shanghai and Ningbo. What preparation. He may have been anticipating that, under the glare of his austere and morally invincible reprimand, I would tremble, confess my errors, and send bourgeois liberalism to its final death. But that didn't happen.

If Wan Li had launched his criticism of me one-on-one, in the privacy of his office inside Zhongnanhai, I would have had no interest in locking horns with him. I would probably have just mumbled a few polite phrases and let it go. But out there in front of an audience of a hundred or so, in the elegant Hall of Rice Fragrance, the teacher's intuition to explain the truth to others took over inside me. Sorry, Your Highness Mr. Vice Pre-mier, but you leave your humble servant no choice. I'm going to contest you point by point and we'll see who wins. Are you ready?

A ferocious debate ensued for the next hour and a quarter. I can't pos-sibly record all the jabs and hooks of every round, but I can attest that both speaking speed and voice volume of the two combatants rose steadily as the debate progressed. The full drama of the melee cannot be captured in words; one would need to watch a videotape for that. But as one mea-sure of the degree to which His Highness was, by the end, incensed, it is enough to record the following exchange, which happened in the bout's final round:

> Wan Li: *"When did you join the Party?"*
> Fang Lizhi: *"Thirty years ago."*
> Wan Li: *"For me it's fifty."*

Touché. He had me. Who wins an argument can be hard to measure. But numbers are numbers, and here he had won—fifty to thirty. The signifi-cance was more than numbers, though. Readers who don't understand Chinese culture might not appreciate how age alone establishes superior-ity. Every child growing up in China knows that when an argument reaches a standoff, it can be decided by asking:

"How old is your father?"

"My dad is thirty."

"Hah! Mine is fifty! I win!"

It is worth noting, though, that even though the Vice Premier had landed a devastating blow in the final round of our match, the Xinhua News Agency sealed the entire match from the public. All of the audio-tapes and videotapes that the journalists had made were stashed away as secrets.

After the debate a number of people came up to shake my hand. Some of them were friends. But some, too, were high officials in Anhui Province.

All of this may not have mattered, however. By now the student move-ment was running on its own momentum.

18. DISSIDENT

On December 5, 1986, five days after my debate with Wan Li, more than a thousand USTC students took to the streets of Hefei in protests. The Wan Li debate was not the reason, but, both then and later, students often invoked one of the concepts that I had stressed in the debate: democracy is not a gift bestowed by higher-ups.

The students' immediate cause was to democratize elections for "district people's representative." The Chinese constitution stated that every three years, at the district level—the lowest level—representatives of the people were to be elected directly by the people. This was the only direct-election right that citizens had. Election law provided further that any person who had the support of ten or more voters could stand for election. In several decades of practice, however, that right had never been exercised. The authorities had always named the candidates, and the voters had merely drawn circles to indicate concurrence.

The election in the district that contained USTC was scheduled for December. The government's election committee had prepared its list of candidates as usual, had announced it on November 28, and had set the election for December 5. On November 30, the day I debated Wan Li, a wall poster went up on the USTC campus asking that the candidates meet with voters to answer questions. A flurry of similar posters followed the next day. The students were refusing to recognize the government-appointed candidates. They said that if the rules of the election law were not followed rigorously, they would boycott the election. A confrontation was shaping up.

Because the students had the letter of the law on their side, the government's election officials were obliged to cancel their plans and begin the nominating process anew. They announced that an assembly at which candidates and voters could interact would take place on December 4. This meeting became an almost unheard-of event in China: several thousand students crowded an auditorium for what was essentially a free political convention.

Even though the authorities themselves had called the meeting, it was clear to me that in Beijing's view, it counted as a "student disturbance" of the kind that a university official is supposed to minimize. This put me in a bind. It was my job to put out the fire, but on the other hand, the students were not wrong and it was my duty to protect them. I decided to sidestep the dilemma by staying away from the meeting and monitoring its progress from my apartment. Perhaps a third way would emerge, I hoped.

My sidestepping didn't work. Around 10:00 p.m. the student convention was showing no sign of winding down. No longer able to resist, I went to take a look. But then, as soon as I set foot inside the hall, I became a sort of prisoner of the situation. The students were still at fever pitch and still, at that late hour, numbered a thousand or more. They seemed ready to explode the place. They waved for me to go onstage and state my view. To refuse to speak would have been wrong (as well as impossible, actually), and to speak against conscience in such a situation was even less thinkable. So I went onstage and said some things extemporaneously, and what I said became the basis for my article "Democracy Is Not Bestowed from Above." I closed with these words:

> *It really is true that democracy will arrive only if we all work for it . . . The only reliable democracy is a democracy that is built on popular awareness and won by struggle from below. A thing bestowed from above, after all, can always be taken back from above (cheers and long applause) . . . What we see here*

this evening—free competition for election, everyone able to express his or her own view—is genuine progress. Once before, six years ago, students at Peking University tried to hold free elections. They elected two representatives. And then what? Those two students were given especially bad job assignments when they graduated (mass groan from the audience). The obstructionists are still with us today, still doing what they can to block the progress of democracy . . . and that is why this evening's event here at USTC, where everyone is free to express an opinion, is so extremely important. Tonight's meeting is democracy in action, and it is why I, as a vice president of your school, am here to say I will defend any person who, tonight, has stood for election, has cast a vote, or has expressed an opinion, no matter what that opinion may have been (lengthy cheers throughout the hall). I hope tonight's meeting will be the starting point of a process of democratization at USTC and I promise again that I will do what I can to protect this sort of activity. If anyone tries to persecute those who have spoken out tonight in the way those two students at Peking University were persecuted six years ago, they will have to fire me first (joyous, lengthy cheers throughout the hall).

The students reached their goal. They successfully claimed the right to nominate candidates for election as the law provided. But they did not want to stop there. They wanted to take their victory to the rest of society. They decided to go to the streets on the afternoon of the next day, December 5, to spread their ideas about how local elections ought to be conducted.

I was not in favor of this move. Going off campus would precipitate problems at another level and, unless there were very careful preparations, might amount only to a big show with no real progress. Besides, as university vice president I felt a responsibility for the students' safety. On campus, I could have some say over that; off campus, what could I do?

On the morning of December 5, I called in six or seven of the student leaders and tried to dissuade them from their afternoon plans. But I failed.

At 12:30 p.m. students were already gathering in front of the USTC library, ready to march. At 1:00 p.m. I went to the library myself, hoping to spend the modicum of prestige I had earned with the students to persuade them, at the last moment, not to go to the streets. My words worked with about 40 percent of them. The rest—more than a thousand—marched off, holding up banners that read, among other things, DEMOCRACY IS NOT BESTOWED FROM ABOVE. They really were too young, I felt. Some of them, in response to my plea, had said, "Please let us go this one time, Teacher Fang! We've never been to a demonstration before!" They saw it as a sort of game. They had no idea how serious the consequences could be under a political system like China's.

Luckily, on that particular march, nothing bad happened. The police had been notified of the parade route in advance, and neither the students nor the authorities caused any trouble. Traffic police along the route facilitated the march and even exchanged some salutes with the marching students. The provincial government authorities were reasonable as well; they announced that the right to demonstrate is provided in the Chinese constitution and that this demonstration was legal. After the march the students gradually calmed down.

This was not the first student demonstration of the season, but it was the first to make a political demand: a call for real elections. The issue had broad resonance. Soon students at other college campuses—in all, 156 campuses in twenty-nine different cities—were out marching as well, and the slogans echoed the ones that had appeared at USTC. If the authorities everywhere had responded as wisely as the authorities in Anhui Province had on December 5, things could have proceeded peacefully throughout the country. But that did not happen.

Shanghai authorities took the lead in the nosedive. On December 17, students in Shanghai went to the streets after applying, as the Hefei students had, for recognition that their demonstrations were lawful. But the Shanghai authorities ignored the application and instead called in police, early in the morning on December 19, to disperse the demonstrators by force. This move enraged students all across the country.

About 3:00 p.m. on December 23, students at USTC took to the streets again, this time in support of the Shanghai students. Their mood, in marked contrast from the last time, was combative. They marched down-town and gathered in the square in front of the Hefei municipal govern-ment offices, where they demanded that the Anhui authorities announce a condemnation of the violence that the Shanghai authorities had used. The Anhui officials rebuffed that demand, and communication between the students and the authorities broke down. Both sides stiffened. Refus-ing to disperse from the square, the students began a sit-in. Crowds of onlookers grew. When evening arrived, the Anhui Party Committee began to consider whether it, too, should use force to disperse the students. The situation was extremely tense.

Guan Weiyan and I made a quick decision to go talk with the students. Around 10:00 p.m., we squeezed through the crowd and into the city government compound, where we found that the east side of the main building had been occupied by the students while city officials continued to inhabit the west side. The two sides were not speaking. The first thing Guan and I did was to run back and forth carrying messages, trying to mediate. After two hours, a compromise emerged: the students would end their sit-in if Hefei officials promised to forward the student demands to their counterparts in Shanghai. But a big question loomed. Would the students outside the building—more than a thousand and still very energetic—accept the compromise that had been reached on the inside? If even a minority of them rejected it, the sit-in would continue. The stu-dent negotiators, hoping to increase the likelihood of agreement, asked Guan Weiyan and me if we would accompany them outside to announce the deal and to urge its acceptance. For me, this was a fearsome challenge. I had no confidence at all that I could address a throng of a thousand agi-tated young people and, with a few words, persuade them to end a sit-in. If I failed, though, violence would be the certain result. There wasn't much time, either. Early morning was the time the authorities normally chose for the application of violence. So, confident or not, I had to go try.

The order of speakers was: student leaders, Guan Weiyan, me. I have no memory of the exact words I chose that night, and even if I could remember them, and were to write them down here, I'm afraid they would strike the reader as incoherent floundering. In that kind of situation—facing shouts of protest, the chanting of slogans, and triumphant cheers, all woven together into one continuous undulating cacophony—logic could hardly be the tool of choice. Only by opening my heart, in full, could I hope to capture even a shred of credibility. I can remember only my last sentence: "So I think it's best if we just end today's protest here and go back to campus."

What happened next seems in my memory something of a miracle. The thousand or more students arose from their sitting positions, one by one, and began to trickle out of the back of the compound. I was stunned. I truly had not imagined that that final sentence would make any difference.

It was 2:00 a.m. when I finally got back to USTC—utterly exhausted, but too excited to fall asleep. A possible disaster had been averted, and peacefully. The next day I heard that the Anhui authorities had commended Guan Weiyan and me for our roles in the matter.

But the central authorities saw things very differently. I began receiving a stream of phone calls from Li Shuxian, who was in Beijing and had heard, on impeccable authority, that Party Central was right then holding a meeting on what to do about the Fang Lizhi problem. One of the alternatives, she had heard, was to arrange an auto "accident" and just be done with it. She wanted me to leave USTC and return to Beijing as soon as possible. I couldn't quite believe everything I was hearing from her, though. Guan Weiyan and I were at the front lines of the problem, working hard to calm things down—and we *had*, in fact, calmed things down. How could Party Central not know this? Besides, my classes were still in session. I still had the teacher's duty to hold class. You can't walk away from someone else's children, as the Chinese proverb says. So I stayed in Hefei until December 30, then left for Beijing.

The following events, from 6:00 p.m. on December 29 to 6:00 p.m. on December 30, occupied the last twenty-four hours (I did not know at the time they would be the last) of my twenty-eight years of working at USTC.

December 29, 7:00 to 9:00 p.m.: I taught my last class. It was on gravitation and quantum physics.

December 29, 9:00 to 11:00 p.m.: I did an interview with Tseng Hui-yen, a reporter from Hong Kong. She was the only non-mainland reporter covering the USTC events at the time, and it turned out that her photos of me, which she took on her little instant camera, were the ones the media later treated as the standard Fang Lizhi photos.

December 29, 11:00 p.m.: The results of the voting at USTC were announced. I was elected as the district people's representative.

December 30, 8:30 to 10:00 a.m.: I did an interview with a reporter from the Associated Press. The authorities allowed the interview— the only one they allowed to a foreign journalist—but would not let the journalist enter the campus. So we met outside, at the Luyang Guest House.

December 30, 2:00 to 5:00 p.m.: I chaired a meeting to evaluate the performance of USTC instructors. Several were promoted to associate professor or full professor.

December 30, 6:30 p.m.: I boarded a northbound train for Beijing.

My principles during those days of student unrest were, on the one hand, to support the just demands of the students, while, on the other, trying to show that the Communist Party still could be open-minded. Whether addressing students or talking with reporters, I did what I could to resolve the binds that the authorities were getting themselves into. Still, it was on that same day, December 30, in Beijing, that Deng Xiaoping finally lost his temper and said, "As for Fang Lizhi, we no longer 'advise to resign'; now we expel."

After the overnight train ride I went to our apartment at Peking University. It was New Year's Eve, but there was no holiday spirit in the air. The next day students went out to march on snow-covered streets. A protest on New Year's Day? Hardly a good omen.

The speech in which Deng Xiaoping said I should be expelled from the Communist Party turned into Document No. 1 of 1987 and was relayed downward through the bureaucracy, nationwide. It also became the first headline news of the year. I had, of course, been expelled once before, in 1958, but the feeling this time, twenty-nine years later, was very different. Might I invoke that famous line from Karl Marx that "history repeats itself, the first as tragedy, second as farce"? If Marx was speaking of my Party expulsions, he had it right. In the days after my first expulsion, some close friends distanced themselves from me—and that, yes, felt tragic. After the second expulsion, though, my stock soared. It was as if I'd won the lottery. Being the subject of Document No. 1 in a new year was, statistically speaking, a less likely occurrence than winning a lottery, and its power to spread one's fame was a thousand times greater than any advertisement could be. So when students asked me, "What do you think of your nemesis, Mr. Deng Xiaoping?" it occurred to me to say, "Well, first, I need to thank him; where else could I have found such a good public relations agent?"

I received another free advertisement on the evening of January 12. National television, in prime time, announced that Guan Weiyan had been removed as president of USTC, that Fang Lizhi's vice presidency had been revoked, and that Fang had been transferred from USTC to the Beijing Observatory. Li Shuxian and I were a bit late having dinner that evening, and I did not turn on the evening news when I usually did. Just past 7:00 p.m. the phone rang and a friend said, "Congratulations!" I had no idea what he meant, and said so.

"You're not watching TV?" he asked. "You got revoked! Your split-family problem is solved! Aren't you happy?!"

So there it was in a nutshell: congratulations on a firing. But he was right, at least, about the reason to rejoice. Our family had been forced to live apart since 1969, and I never dreamed that one by-product of the student demonstrations that arose in Hefei would be the fulfillment of my eighteen-year wish to be reunited with my family.

I was in the newspaper headlines again on January 19, 1987, when it was formally announced to the nation that I had been expelled from the Communist Party. As noted in chapter 8, the Communist Party charter provides that the process for expelling a member begins with discussion at the local branch and that the decision is then sent to higher levels for approval—except during dire emergencies like wars or earthquakes. Yet this time, like the last, neither discussion nor earthquake proved to be necessary. I received a high honor—personal expulsion by the Party's supreme authority.

Once again my fame got a major boost. It was highly unusual for the regime to lavish this much attention on a scientist, and yet the authorities seemed to feel my boost needed to be even bigger. They pulled together a two-hundred-page book of excerpts from my speeches, listed the editor as "Party Central," printed half a million copies, and then sent copies to every Party branch in the country. The goal was to provide material for use in denouncing me, but the actual effect was the opposite. Nothing before or after has ever spread my ideas more effectively. Many people heard about me for the first time because of this little book, and quite a few apparently liked what they saw. When Party Central figured out what was happening, an urgent order went out to retrieve all those errant arrows. But it was hard to do. Pirated copies of the book were already for sale on the black market.

When news of my expulsion appeared, I started getting letters of support from all across China. Then, when the little book of wrong opinions appeared, there was a flood of them. One day I got 157 letters. They came from people of many kinds: college students, high school students, and a wide range of intellectuals, as well as some workers, soldiers, and officials— even officials in the central government. Some wrote to endorse my views, others to comfort me, and still others to rail against the stupidity of the regime. I received poems. Some were copied lines from ancient works, and some were original. This one sticks in my mind:

> *Leaving office, a person learns*
> *The stars still shine, the sun still burns*
> *But every hero always yearns*
> *For the day when he returns*

The poem got me right on the part about shedding official duties in order to return my attention to bright objects in the sky. But it got me wrong, I have to say, about the yearning to return. My youthful passion for the Communist Party had been but a distant memory when 1987 began, and by now even those faintest of vestiges were gone. I had friends who were indignant on my behalf; they said that Party Central had made a mistake and that I should be "rehabilitated" and my Party membership re-restored. The goodwill of those friends moved me considerably, but their idea did not. It no longer mattered to me whether my expulsion was "correct," or whether "rehabilitation" was warranted. I had no interest whatsoever in being a member of the Communist Party of China again. Good-bye, great, glorious, correct Party! Good-bye for good.

So what was I now? In the regime's eyes, a "dissident." The word was another foreign import to China. In Europe it had referred, originally, to adherents of unorthodox religion. Chinese society did not have religion in quite that same Western sense, and as a result there was no ready-made term in Chinese waiting to translate the word *dissident*. During forty years of Communist rule in China there had been, to be sure, plenty of people who did not subscribe to the officially enshrined ideology. In that sense I was no pioneer. But those other people had been called "counterrevolutionary elements," "alien-class elements," "bourgeois-rightist elements," and the like. Not "dissidents." One of the positive contributions of Deng Xiaoping's opening of China in 1979 was that it allowed this concept of "dissident" to enter China. Under that label I *was* a pioneer. I was arguably the first open dissident in China.

For the regime, dissidents were a new breed and posed a new problem. How should they be handled? The authorities knew exactly what to do with all those counterrevolutionary elements, alien-class elements, and bourgeois-rightist elements, but what should they do with a dissident? Repress? Smash? Annihilate? Tolerate, in order to seem broad-minded? Try to buy off? For a time the regime seemed genuinely confused about what to do.

What happened to Li Shuxian and me in August 1987 illustrates the problem very well. An international conference on experiments in gravitational physics was to be held in Guangzhou that month under the auspices of Zhongshan (Sun Yat-sen) University. I was chair of the board of the Chinese Association for Gravitational and Relativist Astrophysics at the time, so it was more or less mandatory that I be invited. It was not very likely that such a specialized conference would draw much public attention, but still, to the Communist Party Committee of Guangdong Province, my pending arrival posed a major threat that the "dissident" virus might spread to Guangzhou. They proposed moving the conference outside the city to a remote county town—for "safety." But that proposal brought stiff opposition from the foreign scholars who were the joint organizers of the conference. Some of them said that if the conference were moved in this way, they would boycott it. At that the authorities backed down, at least partway, and negotiated a compromise: the conference could stay just barely inside Guangzhou. It would be at the Nanhu Guesthouse in a suburb.

On August 2, Li Shuxian and I flew from Beijing to Guangzhou and settled in at the guesthouse. No problems. Everything was calm, and the conference began the next day. The day after that, though—August 4—Hong Kong journalists somehow figured things out and got my room number. I was scheduled to give a talk that morning—on gravitational waves and cosmology—and as I was going over my notes the phone kept ringing with requests for interviews. The meeting organizers reported that the lobby in the guesthouse was filling up with Hong Kong journalists and that some camera trucks were parked outside. All this bustle was over me, the dissident.

The Chinese organizer of the conference, Professor Hu Enke, was a colleague and a friend of mine. Not wanting my politics to upset his conference, I went to him and invited him to decide: "Should I do these interviews or not?" But this was not, unfortunately, a matter for someone at Professor Hu's level to decide. Not even the president of Zhongshan University could decide it. It was an "emergency issue" that shot all the way up to the provincial Party Committee. There, we got a clear, if predictable, decision: no interviews, period.

But that word hardly stopped the Hong Kong reporters. Indeed, it seemed to attract more of them. The conference banquet was scheduled to be held that evening, and the reporters apparently calculated that I would have to emerge from my room around the banquet hour. That would give them, at a minimum, some photo opportunities. By afternoon the area outside our room was besieged by journalists. Mounted television cameras were trained on our windows. Any appearance by me at any door or window would yield footage. This scene produced another emergency report to the provincial Party Committee, who replied quickly with an order to pull all the curtains in the room and to unplug the telephone. After that, our meals were brought to our room—"every need filled at our feet," as the Chinese saying has it—but we were not allowed to attend the banquet. The reporters were frustrated again.

Still they did not give up. It was printed on the conference schedule that I was to give a presentation the next morning, August 5. Quite a number of them decided to camp out in the woods near the guesthouse to wait to see, when the crunch came, whether the regime would let me out of my room for a scholarly presentation.

The authorities faced an excruciating dilemma. I learned later that on August 4 the Party Committees of Guangdong Province and of Zhongshan University stayed up all night trying to think the question through. In the end they decided to relent and to allow the journalists to do interviews and to make recordings for television and radio, but only during the time it would take me to walk from my room to the conference site. The next day that ten-minute walk took place as planned, but, for the reporters, it was over far too soon. Some who wanted more time tried to mix in with the conferencegoers to get inside the building, but none of them succeeded. The authorities had assigned about seventy highly experienced security personnel to guard the doors. These guards were very good at spotting journalists, and one by one they sent them on their way.

Right after my presentation, Professor Hu Enke informed me that Li Shuxian and I would have to leave the conference immediately. The Communist Party Committees of Guangdong Province and of Zhongshan University were jointly "inviting" us, as "honored guests," for a deluxe tour of the Pearl River Delta. We understood, of course, that it was not up to us to decide whether we wanted to be honored guests. Professor Hu led us into a room adjacent to the conference meeting room. This room, it turned out, was connected to a secret underground tunnel that had been built for emergency escapes. (In foreign countries, the rooms in which scholarly meetings are held are equipped with normal fire escapes; secret underground tunnels are wholly a "Chinese characteristic.") A car was waiting for us at the mouth of the tunnel. As we sped along—the tunnel was wide enough to allow cars to pass in two-way traffic—we could see lights of different colors flashing on the two sides. These seemed to be intersections with other tunnels. It was a separate underground world.

After about ten mysterious minutes, the car emerged into daylight. The

Nanhu Guesthouse was nowhere in sight. We were in a large garden compound whose buildings were sequestered in foliage. There were soldiers guarding the grounds. We were met by a manager who explained that this was one of the sanctuaries for the very highest leaders when they visited Guangzhou. *My goodness*, I thought to myself, we were indeed "honored guests." The staff at the compound were obviously unaware of our actual status; they must have assumed we were big shots from another province or maybe among the newly rich in Beijing, here in Guangzhou on tour. They eagerly reported to us about the Vice Premier of China who had just left, the chair of the Chinese People's Political Consultative Conference who spent the winter here every year, and so on.

Our short stay was very worthwhile—not because of the lovely setting or the great food, but because it gave us a glimpse into the lifestyle of the people who claim to represent the impoverished proletariat. We stayed in a suite for top Party officials. The bedroom alone was more than a thousand square feet. But what really puzzled us, as newcomers to all this, was why the bathroom, too, had to be so large. It was nearly 650 square feet. Was this so that, if both nature and nation called at the same time, a meeting of Party Central might convene here? The walls around the compound were more than ten feet high, impossible to jump over, and were more than three feet thick, enough to thwart a standard-caliber artillery shell.

For our three-day "honored guest" tour of the delta, we went to the small cities of Zhongshan, Xinhui, and Jiangmen. In each place we were "fortunate" to stay in the palace-villas of high officials. Some were French style, some American style. One had a golf course, and all three had separate quarters for retinues of servants and assistants. Local officials of the highest ranks came out to meet us at every stop. In Zhongshan, the mayor himself ate every meal with us, even breakfast. On our way back to Guangzhou from Jiangmen, we had to cross the West River, over which there was no bridge, only a ferry. When we reached the ferry about 180 vehicles of various sizes were waiting to cross. If we had stayed in line, the wait would have been at least an hour. But suddenly, as if from nowhere, a police car appeared in front of us. It cleared the way for us to drive past all of the waiting cars, trucks, and buses, straight to the ferry.

Why had the authorities decided, at this particular juncture, to regale Li

Shuxian and me with this deluxe entertainment? This is hard to say. The whole thing may have been an experiment to see if "honored guest" treatment could soften dissidents in the way that, in the past, the method had worked on certain prisoners of war. It is undeniably true that when a person is whisked past a line of more than a hundred waiting vehicles, he or she can sense how wonderful it is to be attached to power, especially to big power.

But if that was the government's calculation, it was fundamentally flawed, because even if it worked, it could hardly be used on every dissident. The authorities were afraid dissidence was going to spread like a communicable disease, and in the spring of 1987, something like that indeed was happening. More and more "dissidents" were popping up. To treat every single one as an "honored guest" would have been prohibitively expensive. Moreover, if the case of Li Shuxian and me were any guide, the treatment did not work.

The failure of the gambit must have irritated Deng Xiaoping, because not long thereafter he came up with an entirely different move. He said that I had libeled him and he was going to take me to court.

The roots of this episode were in a trip Li Shuxian and I took to Australia in August 1988. We went first to Perth, for the Fifth Marcel Grossmann Meeting on General Relativity, then to Canberra, Sydney, and elsewhere. We came home via Singapore, Hong Kong, and Macao. Along the way I gave talks on physics, but the Chinese students in Australia asked me to talk about current events in China as well. In Canberra and Melbourne, students specifically asked what I had seen on wall posters at Peking University. I answered as well as I could, noting that some posters had charged that central leaders or their families were keeping money in foreign bank accounts. That is the point on which Deng Xiaoping later claimed that I had libeled him. He said his family had done no such thing.

The regime set to work on the libel case immediately, before we had returned from abroad. In Hong Kong, two reporters from the Xinhua News Agency asked for an interview with me. They had only one question: "Did you say the leaders have overseas bank accounts?" I did not immediately perceive the purpose of this "interview," but later it was obvious. They were recording evidence for use in the libel suit.

In September, back in Beijing, friends in the legal field told me that

Deng Xiaoping had already instructed lawyers to prepare the case. High-level circulars in the Party had already announced that Fang Lizhi's libel would be dealt with according to law. Then an article appeared in *Reference News*, a national bulletin with a circulation even larger than *People's Daily*, explaining that what Fang Lizhi had said constitutes libel. All the signs were pernicious.

Friends began to sweat for me. The topic of foreign bank accounts was pretty common in those days, and what I had said in Australia was hardly unusual. But my friends were afraid that Deng Xiaoping had developed a particular animus toward me and that he might use this issue to purge me once and for all. So I got plenty of volunteer help. Lawyer friends assembled a defense team. Strangers wrote in offering arguments and evidence that I could use in court. Some people even carefully went about collecting evidence of the foreign bank accounts of leaders and their offspring, so that truth could be my defense.

The tension reached a peak when rumors began flying that the Beijing Intermediate People's Court was about to issue me a summons. That made me feel a bit uneasy, of course; but it also occurred to me that the chance to do combat with Deng Xiaoping in court, even if I lost, might be the experience of a lifetime and something I could write about later. My penalty would likely be a sum of money payable to Mr. Deng to compensate for my libel. But to judge from the responses around me so far, money would not be much of a problem. There would be plenty of people offering donations, and even wanting their names associated with the effort.

But a month passed, and another month, and the summons never arrived. I never got to see Deng or any person representing him in court. All of the arguments I had gathered in my mind, and was ready to use, went for naught. That was disappointing.

It's too bad Deng Xiaoping has written no memoirs. We can never know for sure what led him to withdraw his idea of a lawsuit. It may have been that he suddenly realized he should not—yet again—be Fang Lizhi's volunteer ad man.

19. SPRING 1989

THE YEAR 1989 IN BEIJING OPENED CHILLY AND WHITE, WITH A SOFT, clean snowfall. Who could guess that within just a few months it would be the scene of cataclysm—or that blood, flesh, and death would replace the falling snow?

It almost seems fated that my first paper of 1989 was about explosions—supernovae in particular. Until then I hadn't really worked much on supernovae, but the appearance of Supernova 1987A had turned the flaming stars into a hot topic. Not just astronomers but other scientists, too, and even the general public, suddenly found them fascinating, and we astrophysicists were flooded with requests to explain them. After a bit of homework, I did my best to respond.

Today supernova explosions are viewed as purely astronomical phenomena. In ancient China, though, as we know from records two thousand years old, they were taken as signs of human events and were valued for their predictive power. Usually they meant nothing good.

There had been about eight or nine spectacular supernova explosions during those two thousand years. One of them, in the year 1006, is described in historical records as shining, at its peak intensity, half as brightly as the moon and giving enough light to read a book by. These spectacular outbursts were always taken to be predictive of some kind of great military or natural disaster—or perhaps the death of an emperor. All the records show, too, that the predictions were never wrong. For example, the official astrological reading of the supernova explosion of 1054 was "heavenly ruler expires"—and, sure enough, the next year the Xing Zong emperor of Liao died. This was a coincidence, of course, but the careful recording of the details (after the fact) shows how important supernova explosions were taken to be. When they were sighted, it was the job of the officials in charge of divination to memorialize the emperor and to urge him to announce a "general amnesty" as a way to induce heaven to soften the impending disaster, whatever it might be, and to bless the state with continued prosperity.

In 1989 I was working at the Beijing Observatory, the modern successor of the imperial institution whose charge had been to scour the heavens, keep the calendar, and divine the future. By now, of course, we astronomers had no formal duties to prognosticate for political rulers, but we felt we did have a duty—and a right—to be concerned for the future of our society. This may be why, as I was writing my piece on supernova explosions, that ancient tradition of "general amnesty" floated into my mind. Was not China today, in fact, very much in need of such a thing?

The arrival of the new year made the point seem more obvious, and a few simple questions occurred to me with a sudden new clarity. Why drag old fights into a new year? Why can't people be a bit more conciliatory, more tolerant, more ready for amnesty? Why is it that we set aside our differences and wish one another the best only on a few holidays during the year, while on all the other days we are constantly at one another's throats?

And what was the reason for holding in prison, for long periods of time, exhausted people who were no threat whatever to society? Was this only to show the power of the rulers? How can it be that people who claim to lead the world's most advanced human society turn out to be less magnanimous than the emperors of a thousand years ago, who could "benefit the world" by granting amnesties?

These questions were on my mind after I finished my article on supernovae, and I wrote the following letter to Deng Xiaoping:*

> Central Military Commission
> Chairman Deng Xiaoping:
>   This year will mark the fortieth anniversary of the founding of our nation and the seventieth of the May Fourth Movement. There undoubtedly will be many commemorative activities. But compared with remembering the past, people might be even more concerned about the present and the future.
>   In order to capture the spirit of these occasions in the best possible way, I sincerely propose that you announce a general amnesty, specifically to include all political prisoners such as Wei Jingsheng, on our nation's fortieth anniversary. Whatever one might say about Wei Jingsheng, to release someone like him, who has already served ten years in prison, would show a humanitarian spirit.
>   This year will also mark the two hundredth anniversary of the French Revolution, whose ideals of freedom, equality, fraternity, and human rights have been gaining ever more respect in the world. So I again express my earnest hope that you will consider my proposal, as a way to demonstrate even greater concern for our future.
>
>   Sincerely, and with best wishes,
>   Fang Lizhi
>   January 6, 1989

I wrote the words "Deng Xiaoping, Party Central, Beijing" on an envelope, put the letter into it, and deposited it in a public mailbox outside the Beijing Observatory about noon on January 6. It later became what the authorities called "the letter that led to the Beijing riot."

When I mailed it I had no expectation that anything would result. The fate of most letters to top leaders—which arrive in the thousands, maybe

---

*Translator's note: The author reconstructed this letter from memory while writing inside the U.S. embassy. It differs in some minor ways from the original text.

tens of thousands, each day—is to sink into silent oblivion, perhaps without even being read. Chinese leaders never answer letters from commoners (except when, in well-selected cases, they publish an exchange in order to spread a certain message). Certified letters mailed "return receipt requested" do not bring receipts. I was a member of the Chinese Academy of Sciences, and my letters to the president of the Academy had never received any acknowledgment; so why should I expect one from Deng Xiaoping?

Still, I felt it likely that Deng would at least notice my letter, if not answer it. For better or worse, I was one of the people he "cared about."

The next day, January 7, two guests came to my home, and their visits made it considerably more likely that my letter would get noticed by the addressee. The first guest was Liu Da, the open-minded former Party secretary at USTC, who followed the practice of "opening one eye and closing the other." Liu read my letter (I had saved a handwritten copy) and expressed his strong approval. "Yes," he kept saying, "yes, those people should be released." He said he would make sure the letter reached Party Central. He had once been a member of the Party's Central Advisory Committee, and he had ways to be sure that letters got delivered.

The other guest was Professor Perry Link, a new friend. Link ran the office of the American Committee on Scholarly Communication with China and had arrived in Beijing shortly before the Mid-Autumn Festival in 1988. He studied Chinese literature, was an editor of the Chinese magazine *Eastern Miscellany*, and had asked me, a few weeks earlier, if I would contribute to it. Now I gave him an essay and gave him, as well, a copy of my letter to Deng, which he said he would translate and release to the international press. When he did this, the letter turned into an open letter, all the more difficult for the addressee to ignore.

I later learned that Deng Xiaoping did indeed read it. True to form, though, he gave no sign of having done so: no acknowledgment, no response.

Then, during the recess for the Chinese New Year, some of my colleagues in the Chinese Academy of Sciences began discussing whether they should write their own letter to Party Central about amnesty for prisoners of conscience. My old friend Professor Xu Liangying in the

Institute for History of Science headed the effort, and the eventual result was a letter signed by more than forty natural scientists and social scientists.

After that some young writers and poets—Bei Dao, Lao Mu, and others—came to visit me. They, too, were thinking about making a call for amnesty. I gave them a copy of my open letter, and on February 13 they drafted one of their own. It called for releasing political prisoners and was addressed to the Standing Committee of the National People's Congress. Three days later they made their letter public. Thirty-three prominent people in cultural fields had signed.

An ancient Chinese proverb says "Things stop at three." And sure enough, three open letters was enough for the authorities. They began to show signs of unease. The first salvo came from the Ministry of Justice, whose formal complaint was that writing public letters about prisoners compromises the independence of China's judiciary. (This made it clear, at least, that citizens of the "People's Republic" did not have the right to write such letters.) The next step by the authorities was to find the people who had signed the open letters and, one by one, give them "education"—or "reeducation." Some were offered sweet talk ("This is not in your best interests"), while others were issued warnings or put under surveillance. The authorities viewed me as a major "instigator" of all that had happened, but for now, anyway, they did not put me in the category of people to "talk to."

The public calls for amnesty had failed in their immediate objective. But the fact that they caused such nervousness shows that "dissidence" had grown into an epidemic that the authorities could not easily be rid of. The regime's absolute power was declining.

Just as this new dissidence was unfolding, a new American president, George H. W. Bush, came to China for a visit. The U.S. government had already had quite a bit of experience with dissidence in the Soviet Union, but apparently had no ready guidelines about how to deal with it in China. The American president had to decide whether to treat Soviet and Chinese human rights in the same way, thereby risking offense to the Chinese government, or, for now, to apply different standards, sidestepping China's human rights issues and preserving the "old friend" relationship between the governments that Bush himself had helped to establish during his stint as chief of the United States Liaison Office in Beijing in 1974–75. It was obviously a dilemma.

In the nick of time, the president's brain trust thought up a way to serve both ends at once: invite some Chinese dissidents to attend the president's farewell banquet in Beijing. In Western culture, awkward topics could be avoided at such an occasion even as it functioned as ceremony. As the Americans saw it, inviting Chinese leaders and Chinese dissidents to the same dinner party could be seen as expressing the president's concern for Chinese human rights and, simultaneously, as doing no harm to the formal authority of Chinese leaders. It seemed a brilliant middle road.

This was the background for a White House invitation, hand-delivered to Li Shuxian and me by the American embassy, to attend the president's farewell banquet on February 26. It was to be a Texas-style barbecue at the Great Wall Sheraton Hotel. We later learned that five hundred guests had been invited, which meant that even if we had been there, we would have constituted only about 0.4 percent of the group. The president's brain trust probably made this calculation.

However correct numerically, the calculation was wrong in theory. The brain trust forgot (or perhaps never knew) about the Chinese tradition of political banqueting. Chinese history teems with stories of grand political banquets that mark weighty historical events. The contrast with the West is sharp. Peking opera is full of political banquets—not so for Shakespeare's plays. Every time Peking opera comes to the line "Let there be wine and feast!" you know that the climax is around the corner.

So how could ancient, magnificent, splendid China stand by as a new president of the upstart U.S. of A. used wine and food for political theater? As China's rulers saw it, the president's Texas barbecue was in the wrong place and had invited the wrong guests. Dissidents to be guests at an event where we ourselves are also guests? Anathema! Even if the dissidents were only 0.4 percent, it was out of the question.

From the moment we received our invitations, I could sense that the stakes were high. Not wanting to take any chances, I called the Foreign Affairs office of the Chinese Academy of Sciences the next day, February 23, to report that we had received the invitations. I wanted to know as soon as possible whether the authorities were going to disapprove, so that if they did, there would be ample time to send our regrets. To be quite plain about it, Li Shuxian and I were not going to feel shattered if the authorities said no. At bottom, the American invitation was for food, wine, and socializing—nothing more. And Texas barbecue would not be a new experience for us anyway, because we had done that once before, in Texas.

I began to take stock in my own mind of what might happen. I reminded myself that—normally, anyway—seasoned politicians conceal their discomfort in public. In this case, moreover, the authorities might see the banquet as an opportunity to present an appearance of broad-mindedness to the world. And if they did want to block us from attending, their most likely choice of ways to do it would be to go through the Beijing Observatory or the Chinese Academy of Sciences to state their instructions clearly. This was, after all, the method they had used with me in the past, whenever they wanted to ban me from foreign travel or other activities.

But, strangely, no prohibitions arrived, either explicitly or subtly, during the three days between our receipt of the invitations and the banquet day. The authorities at the Beijing Observatory even said that they would provide a car for us. It was a bit eerie. Exactly what medicine were the authorities brewing inside their covered pot? There was no way to tell.

What they did do, in the end, was something no person of normal intelligence could ever have anticipated. In order to reach one simple goal—blocking two people from a banquet—they rolled out five stunning countermeasures.

Countermeasure One: Martial law traffic control.

At 5:30 p.m. on February 26, Li Shuxian and I, together with Perry Link and his wife, got into a car in Zhongguancun in northwestern Beijing and headed east across the city toward the Great Wall Sheraton Hotel. Our driver told us later that he had noticed, as we pulled out, that another car fell in behind and was tailing us. The rest of us didn't notice this.

Around 6:00 p.m., where the Third Ring Road passes near the Great Wall Hotel, Countermeasure One kicked in. Hundreds of police appeared as if from nowhere, eyes flashing, and bringing traffic to a standstill. We thought, at first, that this must have been part of security for the Bush entourage as it arrived at the banquet. But no. Once the police had spotted our car, a swarm descended to surround us, while the others disbanded. All of this activity had been for us.

Countermeasure Two: On-the-scene control by the top special agent.

With our car unable to move, we decided to get out and walk the remaining short distance to the Great Wall Sheraton. After only a few steps, however, a bevy of plainclothes police surrounded us to block our way. Their leader was a swarthy man with a rough manner—the very image of the "hit man" used by police. He stepped forward, hooked his arm roughly under mine, and said, "I am the special agent in charge of all security for the Bush visit. The invitation list that the U.S. Secret Service gave to us does not include your two names, so you cannot go to the banquet."

This told us several things. For one, it showed that the highest priority of the highest-ranking agent in charge of security for the U.S. president was not the security of the U.S. president.

Countermeasure Three: Suspension of public transportation.

With advance impossible, retreat was our only option. We decided to go to the U.S. embassy to seek a determination about the alleged "Secret Service name list." Our car and driver were by now nowhere to be seen. We lined up for a taxi at another nearby hotel, but after a few hundred yards police forced that car, too, to stop. Next we tried the public bus system, but once again the police were a step ahead. As we waited at a bus stop, we could see police flag down buses before they arrived. Something was said to the drivers, who then drove past our stop without stopping. No one could get either on or off. Passengers on the buses and would-be passengers waiting to board were of course puzzled and frustrated. Our plight (if not our taint) had spread to them.

Countermeasure Four: Accompaniment on a nighttime stroll.

We abandoned the idea of boarding any sort of vehicle and set out toward the embassy on foot. It was already 7:00 p.m. or so; the sky was dark and the temperature was falling. But we were never alone: in front, behind, and on both sides, police were always "accompanying"—some in uniform, some in plainclothes—and a police car always tailed. At each intersection an armed motorcycle with a sidecar awaited, engine humming, ready for action. The visible police that night must have numbered at least a hundred; the number behind the scenes, invisible to us, must have been that many or more. So there you have it: a single dissident, just one person who says, "I will be free," is reason to deploy more than a hundred armed police.

We reached the embassy district around 8:30 p.m. By chance we met a Canadian diplomat, David Horley, who was out with his wife for an evening stroll. When they learned of our predicament they invited us to their apartment. We accepted, and this move stymied the police, who could not enter the home of a diplomat and therefore could no longer "accompany" us. But police vehicles pulled right up to the gate of the Horleys' apartment building, where they waited, at the ready.

Countermeasure Five: A police escort to a press conference.

This was the most baffling of the countermeasures. During the hour between 8:30 and 9:30 p.m. at the Horley apartment, we received calls from journalists. They had noticed that the seats for Fang Lizhi and Li Shuxian at the banquet were empty and they had called our residence to find out why. Our son Fang Zhe, who was at home, knew we were at the Horleys' because we had called him from there right away, just to assure him that we were all right. He gave the Horleys' number to reporters, and the stream of their calls was incessant. We decided to go to the Shangri-La Hotel, where hundreds of international journalists who had come to Beijing to cover the Bush visit were centered. This would be more efficient: we could answer everyone's questions at once. We had to assume that the authorities were listening in when we mentioned the plan on the telephone, and we worried that police might once again appear to prevent us from seeing the journalists. Horley volunteered his car, and we indeed were followed—but not blocked. We reached the Shangri-La with no problems.

Why did they let us go? The most plausible explanation for the peculiar forbearance is that the authorities, in drawing up their plan for the evening, had omitted the journalism question. The job of Chinese police is to carry out plans; if something is not in a plan, they do not take initiatives on their own.

Let me insert an anecdote to illustrate this mentality. In October 1987 a researcher at the Beijing Observatory was killed in an automobile accident. The traffic police requested, repeatedly, that the death be recorded as "accidental," not as a "traffic death." They wanted this because the quota for traffic deaths in their annual plan was nearly full. If the number of traffic deaths were to exceed the number in the plan, they would not get their bonuses for plan fulfillment. Their problem was that the bereaved family would not honor the request. The family insisted that the death be truthfully recorded as a traffic death while the police continued to make up reasons why "accident" was a better label. The family eventually prevailed, but in January of the new year, the police unfurled a splendid banner in front of the Beijing Observatory. I can't remember it word for word, but it was something like STRUGGLE HARD TO FILL THIS YEAR'S PLAN FOR THE NUMBER OF TRAFFIC DEATHS!

In any case, at 11:30 on the evening of the banquet, at an impromptu press conference for international journalists, we explained what had happened. The reporters were excited. From the police point of view, the work plan of several hundred personnel had been successfully executed. But the success had stolen from President Bush the headlines in the next day's newspapers all around the world.

After the banquet affair, the authorities redoubled their "care" for me.

On the evening of March 6, 1989, I boarded the Beijing–Shanghai Express to go to the annual meeting of the Chinese Astronomical Society in Suzhou. Three colleagues from the Beijing Observatory traveled with me, as did a graduate student who had been my assistant when I served as vice president of the University of Science and Technology of China. The trip was uneventful, and we arrived on time the next morning at the New Shanghai station.

Three people were there to meet us—or to meet me, I should say, because they paid little attention to the others. The chief greeter was Yang Yiquan, deputy director of the famous Purple Mountain Observatory in Nanjing. It was clear that the authorities had deputized him to "care" for me. I knew Yang as a colleague and, not wanting to cause him trouble, readily accepted his care and got into the car that was waiting for us. We departed Shanghai, where "problems" in the wake of the banquet affair were still rife, and headed for Suzhou.

Yang was straightforward. As soon as our car had left the station, he turned to me and said, "Do you think we could avoid setting off any atomic bombs in Suzhou, my good fellow? We're old friends; please promise me this."

I knew, of course, what he meant by "atomic bombs."

"I'm here for the Big Bang in the cosmos, not for any other," I answered.

This reply accorded with my general policy. Ever since that conference on gravitational physics in Guangzhou in 1987, I had made it a point to limit my activity at scientific meetings to the reading of scientific papers and to say nothing about political or social questions. I did this to save trouble for my colleagues, and the meetings in Suzhou would be no different. I would read my paper on the origins of the universe. My only other goal would be to visit Guanqian Street to buy some of the dried tofu for which Suzhou is famous.

The main difference between the situations in Suzhou and Guangzhou was that here, for five days, every single one of my activities got special care. (This included even a special car and special companionship for my stroll along Guanqian Street.) The other astronomers, through their association with me, received care as well. For the duration of the conference, no one but formal participants was allowed inside our hotel. The manager had orders that the hotel receive no guests other than astronomers and that no outsiders be allowed to visit any guest. The official reason offered for this policy was that the stars and the universe that the scientists were studying were extremely sensitive secrets that had to be protected at all costs. The astronomers, bemused at this dramatic elevation of their status, felt an odd elation.

Certain others, though, experienced train wreck. Two editors from the Education Publishing House in Shanghai, for example, were staying for a few days at Suzhou University, and one of them had been the editor for my book *A Bird's-Eye View of the Frontiers of Astrophysics*. When they heard that I was in Suzhou, they invited me to dinner at the Suzhou University dining hall on the evening of March 8. I accepted. No one else was present when we spoke, and yet, less than three hours later, authorities at Suzhou University summoned the two editors for interrogation: How had they made contact with Fang Lizhi? Why were they inviting him, of all people, to eat at Suzhou University? And so on. My two friends answered the questions, one by one, with the plain truth, and in the end their punishment was thankfully light: it was that they must leave Suzhou University immediately, and never, ever, try to eat there again.

Astrophysicists are fond of puzzles, and when word of this episode spread among the conference participants, the question of the day became, "Exactly how did the authorities know within only three hours that Fang Lizhi was going to Suzhou University for dinner?" The theoretical astrophysicists applied their rigorous methods of logic to rule out a number of possible explanations, while the observational astronomers invoked the methods with which they were most familiar: detection of which personnel in the hotel were the most likely moles for State Security.

With heaven's favor, and despite the minor distractions, the five-day conference ended in success. When we said our good-byes, Yang Yiquan was effusive in his warmth. Clearly grateful to me, he noted that "no atom bomb went off."

But there was, alas, another atom bomb whose explosion was edging ever closer in that season.

As it happens, atomic explosion provides a surprisingly apt metaphor for Chinese society in the spring of 1989. Three elements, basically, are necessary for the detonation of an atomic bomb: (1) fissionable material in sufficient amount, (2) a means to coalesce the fissionable material into a critical mass, and (3) timely neutron bombardment. China in 1989 had, metaphorically speaking, all three.

First, the supply of fissionable material: Ever more obvious corruption, stalled political reform, and tight constraints on freedom of speech and of the press were producing anger, frustration, and resentment among students, intellectuals, workers, small-time entrepreneurs, Party functionaries, and even some high-ranking officials. The potential for explosion was growing steadily.

Second, factors that could bring the fissionable material to a critical mass: The several anniversaries in 1989—the seventieth of the May Fourth Movement, the fortieth of the People's Republic of China, and the tenth of the Democracy Wall movement—could become vortices in the sea of unorganized popular resentment.

Third, neutron bombardment: Flying neutrons were in pretty steady supply. Small skirmishes kept popping up, now here, now there, in response to various ham-handed moves by the government. The clumsy handling of the "open letters on amnesty" was one of those bombarding neutrons.

The death on April 15 of Hu Yaobang, the reformist former General Secretary of the Communist Party, accelerated the coalescence of the fissionable material and eventually exceeded, by a considerable margin, the threshold for a critical mass. Next: explosion!

When the student demonstrations began, my daily life fell into a pattern: in the mornings I went to work at the Observatory, in the afternoons I stayed at home receiving various visitors—mostly friends and students, but also reporters—and in the evenings I did my writing. Between April 16, when the student movement started, and May 20, when the regime declared martial law, I finished a paper called "Biased Clustering in a Universe with Hot Dark Matter and a Cosmic String." I met with reporters a total of fifty-seven times.

I always expressed support for the student movement when reporters asked me about it. But I never joined the demonstrations and never went to Tiananmen Square. My reason for staying away was that on April 20, just a few days after the demonstrations began, municipal-level authorities were already issuing internal memoranda saying that the uprising was the personal handiwork of Fang Lizhi and his wife. It was their justification-in-waiting for the moment when an order to crush the movement might arrive from the top.

I owe a debt of gratitude to my colleagues at the Beijing Observatory for finding ways during those days to shield me from the thrusts the authorities were delivering. An important example came on April 27, when students organized a large demonstration to protest an editorial in the previous day's *People's Daily*. That editorial had labeled their movement "turmoil" and said it had been instigated by "a tiny minority" of people with "ulterior motives." The language was obviously intended to prepare a case for suppression. It was a standard tactic, which had been used many times before, and my astrophysicist colleagues had little trouble guessing that the iniquitous "tiny minority" included me. Sure enough, when people came back from the demonstration that evening, they reported that word had been passed through the crowd that Fang Lizhi was mixing with the demonstrators—"running around giving orders." This was a bad sign.

I was lucky that my colleagues at the Observatory were such astute readers of official tactics. An event at the Observatory had long been scheduled for the morning of April 27—the French astrophysicist Jean-Marc Bonnet-Bidaud was to speak on "Millisecond Pulsars." Should my colleagues cancel the event because of the "turmoil" on the streets? Not only did they not cancel it; they assigned me to chair it. Then, as they walked into the seminar room, quite a number of them said things like, "We can be witnesses: Fang Lizhi was not on the streets with the protesters today." That was *before* anybody had reports about the Fang Lizhi rumors running through the streets; my colleagues had divined the authorities' plan in advance.

April 28, the next day, was the first time anyone advised Li Shuxian and me to leave our home and go into hiding. A group of younger colleagues came to us with this proposal, and they put it to us in no uncertain terms. They had heard, from well-placed sources near the pinnacle of state power, that "the relevant offices" were drawing up concrete plans to "deal with" Fang Lizhi. My movements were already being closely monitored, they said. (One piece of evidence that they were right about this is that the film the government later released to show that I had been a turmoil instigator included footage of me going to work at the Observatory during those days.) My young colleagues had already prepared a hiding place for us and had devised some special ways to communicate (which included, for example, picking up the telephone only after the eighth ring). They also offered training in how to throw off tailers on bicycles.

I respectfully declined their offers. I did not feel that the situation had deteriorated to the point where hiding would be necessary, and I felt reluctant to pull out so abruptly from my work at the Observatory. But I did heed the warnings: I paid more attention to who was following by bicycle, and I avoided walking outdoors at night. One never knew.

On May 12 the protesting students began a hunger strike, and a few days later, when the strike was at high tide, it so dominated the news that even the visit to Beijing of Soviet leader Mikhail Gorbachev was bumped from the headlines. The protesters in Beijing had riveted the attention of the world. For a few days it seemed that a brighter day for China was just around the corner, and those were the days when I really did wish that I could go down to Tiananmen to have a look at the stirring scenes. A number of students and friends—especially overseas friends—urged me to do it. "It's time!" they kept saying. "You should go!" But colleagues who were closer to the realities at home were unanimous in insisting that I not appear at any public occasion. The road ahead was not nearly that bright, in their view, and the danger that "an unfortunate accident" might befall me was still very real. My colleagues at the Observatory, as they gathered to head out to the demonstrations, sometimes stopped by my office to say, "You stay here, and don't worry—we will represent you."

On May 18, Professor Zhang Wuchang of Hong Kong University telephoned me with an earnest plea that I go to Tiananmen Square to persuade the students to end their hunger strike. I, too, felt that it would be better to end the hunger strike, and Zhang's passionate appeal was almost enough to nudge me into action. For a moment I thought I should try. But on second thought, I stifled the impulse and stayed home. My experience of December 23, 1986, when I persuaded the USTC students to end their sit-in at Hefei, had shown me the furthest limits of my influence. There was no way I had the power to persuade the students at Tiananmen Square to end their hunger strike.

In the days after martial law was announced on May 20, rumors of arrest lists spread through Beijing. Who were the people the government was ready to nab and "rectify"? These lists came in several versions, but my name was on every one—sometimes higher, sometimes lower. My friends at the Observatory all thought that I should leave Beijing, perhaps by finding some scholarly meeting to go to.

The mood in the city was abnormal in those days. Even traffic was odd. Many scholarly meetings were simply canceled. The world of astronomy soldiered on, however, persisting with a plan to hold a meeting from May 24 to 29 in Datong, Shanxi Province, on "high-energy stars." Was this an atavism of the habits of ancient Chinese astronomers? For them, the more unstable society was, the harder they worked, because troubled times were exactly when society most needed their astrology.

In any case, on the evening of May 24, a colleague and I left Beijing by train for Datong. At the Changping station on the northwest outskirts of Beijing, our train had to thread its way through the station on the only available track, because all the other tracks were crowded with military carriages. These were the cars that would carry the troops who, a few days later, would kill their way eastward into the heart of Beijing.

Despite its perilous context, the meeting of astronomers in Datong went off without a hitch. My paper was on "High-Energy Processes in Supernova 1987A." On May 26 the conference had a day off, and some of us went to visit the famous nearby Hanging Temple, whose construction is truly stunning. None of its several dozen halls of various sizes rests on a foundation in the ground; the whole edifice clings to the side of a towering vertical rock wall. The philosophical point that the construction suggests is that in order to cultivate oneself into Buddhahood, one must leave the earth, must transcend, must rise above the troubles of mundane human life.

As I looked down from the Hanging Temple on the people below, I saw them there still: plainclothes police—watching, waiting.

20. THIRTEEN MONTHS

PRECISELY TEN DAYS AFTER COMING DOWN FROM THE HANGING TEMPLE, I walked into the United States embassy in Beijing to take refuge. Who could have imagined such a turn of events? I daresay that almost no one in Beijing, almost no Chinese person anywhere, and almost no television viewers around the world were ready to believe that what was about to happen during those ten days could ever happen. Here's what happened: the central government of China mobilized two hundred thousand regular troops, supplied them with regular military weaponry (tanks and submachine guns), and used regular military formations and tactics to force an entry into its own capital city—territory that it already held.

Then, about 9:00 p.m. on June 3, a massacre of students and other citizens began. At 9:30 Li Shuxian and I received a phone call from a student at Muxidi, the first of the massacre sites. The caller urged us to flee. We could hear gunshots in the background.

The outbreak of killing, horrible in itself, was also a sign to Li Shuxian and me that our own situation had taken a sharp turn for the worse. We felt this because a few days earlier the Chinese authorities, in preparing the ground for what they were about to do, had organized a "demonstration" in a Beijing suburb. They issued straw hats to farmers, paid them 15 yuan apiece, and ordered them to go out and chant

"Down with Fang Lizhi!" At the end of the demonstration the farmers burned a paper effigy of me.

Some of my colleagues overseas were intensely worried when they saw this news. Remo Ruffini called from Italy about twice a day. He just wanted to hear my voice in order to assure himself that I had not been arrested and that some kind of unpredictable thing had not happened. I myself, preoccupied by immediate events, did not sense that much danger. Seeing the effigy burn actually gave me a sense more of ludicrousness than of terror.

A journalist asked one of the protesters, "Do you know Fang Lizhi?"

"No."

"Then why do you want to knock him down?"

"They said he won't let us go into the city to sell watermelons."

After the massacre, though, no humor of any sort was appropriate. We got quite a few phone calls. They were all short, like the one from the student at Muxidi: "Run." "Get out now." "Save yourselves." Still I felt hesitant. Flee our home during peacetime? Something seemed wrong with that. About 11:00 a.m. on June 4 we got a phone call from an old friend, a man who used to work in an organization at the highest level of the government. Afraid that the police who regularly tapped our phone might recognize his voice, he substituted the dialect of his hometown for the standard Mandarin that he normally used with us.

"I'm using a public telephone on the street to call you," he said. "What are you waiting for? Why aren't you out looking for a clean place to stay?"

In the past, his information had always been reliable. His call made us realize that we really did have to consider leaving home.

We had four alternatives. Two were to go hide for a while in nearby homes of friends. The two friends who made this offer both came to see us on the afternoon of June 4. The third alternative was to go to the home of a professor who lived rather far away; a friend had already arranged a car that could pick us up at 8:00 p.m. The fourth alternative was to go to the U.S. embassy. Professor Perry Link had said he could help.

After thinking it over we ruled out the first three alternatives. We did not want to pull friends down with us in our ill fate. But we did not want to go straight to the U.S. embassy, either, because we worried that once this fact was known, the regime could use it to "show" that foreigners had instigated the whole student movement. So we chose a compromise. We went to the Shangri-La Hotel, where CBS Television helped us, and spent a night there.

At that point we were still underestimating the seriousness of the matter. We still thought that after a few days of flying bullets and prowling soldiers, it might be safe to go home again. That's why, when I left home, I carried only a small briefcase holding a few daily-use items plus partial drafts of two articles. A half hour before we left home, I asked a friend to come pick up some research manuscripts and letters and take them to the Beijing Observatory, where I thought I could use them when I returned to work after a few days.

But the next day, June 5, conditions got no better. Sporadic gunfire continued. It was clear that we couldn't stay very long at the Shangri-La. Around noon, we headed for the other side of the city, to the U.S. embassy, accompanied by Professor Perry Link and a CBS employee who carried an emergency telephone. At the embassy we made two requests: that we be allowed to stay a few days, and that our presence be kept secret. The embassy people told us frankly that the second request would be almost impossible to meet.* So, still not wanting to create news that the regime could exploit, we left the embassy around 5:00 p.m.

We went to the nearby Jianguo Hotel for the night. Beijing remained in a warlike state. Cannon fire was audible in the distance, and as midnight approached we still could not sleep. Suddenly there was a knock at the door. It was Raymond Burghardt and another official from the U.S. embassy. They were dressed in casual clothing but seemed burdened and tense. Was their workload too heavy? Were the streets under martial law too gloomy? What was it? In any case they lowered their voices and said, very formally, "We invite you to our embassy as the guests of our president; you may live there as long as you need."

Matters had clearly escalated. By now it would be hard to make any

---

*Translator's note: The U.S. diplomats pointed out that Fang had already been "noticed" by Chinese staff who were supplied by the Ministry of Foreign Affairs; they noted, too, that the room in which Raymond Burghardt (deputy chief of mission), Russell McKinney (head of the embassy's USIA office), Fang Lizhi, Li Shuxian, Fang Zhe, and I were talking was "not secure" from listening devices.

other choice, so we accepted. A few minutes later we got into an embassy car that was waiting at the back of the hotel. Like other formal guests, we were driven straight to the ambassador's residence. We arrived at midnight on June 6, 1989, and that moment began our thirteen months (384 days and 10.5 hours, to be precise) of life in refuge.

That same day a White House spokesman confirmed our location. The fact was public now, and this was both good and bad. The good part was that our friends all knew where we were and that we had protection. In the next twenty-four hours we began receiving sympathetic telegrams and faxes from both inside China and overseas.

The bad part—the dangerous part—was the risk of precipitating a forced entry of the embassy by Chinese soldiers. Diplomatic protocol forbids this sort of thing, but for a regime that had just carried out a massacre, who could say? Protocol was no guarantee. In 1967, rampaging Red Guards had burned the British embassy to the ground. In 1989, might an irrational regime crash in to grab Fang Lizhi? It could have happened.

The first three weeks were the tensest. James Lilley, the U.S. ambassador, had just been appointed and had not yet moved into the ambassador's residence, where we were housed. The building was basically unoccupied. The daylight hours seemed safe enough, but at night only a lone watchman was there, and under cover of darkness it would not have been hard to break in and whisk two people away. The regime could thumb its nose at diplomatic objections and just say "the angry masses" had demanded it.

The best defense, the Americans told us, was to make it seem that the entire building was empty. This meant avoiding any sign on the outside that anyone at all was inside. Tactics included: make no phone calls, and do not answer the phone; allow only the ambassador and one or two other people to have contact; at night, keep any interior light far dimmer than the exterior light in the adjacent streets; in the toilets, flushing and drainage must be soundless; in sleep, no sleep-talking or sleep-singing. That last item was the most difficult, but we managed.

We felt constantly on edge. The tension reached a peak on June 12 when the authorities published warrants for our arrest. Even the night watchman, who was afraid of a replay of the incineration of the British embassy, wore a haggard expression. We made contingency plans, just in case. But two weeks passed and nothing happened. There were not even any staged protests—no burning of effigies—outside the embassy gates. The danger seemed to be subsiding.

Was this forbearance on the part of the authorities, or pursuit of their own interests in another guise? It was the latter, I'm sorry to say—it is always the latter. Consider the following story, which was relayed to us by Ambassador Lilley: In the days right after the massacre, the number of applications for U.S. visas from the children of the top leaders remained the same or was even slightly higher than it had been before. One day in July, Teng Teng, the vice chair of the State Education Commission, summoned Ambassador Lilley to deliver a stern protest of the recent decision by the U.S. Congress to allow Chinese students in the United States who had spoken out against the massacre to extend their U.S. stays indefinitely. After the denunciation, the ambassador returned to his residence and, in less than an hour, received a telephone call from the secretary of the same Teng Teng. The reason for the call was to entreat the ambassador to see to it that Teng Teng's wife's application for a U.S. visa be approved. In addition, could he please arrange that Madame Teng Teng be given "indefinite residence" status? It turned out that the couple's four children were already in the United States and already had this status. Now let's ask this: How likely is it that officials like these, so intensely focused on getting their families out to America, would be so stupid as to risk all by breaking into an embassy to grab a couple of criminals? Many a weird thing has happened in human history, and here, certainly, is one: the psychology of the shameless bureaucrat had become our first line of defense.

But we couldn't, of course, put too much trust in a defense built on people to whom fundamental morality was alien, and that is why, for the entire thirteen months of our stay in the embassy, our location had to remain just as secret as it was on the first day. The windows of our "apartment" were nailed shut with thick boards, a security alarm was installed on the door, and we never dared to walk in the courtyard.

Underground tunnels were a considerable worry. In the early 1970s, during the Cultural Revolution, a web of tunnels about six to ten feet below the surface had been built all across Beijing. Entrances to this tunnel maze were everywhere, and some, although now blocked off, had already been found inside the ambassador's residence. One had to wonder: Had they really been blocked off? And where did they lead? There were no maps for this sort of thing. Deep at night we could hear, quite clearly, the muffled sounds of footsteps—plunk, plunk—somewhere, and it was frightening. It was only a modest comfort to realize, when we thought about it, that since those sounds were so audible, if someone really were to try to dig an illegal tunnel to us it would not be hard to hear them coming.

In any case, our blanket of protection extended from the skies above into the earth below. The regime, too, watched everything between heaven and earth to prevent us from slipping out. During August and September a rumor spread that Fang Lizhi and Li Shuxian had been spirited out of the embassy by some secret means and now were already living outside the country. The Chinese authorities gave some credence to these rumors and made a number of formal demands through diplomatic channels that Ambassador Lilley promise that the Fang couple not be transported out of China secretly. The ambassador declined to respond to those inquiries, and his nonresponse fed further speculation that the Americans were preparing (or perhaps had already accomplished) a secret evacuation of the Fangs from China.

On October 28, 1989, the U.S. embassy hosted a Halloween party. By custom, at such events, invitees wear masks, and some Americans that evening had the bright idea of wearing Fang Lizhi masks. When the Chinese authorities heard this, they panicked. They ordered the Ministry of Foreign Affairs to summon the U.S. ambassador and to deliver a stern warning that the Fang Lizhi couple not be smuggled out of the embassy using Halloween disguises. To this the ambassador did respond. He guaranteed that he would not choose Halloween as the day to see his guests off.

We ourselves never had any impulse to sneak out. We were guests. Should guests have to steal out a side door? But we cooperated in the secrecy, which of course was necessary. At one point the embassy ran a test to see how the secrecy was doing. Since all of the non-American embassy staff had been assigned their jobs by the Chinese Ministry of Foreign Affairs, it was impossible to know which of them had covert espionage duties. The embassy's test was to put out an item of false news about asylees in order to observe the reaction of embassy staff. The result of the test showed that the authorities did not know which area of the embassy compound held asylees and did not know how many there were.

At least three foreign embassies in Beijing protected people after the Tiananmen massacre, but our case was the only one the media and the public knew about. In matters like this, negotiations between two governments are normally easier if the media are kept out, because that leaves more room to maneuver. In our case, the Chinese government had to worry about saving face, and the U.S. government felt pressure to be seen as upholding principle. Room to maneuver shrank on both sides. The other post-Tiananmen cases, which did not hit the media, were all resolved within three months, but ours remained locked in stalemate.

Asylum in embassies elsewhere, in earlier times, had sometimes lasted five or ten years. We were prepared, therefore, that the stalemate in our case might hold for some time—something like three or five years, until the people who had ordered our arrest had stepped down, or perhaps had died.

I felt fortunate that my professional work was a kind that could survive through long-term solitude. One day, during an informal visit by the ambassador, he said he felt sorry that "you're an astrophysicist but we can't even give you a room from which you can see the sky."

"That's okay," I answered. "I'm a theoretical astrophysicist. I don't need to see the sky in order to tell you what's going on there."

What I needed was a computer. Again I was fortunate, because one of the diplomats, who originally had been a student of mathematics, was being transferred back home and was ready to part with his first-generation Apple computer. It was an old machine, not as good as the one I had left at home—which by now had been confiscated in a police raid and could not be retrieved in any case. That old Apple was less than ideal but it would do. I could study the universe with it. I reflected on the fact that the great physicists who had designed the first atomic bomb did not even have calculators. I programmed the Apple so that it could run all night doing calculations. I think the regime's surveillance equipment could probably detect the ultra-high-frequency signals that the machine was emitting, but I seriously doubt that they could understand that what they were hearing was a model for a multiply-connected universe.

Shortly after we entered the embassy, astrophysicist friends around the world began sending me materials—books, articles, and copies of the major professional journals. These grew to be so numerous that the man who delivered mail at the embassy joked with us, "Your mail is overloading the diplomatic pouch—you should ask your physicist friends to pay postage to the State Department." We felt better when an American physicist wrote to us saying, "I paid my taxes today and felt okay about it—with you living in our embassy, at least my government is getting something right."

The first article I finished inside the embassy, which I sent out for publication in September, was called "An Upper Limit to the Intrinsic Velocity of Quasars." The Fermi National Accelerator Laboratory in the United States then began distributing preprints of my articles, and colleagues inside China could obtain them that way. This was important for more than scientific reasons. Our entry into the embassy had meant that we were completely and abruptly cut off from our friends in Beijing. My scientific articles at Fermi were the first new signs they had of us. One colleague who figured out a way to get a letter to us in the embassy wrote, "We were relieved to see your article; it gave us confidence that you could hold out until those people die off."

This colleague had it right. We could hold out. There was no problem at all with our spirits. Our problem was physical—we didn't have enough space for activity. For thirteen months, the area in which we could move was only forty-two paces at its widest. But we were prepared to be patient. A year? Two years? Three? Five? We could wait.

The men who ruled China, though, could wait only four months. When we entered the embassy they at first were elated. They had been dealt wonderful cards to play both internationally and domestically. To the world they could say, "Look how the United States is meddling in our domestic affairs," and to the Chinese people they had "evidence" that the student movement had been manufactured and directed by the Americans working through Fang Lizhi. Apparently judging that this card would be useful for quite some time, the authorities brushed off several early proposals from the Americans to resolve the crisis by sending us to a third country. Brent Scowcroft, the U.S. National Security Advisor, who was sent by President Bush as a special emissary to China, ran into a brick wall on this issue. Chinese authorities told him that Fang Lizhi was now a burden on America's back that the United States would just have to bear.

Meanwhile the official Chinese press was busy denouncing us. Its message was monotone: anyone under protection in a foreign embassy is a "traitor." The authorities were apparently calculating that if they just kept repeating, "Fang Lizhi is a traitor, a traitor, a huge traitor," the United States would eventually come to feel that the burden was indeed too heavy to bear and would turn Fang and Li over to the Chinese government to face punishment. What they didn't realize was that the thief's tactic of crying "Stop, thief!" could work only inside their own country; it didn't work in other countries. In fact, the more loudly we were denounced as traitors in China, the more mail we got from U.S. citizens who wrote that the Chinese government's repression and persecution of us increased the pride that they felt in our being guests in their country's embassy. Perhaps because American administrations are beholden to voters who have sentiments like this, it seemed that the more the Chinese government shouted "Traitor!" the more the American government felt that the "burden" was becoming valuable. After each new volley of invective from the Chinese press, our treatment from our American hosts seemed to improve. At one point, when Li Shuxian got a toothache, the Americans flew a top-quality dentist all the way from Tokyo to pull the tooth and fix the problem.

In September the shouts of "Traitor!" receded and then disappeared altogether. One reason for the decline was that the Communist Party needed to mark the approaching hundredth anniversary of the birth of Li Dazhao, one of its founders. Li, a hero in the Communist pantheon, was hanged in 1927 by the Beiyang warlord government. His martyrdom was always a shining star in the Party's historical record, but now, by very bad luck, one point in his résumé was making people think of Fang Lizhi. Shortly before his execution, Li had taken refuge in the embassy of the Soviet Union in Beijing. After roundly denouncing him as a "traitor," the warlord authorities had sent soldiers charging into the embassy to grab him by force. These facts were now presenting a dilemma for Chinese propaganda officials. How could one denounce a person who had fled to the American embassy as a despicable traitor while at the same time praising a person who had fled to the Soviet embassy as a "great pioneer of the Communist Party"? What a dilemma! I almost felt sorry for them. In the end, they took two measures: none of the many articles on Li Dazhao should mention his embassy stay, and the mantra of "fleeing to embassies is traitorous" should dwindle and die. I owe a debt of gratitude to Li Dazhao. My fellow "traitor," seeker of asylum, I hereby direct a bow toward your spirit in heaven!

From that point on, the Fang Lizhi burden shifted from the U.S. government to the Chinese government. On October 1, 1989, China's National Day, the Chinese side made its first move toward "solving the Fang problem." Xie Xide, the president of Fudan University in Shanghai, approached the American consul general in Shanghai to ask, "What can we do to solve the Fang Lizhi problem?" The regime's choice of Xie to make this overture seems to have been carefully considered. Professionally, Xie was a physicist, had once been Li Shuxian's teacher, and knew the two of us well. Politically, she was a member of the Central Committee of the Communist Party of China. Moreover, she had ties with the United States—she had studied there and had been a frequent visitor in recent years.

Shortly thereafter, the president of the Chinese Academy of Sciences, who was also a member of the Communist Party Central Committee, revealed to the president of the U.S. National Academy of Sciences during a visit to the United States that it was his "personal opinion" that "the Fang Lizhi problem can be solved."

Next, Hu Qiaomu, a member of the Party's ruling politburo, made a cameo appearance. He told Kenneth Lieberthal, an American professor with ties to President Nixon, that he was ready to mediate the Fang Lizhi problem in an unofficial capacity.

Here again we can observe that "things stop at three." The Chinese government calculated that three "unofficial" gestures would be enough to get the Americans, who presumably were desperate to solve this problem, to come up with a response. And in November, the Americans did.

Two important Americans, Richard Nixon and Henry Kissinger, had already been scheduled to pay unofficial visits to Deng Xiaoping in

November. Nixon indicated that he would be willing to assist the U.S. government on the Fang question, but Kissinger refused. He said he wanted no part of the problem.

Deng Xiaoping received Nixon and Kissinger, his "old friends," on November 2 and November 14, respectively. The Fang issue came up both times. Kissinger had not wanted to touch it, but Deng brought it up on his own and left Kissinger with no alternative.

With both men, Deng made two points: (1) Fang Lizhi can leave China; and (2) Fang must confess his wrongdoing and promise never to oppose the Chinese government again. Deng's goals were obvious: he wanted to restore an "old friend" relationship with the U.S. government while also getting rid of an "old thorn in his side"—me. His primary tactic was clear as well: pass the problem of getting me to "confess" over to the U.S. side.

On November 15, Ambassador Lilley dutifully presented me with this imperial admonition from Deng Xiaoping:

> *A spokesperson for the relevant offices has published a speech urging that Fang Lizhi and Li Shuxian seek lenient treatment by surrendering themselves as soon as possible.*
>
> *The spokesperson stated that, with the enthusiastic support of the people of the entire country, we have already won a decisive victory in curtailing the turmoil and pacifying the counterrevolutionary riot. Social order in the present stage has already been returned to normal and the domestic situation is more stable than before. Inspired by the policies of the Party and the government, many people who committed crimes during the turmoil and the riots have surrendered to public security organs and have received generous treatment.*
>
> *The spokesperson further stated that, after the pacification of the counterrevolutionary riot, a number of Chinese at different times hid inside the embassies of foreign countries in China. At present, except for the two people Fang Lizhi and Li Shuxian, who remain inside the embassy of the United States, all of the others have earlier or later left the organizations of foreign countries in China and have received generous treat-*

ment from the Chinese government and forgiveness from the
Chinese people.

The spokesperson urged Fang Lizhi and Li Shuxian to mend
the errors of their ways, leave the U.S. embassy in China with-
out delay, and seek generous treatment.

I interpreted this letter inviting me to surrender as Deng Xiaoping's answer to my letter to him of January 6. Even the word count of the two missives was about the same.

The first formal meeting between the Chinese and American governments on the Fang Lizhi problem took place on November 18, and it was followed by several more. In early December, President Bush again dispatched Brent Scowcroft to Beijing, and after that, things seemed to be reaching a head. We were guardedly optimistic that we could be out by Christmas.

Then, just as suddenly as hope had risen, it crashed. It turned out there were two things that Deng Xiaoping wanted from the Americans that even an American president could not deliver: one was a lifting of the economic sanctions on China that the U.S. Congress had imposed after the June Fourth massacre, and the other was a confession from Fang Lizhi. Deng's miscalculation of what he could get was rooted, fundamentally, in his inability to step outside the worldview of an emperor. Inside China, the top ruler can decide who is guilty of a crime without any need for legal procedure (or, at most, in advance of legal "procedure" that confirms decisions after they are made). Deng truly did not understand that some other parts of the world do not work this way.

At one point I suggested to Ambassador Lilley that he ask the Chinese authorities exactly what law I had broken. After all, it would be easier to write a confession if I knew what to confess to. A few days later the ambassador returned to say he had put the question and heard a response. A deputy minister of foreign affairs had replied that "Fang's crimes are obvious." So what was I supposed to write down? That I am guilty of "everybody-knows-what"?

The exchange did clarify one point, though. It showed that six months after the regime had issued a warrant for our arrest, it still had not figured out what the charges were. More than a month later, the same deputy minister finally agreed to read to the ambassador a "statement of facts" concerning "fourteen points" in the criminal behavior of Fang Lizhi and Li Shuxian. The ambassador told us that the deputy minister read the statement in a tone of voice that suggested it was a legal indictment. But the language itself floated well above the law—never referring to which provision of what law had been violated. The official declined, moreover, to give the ambassador a written copy of his statement. It was for ears only. Perhaps he himself did not have much confidence in the accuracy of what he was orating and did not want it to turn into a diplomatic document.

When the ambassador, speaking from notes and memory, recounted to us what he could recall of the "fourteen points," the deputy minister's wisdom in withholding a written version became more apparent. Two examples will suffice to illustrate the low quality of the material.

According to the "points," one of Li Shuxian's crimes was that on April 18, 1989, she issued an order to the Autonomous Federation of Students at Peking University. But according to the regime's own newspaper, *People's Daily*, that student group was founded on April 19. From a lawyer's point of view, this would be like charging a person with a murder on day X of a person born on day X+1. Example two: One of Fang Lizhi's crimes was that he manipulated speakers at the Peking University democracy salon in order to propagandize counterrevolutionary ideology. But according, again, to *People's Daily,* two of the main speakers at that salon were the former U.S. ambassador, Winston Lord, and his wife, Bette Bao Lord. It would follow that Fang Lizhi committed the crime of manipulating the U.S. ambassador and his wife. Should this be a violation of Chinese law or of U.S. law?

We decided to write "An Answer to the Fourteen Points." It consisted of fifteen points, the fifteenth of which was that Fang Lizhi would be happy to give open testimony—for example, in the newspapers or on television—on the fourteen points. But the authorities ignored the offer, just as they had in the "libel case" about foreign bank accounts in 1988. And with that, the first attempts to solve "the Fang Lizhi problem" ground to a halt.

The government went on New Year's break in February 1990 and was preoccupied with other matters in March, so it wasn't until April that they got around to trying something else on the Fang front. Their new tactic was to ask the Americans just to bracket the problem and not let two little asylees get in the way of great-power relations. (They did this partly in response to a comment that I had made in a letter to a famous American television reporter. I had observed that Li Shuxian and I were "stuck between the governments of two superpowers," and the foreign media had found the notion of "stuck between superpowers" to be fascinating.) But the regime's new tactic didn't work. The U.S. Congress in those days was monitoring Chinese human rights issues closely, and there was no way the issue could be "bracketed."

After this and a few other frustrations, the Chinese authorities returned to the "confession" route. But now they set the bar lower—much lower. The "fourteen points" were gone. All they asked for now was a statement from Fang Lizhi that—one way or another—contained the two words "I confess." As it happened, I had already written a statement during the first round of negotiations in November 1989 and had revised it several times since. None of my versions, alas, included the words "I confess." Should I add them now?

In April and May, the authorities went on an offensive. Every time their spokespeople met the media, they made a point of saying that Fang Lizhi would be allowed to leave China if he confessed. Their effort bore fruit. Friends overseas began writing to us recommending that we take this deal. Some advised us simply to lie. Just say "I confess"—that will at least get you out where you can do some good in the world. It's worth it! Some of them assured us that if you cross your fingers when you lie, God forgives. Friends from Rome wrote that false confession is not officially a sin if it is spoken under duress. Even the great Galileo had once written a "confession"—so what, they asked, was I worried about? They mailed me a copy of Galileo's confession for reference. The more panicky among them drafted some actual language I could use in confessing. Before it was over I received three complete drafts of ready-to-go confessions.

And I might, in the end, have picked one of these if the Communist authorities had opted to let things keep dragging on. But they did not. For some reason they moved decisively to wrap things up. It took ten days, as follows:

Saturday, June 16: American and Chinese diplomats conferred, after which the Chinese Foreign Ministry made it clear that Fang Lizhi and Li Shuxian would be permitted to leave China and that the condition would no longer be confession. There need be only a written request to go abroad for medical treatment, couched in language that somewhere included the word "lenient." There would also need to be a guarantee of nonparticipation in any overseas activities that oppose the Chinese government.

We accepted the medical parole idea but refused to ask for "leniency." We agreed to promise to do nothing that opposed China, but could make no promises about opposing the Chinese government.

Sunday, June 17: The U.S. ambassador visited us again to say that the Chinese authorities would not insist on a "request for leniency"; the key phrase could now be "for humanitarian reasons." It was all right to drop the guarantee against opposing the Chinese government, but Fang and Li should not be released directly to the United States. The preferred destination would be a small, isolated island.

We accepted the word "humanitarian." We also accepted the condition that our first stop be a small island. We chose England.

Monday, June 18: I wrote a statement.

Tuesday, June 19: The diplomats met again. The Chinese Foreign Ministry reverted to asking for a confession, saying this time that the key phrase could be "admit error"—it did not have to be "admit crime."

We refused.

Wednesday, June 20: The diplomats met again. The Chinese side dropped the requirement to "admit error." With that the negotiations were declared a success and the two sides toasted each other at a state guesthouse. Right before the toast, though, the Chinese side presented a new demand: Li Shuxian would also have to sign the statement. She thought it over and decided to half-comply (see below for what that meant).

Thursday, June 21: Choosing our words carefully, we submitted this final version:

1. *I oppose the Four Basic Principles that are contained in the Preamble of the Constitution of China, because these principles function to uphold a political system of "class struggle." I am aware that the foregoing political opinion violates the Preamble of the Constitution of China.*
2. *This is an application to leave the country for travel in order to visit friends and relatives overseas and to obtain needed medical treatment and is written in expectation of humanitarian consideration by the Chinese government.*
3. *Our goals outside the country will be concentrated in areas of scholarly exchange and joint research. We will welcome and take pleasure in any activity that serves the interests of progress in Chinese society and will refuse to participate in any activity that does the opposite, i.e., that opposes China.*

June 22, 1990, Beijing

Li Shuxian and I both signed. But note: point one uses the singular pronoun *I*, point two contains no personal pronoun, and point three uses the plural *we*. So Li Shuxian officially subscribed only to point three (and arguably point two).

Friday, June 22: The diplomats met once more. The topic was technical arrangement of the departure.

Saturday, June 23: Ambassador Lilley visited us in the morning. The purpose was to take photos with which to process Chinese passports and visas for England.

Sunday, June 24: We packed our belongings. In the afternoon, local Party committees across China notified Party members that "the Fang Lizhi couple are going to leave the country for medical treatment." In the evening, the ambassador held a farewell party for us at his residence. Strict secrecy was still in place. Other than Li Shuxian and me, only six people were there.

Monday, June 25: With the summer solstice just passed, dawn arrived early.

8:00 a.m.: A hundred or more police and plainclothes agents converged around the U.S. embassy buildings.

10:30 a.m.: We walked out of the ambassador's residence. The ambassador accompanied us as we boarded the same car that had brought us into the embassy a year earlier. The car exited through the front gate of the embassy compound and headed for the Beijing Nanyuan Military Airport.

Martial law was in place along the entire route. All other traffic was blocked. A car from State Security drove in front of us. Its license plate, GA11-0001, identified it as police vehicle number one. Two other police cars followed behind "for protection." When the police who lined the route saw car 0001 approaching, they knew it must contain a "personage" and reflexively delivered salutes.

11:05 a.m.: We reached the airport. An American military aircraft was waiting.

11:30 a.m.: A Public Security officer, protected on his left and his right by two other policemen, delivered two Chinese passports to us. The man in the middle, who handed over the passports, was perspiring profusely. Perhaps he felt the weight of these two passports was just too much.

12:40 p.m.: The U.S. aircraft taxied and took off in normal fashion.

So there it was. The Chinese government had allowed an American military aircraft to fly away with two Chinese who topped a wanted list for crime. Absurd? Yes, but the world has long seen absurdity.

ABOARD THAT AMERICAN MILITARY AIRCRAFT, FANG LIZHI AND LI Shuxian headed for the "small island" of England and then to Cambridge University, where Fang had spent many pleasant days in 1979–80. When they arrived, they were met by activists from the overseas Chinese democracy movement who hoped that Fang would take a leading role with them, but Fang, adhering to his lifelong principle of being a scientist first, politely declined. It was not that he saw civic duty as a "number two" priority; he saw it as a universal value that should apply to any person in any line of work. He would continue, he said, to speak out about justice and fairness in the world while working as a professional physicist. For now, he was looking forward to "a period of quiet" for a few days.

The international press was in no mood to leave him alone, however: *How does it feel to be free? Was the crushing of the Tiananmen movement a fatal blow to Chinese democracy?* And so on. Tom Brokaw of NBC News asked Fang if U.S. human rights policy still suffered from a double standard. (Fang had said in the late 1980s that the West viewed Soviet dissidents differently from Asian dissidents; now, though, the U.S. government had given Fang and his wife thirteen months of protection in its Beijing embassy. Did that make things different?) Fang, ever the scientist, sought to answer objectively. "Without doubt there is still some double standard," he told Brokaw, even though things "are better than before." President George H. W. Bush, hearing Fang's surprising words, commented the same day, "I'd say he's wrong."

In September 1990, Fang's intellectual independence showed again in an essay he wrote for *The New York Review of Books* called "The Chinese Amnesia." Robert Silvers, editor of the *Review*, had solicited the piece, and Fang had drafted it while still inside the embassy. Silvers asked me to translate it, and when I read it I was startled. Fang had written that the 1989 democracy movement and the June Fourth massacre might soon be forgotten in China. What? How could that be? The shocking events had been broadcast to the entire world and the reverberations were still strong. Forgotten? Fang's analysis was that Chinese demands for liberalization had risen in prerevolutionary Yan'an in the 1940s, in the 1956 Hundred Flowers movement, in the 1979 Democracy Wall movement, and again in 1989—and in each case the protesters began anew. No group knew the history of protest in its country or about the progress that its predecessors had made. This happened, Fang wrote, because the Chinese Communist Party has a program for erasing the memory of protest— and it works. Party leaders will be applying it again, he predicted, and it will likely work again. I set my skepticism aside and translated the essay.

It turned out that Fang was right. Many young Chinese today have only vague impressions that something happened in 1989, and when they do feel that they "know" something, it is often colored by their government's grotesquely distorted version of events. Fang wrote his amnesia essay at a time when most people, including me, were writing about indelible memories. It was the scientist's empiricism, not sentiment or mystical vision, that had given him clairvoyance.

The agreement between the Chinese and American governments in releasing the Fangs provided that after six months on the small island they could move elsewhere. They loved their stay in Cambridge, but they left England in January 1991 and traveled to Princeton, New Jersey, where they had a long-standing invitation to return to the Institute for Advanced Study. They had visited there five years earlier and this time stayed exactly a year, until January 1992, when they moved to Tucson, where Fang had been appointed professor of physics at the University of Arizona.

In his twenty years at the University of Arizona, Fang would publish 162 papers on astrophysics. (Most were coauthored with others, usually his students.) He resumed teaching as well, and to judge from tributes that colleagues wrote after his death, he taught with gusto. He even volunteered to be a freshman adviser. Once, when his department came up short of teaching staff and needed to cover another course, he simply volunteered to do it outside his normal teaching load. His department chair, Sumit Mazumdar, recalls a hospital visit to Fang in 2011. Fang had been suffering from "valley fever," a rare lung disease caused by a fungus found in the deserts of the American Southwest. The medications that are the standard treatment for the malady have side effects, and patients often need several months, or even a year, to recover, after which residual effects can linger. Fang had a severe case of valley fever, and he had to make several visits to emergency rooms and ICUs through the late summer and fall of 2011. At the time Mazumdar visited him, he had lost sixteen pounds in less than a week and could barely walk. Yet Mazumdar found it hard to divert his conversation with Fang to any topic other than "Can you find a substitute teacher?" After he was released from the hospital, Fang spent two weeks in a nursing home and went home in late November. He began to feel a bit better over the Christmas break and, optimistically, signed on to teach full time again beginning in January 2012. Mazumdar reports that simply to walk from the parking lot to his classroom was leaving Fang short of breath, yet he still didn't want to hand off any teaching.

An anecdote from another of Fang's colleagues, Alexander Cronin, shows how Fang's intelligence and creativity—and his puckish wit—extended to his teaching of physics. During an oral exam for a Ph.D. candidacy, Cronin writes:

> *[Fang] had a twinkle in his eye. He clearly enjoyed phrasing simple, elegant questions that gave students a chance to show what they knew. He asked about the electric field inside a uniformly charged sphere. Then he asked a classic question about the electric field inside a spherical cavity (a void) with no charge that was arbitrarily located somewhere off-center but inside the*

*uniformly charged sphere. After some vector addition, this ques-
tion has a simple answer: a uniform field is found in the void.
Then came Fang's gotcha: please repeat this analysis for two
voids. The student asked for clarification, then went on to reach
a correct but cumbersome answer. The punch line as Fang
ended the session was that "two voids" is not the same as "one
plus one void." It struck me as a deep question about how and
when to apply the principle of superposition. Fang enjoyed this
and the student did, too.*

Fang could not publish inside China at any point during his time in
Arizona. Even his articles on pure science were banned. The three
Chinese characters "Fang Lizhi" could not appear in juxtaposition in
any book or article. He could have used a pseudonym but chose not to.
Despite these barriers, he maintained close contact with physics colleagues
in China. He mentored graduate students and young professors at a distance, using Skype and other electronic means, and he welcomed the
applications of Chinese graduate students to work with him in Arizona.
Some of those students have gone back to China and are now leading figures in their fields.

Finances could be a big problem for Chinese graduate students in the
United States in the 1990s. In addition to living expenses and school fees,
there were subventions that had to be paid in order to publish scientific
papers in international journals. These subventions could run to as much
as one or two thousand dollars per paper, and Chinese students had little
choice but to pay them, because they were the lifeblood of future careers
back in China.

Fang looked for ways to help his strapped students, and one of his
methods deserves special note. His younger son, Fang Zhe, came to the
United States not long after his parents arrived.* Shortly after his arrival
in the U.S., a group of friends and admirers of the family donated to a Fang

---

*Fang Zhe had been with his parents when they entered the U.S. embassy on June 6, 1989, but after only
a few days found the captivity hard to take, decided on his own to leave, and returned to the family apartment. It was nearly two years before he saw his parents again.

Zhe education fund and presented it to the parents. But Fang Lizhi reasoned that his own son did not need the money as much as others did. "If other Chinese students can do on-campus work, our son should, too," he told Li Shuxian. "Besides, Fang Zhe has us to back him up; parents in China can't do backup." With Li's agreement, Fang went back to the creators of the Fang Zhe fund and persuaded them to establish a general scholarship for students from mainland China: one student, for one year, would get about $15,000. The donors agreed and the plan went ahead. Fang and Li decided for the time being not to tell Fang Zhe what they had done. When Fang Zhe died in a car accident in 2007, he still had never heard.

Meanwhile, Fang continued with his human rights activity. In the 1990s he served as cochair of Human Rights in China (HRiC), a group based in New York whose director was the physicist turned rights activist Xiao Qiang. Xiao had been a student of Fang in the 1980s at the University of Science and Technology of China. A number of other distinguished Chinese dissidents in exile—the journalist Liu Binyan, the writer Su Xiaokang, the law professor Guo Luoji, and others—joined Fang on the board of HRiC. In the early 2000s, though, the executive leadership of the group changed hands, and the new leaders turned toward a focus on international activities such as lobbying foreign governments, attending conferences around the world, and so on. They seemed, in the view of the Chinese board members, to be losing contact with the people struggling on the ground inside China. Some of the board members felt awkward that their reputations were being used to raise funds that were not being well spent. In a tribute to Fang after his death, Su Xiaokang put it this way:

> [HRiC], perched in its offices high in the Empire State Building, was bringing in ever more funding, year by year, and paying corporate-level salaries to its staff, but was also becoming ever more separated from actual human rights conditions in China. Fang was not the sort of person who wanted to be an ornament. One day he gathered me and the other board members from China and said, "They don't seem too willing to work

*with us, so there's not much reason for us to hang around." That
led to a mass resignation of the Chinese board members, who
set up a new group called China Human Rights Defenders
(CHRD) and began running it on a shoestring.*

The CHRD shoestring thrived, primarily because it soon became the
overseas office of the network in China called the "rights support web"
(*weiquanwang*), a loosely linked group that reported on human rights and
sometimes took action as well. CHRD and *weiquanwang* conceived,
wrote, and disseminated Charter 08, the pro-democracy manifesto that
was published in December 2008 and eventually led to both a long prison
sentence and a Nobel Peace Prize for the literary critic and human rights
activist Liu Xiaobo.

Fang Lizhi and Li Shuxian traveled to Oslo in December 2010 to
attend the award ceremony for Liu Xiaobo's prize. Liu was in prison
then, and the Chinese government denied travel permission to any of
his friends and relatives whom they suspected of heading for Oslo. But
Liu Xiaobo's wife, Liu Xia, was able to send out an invitation list of people
who were living overseas, and Fang and Li were naturally included. The
day before the ceremony, in frigid weather, a group of people from Human
Rights Watch, Amnesty International, CHRD, and elsewhere—I among
them—went to the gates of the Chinese embassy in Oslo to deliver a letter
of protest. Fang declined to join. "You will meet, at most, a minor factotum, a person with neither will nor ability to make any difference," he said.
Fang preferred to use his time in Oslo to learn about the Vikings. Bold
pirates, they. What did they do? How, so early in technological history,
could they do it? Readers of this book will understand how these inquiries
arise from Fang's sometimes Olympian view of human history, and especially from his interest in the history of technology. Much more worthwhile
than a factotum. The day after the Nobel ceremony, Fang led Li Shuxian,
Su Xiaokang, CHRD chair Renee Xia, and me on an expedition to the
Viking Ship Museum outside Oslo.

The generally smooth course of Fang Lizhi's and Li Shuxian's lives in
Tucson was marred by one horrible tragedy. On October 25, 2007, their
son Fang Zhe was killed at a highway intersection when an elderly driver

ignored a stop sign. Thriving and handsome one moment, gone the next. Li Shuxian later wrote a long poem called "A Roadside Shrine for My Son Zhe," the final lines of which are:

> *Clouds, low on the horizon, of a kind you seldom see in Arizona,*
> > *silhouette my heart*
> *On a country road in Pinal County*
> *At that heart-searing crossroads*
> *Next to a horse-farm fence*
> *I see the telephone pole; it's made of wood*
> *On its southeast edge, a scar from the crash remains*
> *And a few steps beyond, tire ruts remain as well, at the bottom*
> > *of a gully*
>
> *Here is where my son's soul departed*
> *Here is where he bled*
> *Here I can hear—can I?—the tiny reverberations of the sound*
> > *of the last breath that he took.*

I flew to Tucson for Fang Zhe's memorial service, and an image of Fang Lizhi at the event is vivid in my memory. As I entered the large hall, I saw Li Shuxian in the first row, seated and weeping. Friends and relatives were seated, also weeping. Soon I, too, was doing the same. But Fang Lizhi, the host of the event, stood at the front of the room—straight, silent, aware. Can there be anything more painful for a human being than the death of one's child? But there he was, tall, unbent.

Less than five years later, Fang's own memorial service took place in that same room. Valley fever normally does not lead to death. When Fang died, he had been out of the hospital for more than four months and, although weak, was working daily on his teaching and research. Beginning about March 20, 2012, he began to feel worse than usual. He visited his primary care physician on April 3. On the morning of Friday, April 6, he reluctantly decided to call the university to postpone a class that he was set to teach. He then went to his computer, opened Skype, and began to work on plans for a conference on general relativity scheduled for July in

Stockholm. He was on the organizing committee and was to give a major address. Suddenly he coughed loudly, then died, still sitting, the conference materials still in his hand. An autopsy could identify no specific cause of death.

News of Fang's passing spread quickly on the Chinese Internet. Students he had taught in the 1980s, along with other admirers of his eloquence, wrote their accolades. Here are two:

> *Some call him China's Sakharov, and that's fine. But to me, Fang and the Communist Party are more like Galileo and the Roman church. An astrophysicist against powerful and arbitrary authority; the authority persecutes the physicist, but the physicist gets the truth right.*

> *Fang shows us a better way to be Chinese in the modern world. To be Chinese does not have to mean "supports Bashir al-Assad at the UN" or "puts a Nobel Peace Prize winner in prison." We can be better. Teacher Fang is our example.*

State Security noticed, and soon all Fang tweets on *weibo* (the Chinese version of Twitter) disappeared after posting. The 1989 warrant for Fang's arrest had never been dropped, so it was still the official government view, when Fang died, that he was wanted for the crime of "counterrevolutionary incitement" and as "the biggest black hand behind the June Fourth riots."

Fang's older son, Fang Ke, invited me to say a few words at Fang's memorial service. Since time was short, I settled for a list of eight of Fang's most salient virtues, pairing each with an anecdote from my personal memory. For the virtue of *independence*, I told the story of how he wrote in 1990 that "forgetting" the Tiananmen massacre would become a problem even though everybody else, including me, assumed the events to be unforgettable. For the virtue of *strength*, I recalled his astounding composure at Fang Zhe's memorial. The other six virtues, with associated memories, were:

Modesty. I had met Fang in the fall of 1988, when I was working in Beijing for the scholarly exchange office of the U.S. National Academy of Sciences. My friend Orville Schell arranged an invitation to dinner on the evening of the Mid-Autumn Festival at the classic old-style courtyard home in Beijing of Zhang Hanzhi, a former English tutor of Mao Zedong and the widow of Qiao Guanhua, who had served as foreign minister for Mao from 1974 to 1976. About eight people sat around an outdoor table. What struck me about Fang was how quiet he was. He seldom spoke—although it was clear that he was listening, because he occasionally sent a peal of joyous laughter through the air. My expectations of Fang may have been shaped by what I knew of Liu Binyan, Fang's fellow victim in the 1987 campaign against "bourgeois liberalism." Liu was handsome, imposing, somewhat Lincolnesque, and had charisma that could fill a room of any size. Or perhaps it was because I knew that Fang had been a high-ranking academic official that I expected someone who spoke with some *guanqiang* ("official flavor") or other stylized self-presentation. But no. Fang had no façade of any kind. "Hi! I'm Fang!" That was it.

Empathy for common people. I recalled again what I had seen on February 26, 1989, when the police blocked Fang Lizhi and Li Shuxian (and my wife and me) from attending President George H. W. Bush's Texas barbecue in Beijing. Deng Xiaoping had made it clear that he would not attend if Fang did. After we were stopped for "speeding" and our car ordered away—and after the taxi that we then boarded was blocked as well (for a "defective taillight"), Fang proposed that we line up at a public bus stop and catch a bus to the embassy. A bus approached, but about a hundred yards before it reached our stop, someone flagged it down and said something to the driver. The bus then swooshed past us without stopping. About thirty other people were waiting at the stop. They shouted at the bus; some cursed. A few minutes later a second bus swooshed by in the same way. Fang looked at me and said, "The problem here is us. We have to leave. It isn't fair to these *laobaixing* ["ordinary folk"]. It's the end of the day and they're trying to go home." With that we left the bus stop and headed for the embassy on foot. So there we were, at the focal point of a drama that involved a U.S. president and China's top leader.

Police were swarming and odd events kept occurring. A few hours later the incident was in headlines around the world. But Fang? He was worried that the *laobaixing* couldn't catch a bus. It was unfair.

Courage. About two hours later that same night, we had arrived by foot at the gate of the U.S. ambassador's residence in Beijing. A clutch of policemen barred the way. What to do? By chance, we met a Canadian diplomat named David Horley and his wife, who were out for an evening stroll. The Horleys, who knew who Fang Lizhi was, invited us to their apartment for a snack, a couch, and use of a telephone. At the gate of their apartment building, a policeman demanded to know the identity of the Chinese visitors. Horley began an explanation of his rights as a diplomat to invite to his residence anyone of his choosing, but it was obvious that the niceties of international law were floating over the head of the Chinese policeman. Fang took a different tack. He removed his Chinese ID card from his pocket, stepped forward right in front of the policeman, held the card in two hands in front of his chest, about four inches beneath his chin, and said in a sharp, clear voice: "Fang . . . Li . . . Zhi!" Even the policeman was startled. We entered.

Wit. In May 1989, while student demonstrators were in the streets of Beijing calling for democracy, I listened as a Western journalist interviewed Fang. At the end, the interviewer asked if he could follow up, if necessary. Fang said "sure" and gave the reporter his telephone number.

"We've heard that your phone is tapped," the reporter said. "Is it?"

"I assume so." Fang grinned.

"Doesn't that . . . bother you?" the reporter asked.

"No," Fang said. "For years I've been trying to get them to listen to me. If this is how they want to do it, then fine!"

Conception of human rights. On June 4, 1989, hours after the worst of the massacre in Beijing, I went to Fang's apartment. Li Shuxian answered the door, trembling with rage. "They're mad! Truly mad!" she kept repeating, in a hoarse whisper. Fang, sitting at his desk, was managing to stay calm, although it seemed a struggle. Friends had been telephoning and urging the couple to flee, because word was already out that their names were at the top of the government's wanted list of people responsible for the "counterrevolutionary riot." But Fang said, "This is my home. I have done nothing wrong. Why should I leave?" In a situation where fear, anger, or confusion would overwhelm most people, Fang could see first principles first: no innocent person should have to leave a home.

Youthful spirit. Not long before he died, I wrote to Fang praising his literary talent and saying I wished he would write more. He wrote back attaching an essay about a boyhood prank—one that does not appear in these memoirs. One of his neighbors at Messenger Alley in Beijing had been the famous opera singer Cheng Yanqiu. Fang and some playmates once had the bright idea of prying some gooey tar from the roadway and inserting it into the casing of Mr. Cheng's doorbell button so that once it was pushed, the button would stick and the bell would not stop ringing. Then they pushed the button and ran away to watch the fun from a distance. I was struck in reading this essay that the boy who pulled that prank and the seventy-five-year-old man who sent me the essay about it were essentially the same person, the same authentic Fang Lizhi. In traditional Chinese literary culture, a "childlike heart" (*tongxin*) is a virtue that one works hard to preserve. Fang had such a heart and did not even have to work much to maintain it.

In my talk at Fang's memorial service, in addition to noting the eight salient virtues, I raised the question of how the world is different for Fang Lizhi's having passed through it. I argued (as I did in my foreword to this book) that popular awareness of the notion of "rights" in China today has come as much from Fang Lizhi as from any other person one might name.

Since then, I have asked others about Fang's place in history. I put the question to Yü Ying-shih, who is arguably the greatest historian of China alive today; to Su Xiaokang, Zheng Yi, and other eminent Chinese writers; and to Xiao Qiang and others of Fang's brilliant students.

Some of them, Yü Ying-shih and Zheng Yi in particular, pointed out that Fang's advocacy of rights in the 1980s should be seen as the resumption of a tradition that began in the first half of the twentieth century and then, with the Communist accession to power, was broken off for a few decades. *Minquan* ("people's power" or "people's rights") was much discussed in the Shanghai press at the turn of the twentieth century, and thinkers like Hu Shi and Luo Longji wrote explicitly about rights during the "May Fourth era" of the late 1910s and the 1920s. Mao and the

Communists obliterated this tradition in the 1950s, so Fang's contribution in the 1980s should be seen more as a resumption than as an inauguration—although Fang's was an especially courageous reprise, since the environment was so much harsher under the Communists.

Nearly everyone I asked observed that Fang's importance lay in his *conceptual* breakthrough. Other courageous dissidents were active in the 1980s, but their criticisms, in one way or another, were usually appeals that the existing system work better. The authorities, for their part, were also stressing constantly that their system had "Chinese characteristics," that China, a unique civilization, is exceptional, and that they, the Communists, were the arbiters of what Chineseness is. Fang's breakthrough was to highlight universal values, which were apparent to him in both science and human affairs. In the May Fourth era, sixty years earlier, "science and democracy" had been held up as twin ideals. Now Fang, who embodied both of the ideals as well as anyone, was saying that they are not twins so much as different aspects of the same thing. "Einstein did not do Jewish physics and I am not doing Chinese physics," he said. Similarly, concepts of human rights did not change when one crossed a political border.

Science was not only the fount of Fang's thinking on human rights but the grounding that gave him both inner confidence and stature in the view of others. People deferred to him because he was a distinguished scientist; more important, though, it was his own mind's grasp of the patterns of the universe that served as the internal rock that gave him confidence. No human authority, of whatever position in whatever hierarchy, could compete with this. Communist Party leaders who tangled with Fang were aware of this grounding and knew that—in science and logic, anyway—Fang had the upper hand. They could demote Fang, and did, but that was not science. Nor could they belittle science. It was named in the Four Modernizations, which in the 1980s was the guiding policy of the day. Moreover, Marxism claimed to *be* science. The leaders might not believe in Marxism in any serious sense, but they had to pretend that they did. Fang's challenge-by-science frightened them more deeply than anything a writer or professor of Chinese might do.

In the late 1980s, thanks largely to the regime's miscalculation of how people would respond to his "bourgeois liberal" sayings, Fang found himself a popular hero across China. In the spring of 1989, the government ran a vilification campaign against him, but it fell largely on deaf ears. The "barefoot lawyer" Chen Guangcheng, working in rural Shandong Province at the time, reports that he heard not one negative word about Fang from ordinary people, who reflexively disbelieved what the government campaign was saying.

After Fang's exile in 1990, however, the government ban on the very mention of Fang's name had its effects. His reputation lived on among colleagues at USTC, within China's larger physics community, and among rights activists, but awareness of him in the broader public declined steadily. In this rise and fall of his reputation, the historian Yü Ying-shih sees a possible parallel between Fang and Hu Shi, the famous May Fourth thinker who proposed a literary revolution for China, more openness to the world, democracy, and other ideas that were, like Fang's, conceptual breakthroughs in their time. Hu's reputation with the Chinese public peaked in the late 1910s and early 1920s and eventually reached a low point with Mao Zedong's denunciation of him in the 1950s, but today, nearly a century after his initial fame and a half century after his death, has seen a major resurgence. The staying power of Hu's ideas could not be kept down, and Yü senses that the same may be true of Fang's ideas. Universal values are, after all, neither Eastern nor Western but universal. The Communist Party's attachment of "with Chinese characteristics" to words like *science*, *democracy*, and *rights* will not endure the test of time. Echoing Yü Ying-shih, Su Xiaokang observes that intellectual breakthroughs have always outlasted the political forces that have sought to repress them. "How many people today remember the name of the pope who persecuted Galileo?" Su asks.

Today, as this book is published, China's rise has brought the importance of Fang's ideas onto the world stage. In the 1980s, a key question was "How can China find its way past a narrow-minded authoritarian regime?" Today that regime is challenging not just China but the entire world. It uses trade leverage, disinformation, intimidation, and other tactics to press its interests while advertising a "China dream" and a "China model" of development. The model borrows words like *democracy*, *rights*, and *law* but continues to claim that there are distinctive ways of conceiving these terms, ways that fit the "special conditions" of China (and perhaps of other places, if authoritarians in other places want to borrow them). Today the globe as a whole needs Fang's wisdom more than ever, and we are lucky for its staying power. Fang tells us, today as before, that we are here together. No part of the world can be sequestered. Truth is universal. There is no "Chinese physics."

ABOUT THE AUTHOR

FANG LIZHI was an astrophysicist and
a vice president of the University
of Science and Technology of China.
A recipient of the Robert F. Kennedy
Human Rights Award, he was a
professor of physics at the University
of Arizona until his death in 2012.

ABOUT THE TRANSLATOR

PERRY LINK, professor emeritus of
East Asian Studies at Princeton
University, teaches at the University
of California, Riverside. He is
the author or editor of several
books on Chinese literature,
culture, and politics, including
The Tiananmen Papers.